THE BU$INESS OF PHILANTHROPY

THE BU$INESS OF PHILANTHROPY

PERSPECTIVES & INSIGHTS FROM GLOBAL THOUGHT LEADERS ON HOW TO CHANGE THE WORLD

BADR JAFAR

HarperCollins*Publishers*

HarperCollins*Publishers*
1 London Bridge Street
London SE1 9GF

www.harpercollins.co.uk

HarperCollins*Publishers*
Macken House, 39/40 Mayor Street Upper
Dublin 1, D01 C9W8, Ireland

First published by HarperCollins*Publishers* 2024

1 3 5 7 9 10 8 6 4 2

A catalogue record of this book is available from the British Library

HB 978-0-00-862095-0
PB 978-0-00-874070-2

Printed and bound in the UK using 100% renewable electricity at CPI
Group (UK) Ltd

To my beloved mother Sawsan, and father Hamid,
who taught me everything I know and are still working on
teaching me everything they know.

The author will donate 100% of all net royalties he receives from the production and sale of this book to the International Rescue Committee in support of children affected by armed conflict.

CONTENTS

FOREWORD

Philanthropy is an act of faith. Faith in individuals, faith in community, faith in our common future. In a world that is marked by war, disease, poverty and climate change, progress can seem elusive. But the promise of philanthropy holds out hope that humanity can meet and overcome these challenges. Philanthropy can have an enormous impact on the issues that affect our societies, such as social injustice, gender and racial inequality, environmental degradation and lack of access to education. However, there is no one-size-fits-all approach to the practice of philanthropy around the world, and different approaches can lead to an equally wide variety of results. That is why there is much that we can learn by examining the business of philanthropy itself.

As a goodwill ambassador for the United Nations Development Programme, I have had the opportunity to travel to many parts of the world, particularly in Asia and Africa, where I have witnessed first-hand the humanitarian needs of communities affected by crisis. In many of these communities, local philanthropy has played a crucial role in meeting needs for immediate support and for longer-term recovery and development. Individual donors in these regions have often demonstrated limitless generosity to their families and neighbours.

However, the immense scale and complex nature of many of the crises that we face today cannot be overcome through personal generosity alone. Philanthropists must connect with each other to accelerate and multiply the impact of their giving. We need to facilitate giving on a broader and bolder scale, and convert that giving into tangible and coordinated action. We simply cannot achieve the UN Sustainable Development Goals without harnessing more of the immense capabilities and resources of philanthropic partners working with business and government.

The opportunity for strategic philanthropy is nowhere more evident than in the emerging and high-growth regions of the world, including Africa, Asia and the Middle East, and North Africa. It is here that we find increasing wealth meeting increasing need. In these regions, we see young populations in need of skills training and sustainable employment. We see agricultural communities facing the impact of climate change. We see girls and women seeking health, security and better livelihoods. We also see more wealth being created, transferred and inherited. A rising group of donors is rapidly expanding its ability and raising its ambitions to generate impact across huge populations by investing in education, supporting entrepreneurs, promoting sustainable farming, and deploying digital technologies and mobile communications, among other interventions that accelerate social and economic wellbeing across multiple fronts.

To take full advantage of these opportunities, we must redouble our efforts to empower more leaders in philanthropy, business and government with imagination, courage and skill. Philanthropy itself has particular importance by virtue of its natural capacity to take risks that will help to bring other partners to the table. To achieve our global goals for sustainable development, we must align all efforts. The philanthropists and international leaders whose voices are featured in this book speak clearly to the multifaceted role of philanthropy as a catalyst, a convenor and a partner in the efforts of communities, regions and nations to counter injustice, inequality and disruption. They underline the growing need and the potent opportunity that exist for deepening collaboration across sectors, if we have the courage to grasp it.

True collaboration relies on common strategy, open communication and mutual trust. As individuals we must have the compassion to care for others, the curiosity to understand a challenge from every angle and the aspiration to do more in order to help solve it. We must also have the patience and the determination to commit to specific goals, and to work and learn with others as we go. In this timely book, you will find the stories of a diverse range of philanthropists from across the world told in their own voices. While their perspectives, experiences and local contexts are different, their inspirational stories hold many of the same characteristics of compassion, curiosity and courage. Together they illuminate the great possibilities of strategic philanthropy for accelerating human development, and contributing to the development of new and collaborative solutions to our world's biggest social and environmental challenges.

Michelle Yeoh
Goodwill Ambassador of the United Nations
Development Programme (UNDP)

PREFACE

This book is based on a series of conversations that took place over several years with over 50 leaders in the business, philanthropic and social sectors across five continents, with a particular focus on the high-growth economies of the Middle East, Africa and Southeast Asia. The individuals whose insights are featured in this book are diverse. Some have been active philanthropists for many years. Others are newer to the space. Some are influential voices in business, or in the public and international governance sectors. Many are entrepreneurs. All share a deep interest in exploring the power and practice of philanthropy.

At the outset, it may help to go over a few key terms. At its most basic level, the term 'philanthropy' generally refers to the giving of money, goods or one's time to benefit the community. Contrary to popular belief, philanthropists don't need to be wealthy or famous. What is more important is that they are motivated by a strong desire to help others.

The term 'strategic philanthropy' is associated with philanthropic efforts that aim to tackle problems at their root. Approaches vary, but for the purposes of this analysis strategic philanthropy tends to involve creative planning, agile execution and diligent follow-through in order to maximise impact over time. A strategic philanthropist will commonly define specific goals, and then create a comprehensive plan to achieve them.

They are actively focused on outcomes, and likely believe in the role that data can play in helping to produce optimal results. In effect, they are acting as an investor, accepting both risk and responsibility to strive for a positive, non-financial return on their philanthropic investments.

It is important to recognise that there is no *right way* of undertaking philanthropy. Strategic philanthropy is one approach, but it is far from the only way of making a positive difference. Moreover, applying 'business-like' principles to giving without appreciating the importance of building trusting relationships with community partners would be unwise, no matter how sophisticated your methods. Trust between donors and beneficiaries is essential to creating sustained impact. In a world in which the social, economic and environmental challenges that we face are increasingly urgent and interconnected, there is a growing interest in models of philanthropy that combine strategic thinking with deep listening, using data-driven insights, developing relationships, building on learnings and seeking to multiply impact in a systematic way.

What has been my own path to this way of approaching philanthropy?

I grew up in Sharjah, in the United Arab Emirates, in a family with a strong belief in giving back to the community. When I began my own journey as an aspiring entrepreneur 25 years ago, I found myself regularly questioning the broader purpose of business. I took inspiration from fortunate encounters with great social innovators like Bill Drayton, who coined the term 'social entrepreneurship', and Professor Mohammad Yunus, Nobel laureate and microfinance pioneer. Over time this evolved into practising what I referred to as 'impact entrepreneurship' – thinking about business through the lens of social needs, without necessarily compromising on financial rigour or commercial sustainability. This is the philosophy that I adopted in the for-profit ventures that I was involved in; from the start-ups I helped launch, to the established businesses I managed. Over the years, this led me further along the impact spectrum to pure philanthropy, as it became clear to me that there are aspects of social impact that business capital is not best placed to address on its own. There are gaps in the social marketplace – so-called 'market failures' – that government or business capital are slow to fill, if at all. This is where philanthropy can thrive.

Today, the simple philosophy behind my own approach to philanthropy is investing for growth, and helping to build the systems and tools that promote and support *more* strategic philanthropy. This wasn't an easy landing point for me to reach, given the many urgent causes and issues I was exposed to. I am passionate about opportunities for social innovation across the Middle East and elsewhere. I've witnessed the power of nurturing youth through entrepreneurship, education and skills development. I am a firm believer in the fundamental roles that creativity and the arts play in social and economic development. I am aware of the power of digital technologies and their all-important role in accelerating learning and growth, especially for the underserved. I have long advocated for effective corporate governance as a pillar of socio-economic progress. I recognise the inextricable links between climate, nature and the human development agenda. I have also had the opportunity to engage with and learn from important actors across the global humanitarian and development sectors.

Equipped with these exposures and experiences, and after much reflection, I determined that my own resources and time would be best focused on helping to build the infrastructure around giving – with a focus on the so-called 'emerging markets', many of which are in the fastest-growing regions of the world. In effect, I decided to dedicate energy and resources to strengthening the philanthropic system itself because of the potential multiplier effect of this form of giving. To borrow from a recognised analogy, I wanted to help provide people with better tools for fishing, not simply to give them a fish or even to teach them how to fish. Back on land, I accepted that it was a good use of my own limited resources to help build a better path for philanthropists to tread. It wasn't so much an epiphany as a deliberate refocusing on ways to improve the overall impact of philanthropic capital in and from these exciting regions of the world. With better philanthropic infrastructure, all donors have the possibility of boosting their impact and connecting more meaningfully with their giving.

Not surprisingly, my journey towards implementing this vision was one of trial, error and discovery. In 2010, I collaborated with the United Nations Office for Partnerships to launch the Pearl Initiative, a private-sector-led non-profit that aspired to be the leading Gulf business-led organisation promoting a corporate culture of accountability and transparency as a key driver of competitiveness and socio-economic growth. This organisation now has numerous programmes across the spectrum of industry and academia in all six countries in the Gulf Cooperation Council. In 2017, in collaboration with the Bill & Melinda Gates Foundation, the Pearl Initiative launched a dedicated Governance in Philanthropy programme to help strengthen the regional philanthropic ecosystem. This included the creation of Circle, a peer-to-peer digital platform for next-generation donors which provides helpful resources such as guides and toolkits to inform and optimise their giving.

In the 2010s, I became fascinated by the potential of digital technologies to shift from a 'one-to-many' model of philanthropy – wealthy donors supporting a vast number of different beneficiaries – to a 'many-to-one' model, where those seeking support can source smaller donations from a vast pool of individual donors. Inspired by these learnings, I worked with a team in 2019 to launch a new digital tool, HasanaH, an online charity platform to provide donors of all faiths with information and impact reports on thousands of pre-vetted projects, campaigns and charity funds in more than 100 countries.

Data and research are also crucial elements of the 'soft' infrastructure that enhances the impact of philanthropy. Despite this, there is a scarcity of relevant data on philanthropy in global growth markets. To help address this gap, I have worked in partnership with academic centres of excellence in key locations to establish research and education centres for strategic philanthropy. The first such centre was the Centre for Strategic Philanthropy, established in 2020 at the Cambridge Judge Business

School at the University of Cambridge. This was followed by a similar initiative in 2021, in partnership with NYU Abu Dhabi, with the aim of creating a trusted reference for the Gulf region's philanthropists, practitioners and policymakers. More centres will be launched in Africa and Asia in the coming years, all of them encompassing the interconnected three tracks of research, convening and training. Research will help address knowledge gaps within the field and create a repository of data and case studies that can guide strategy and deployment. Convening will build networks of individuals and organisations who can share ideas, practices and resources. Education and training will develop skills and capacity within the sector itself. Of course, these tracks are all interconnected. The ultimate goal is to create a thriving network of such centres, collaborating with each other to exchange ideas, accelerate learning and enhance practices across their respective regions.

In philanthropy, as in so many disciplines, regional variations cannot be ignored. To date, most studies on philanthropy are written through a Western lens with insufficiently rigorous analysis outside of North America and Europe. The story of the rise of strategic philanthropy across growth markets must be told. One way to do this is through the power of media – another important but often overlooked part of the philanthropic infrastructure. With this purpose in mind, I had the opportunity to partner with *Alliance* magazine, a leading non-profit publication covering philanthropy and social investment since 1998, to help drive wider coverage of philanthropy in global growth markets. Our partnership has seen the recruitment of local champions across the Middle East, Africa and Asia. The many hundreds of stories they have published to date are bringing innovative ideas and approaches from these regions to a wider audience of next-generation philanthropists, institutional givers and policymakers around the world. The rise of more well-informed, independent journalism on philanthropy is shedding new light on the changing nature of philanthropic practice across these regions and telling the untold stories of many local social innovators.

I share these examples of my own philanthropic journey for two reasons. First, I hope that telling my own story provides some context for the approach that I have taken in conducting the conversations included in this book. Moreover, I genuinely believe that we can all see our own paths more clearly when we share our stories with one another. In other words, I would like to give you an idea of where I am coming from, but also where I hope that we can go together as a sector.

My journey so far has convinced me that deploying philanthropy as catalytic capital to create solutions for sustainable and inclusive growth is vital to addressing inequities in our world. I strongly believe that the adoption of more structured and strategic methods for the deployment of philanthropy, including the combination of philanthropic capital with business and government capital, can multiply the impact of these investments. Hence the naming of this series of conversations *The Business of Philanthropy*.

What I aim to do in sharing these conversations is to encourage readers to reflect on their own approach to giving by getting a behind-the-scenes look into the insights and experiences of others. This book is also for those who may be inspired to do more with their time and talent, as well as their money, and who are eager to learn about different methods of generating impact. Above all, *The Business of Philanthropy* addresses the need for fresh, new perspectives on our shared global problems, and offers a much-needed dose of hope and optimism that through a more strategic and collaborative approach, we can indeed address these challenges successfully.

Badr Jafar

ONE

THE BUSINESS OF PHILANTHROPY

The need for strategic philanthropy in the world today is greater than ever. The geopolitical fractures that constitute the headlines every day – regional conflicts, political extremism, and the resulting refugee and humanitarian crises – are compounded by environmental challenges, including climate change, biodiversity loss, energy and food shortages, and global health crises, such as the COVID-19 pandemic. Public- and private-sector leaders in all countries are grappling with these issues daily. More than ever, strategic philanthropists across the world have an opportunity to step up to help meet these challenges.

Trends Shaping Global Philanthropy

There are several strong trends pushing in favour of the growth of global strategic philanthropy. These trends are evident in Europe and North America, but they are particularly important in the high-growth areas of the world, which include parts of the Middle East, Africa, India and Southeast Asia. Among these trends, the most significant are:

- a young and growing population, which is highly connected through access to digital technologies and which is increasingly focused on impact and evidence;
- a historic increase in personal wealth and the opportunity to transfer significant resources to the next generation;
- the increasing involvement of businesses in social issues, not just through corporate social responsibility but through active cross-sectoral collaboration and partnership;
- the accelerating introduction of new technologies, including artificial intelligence, enabling ongoing breakthroughs and innovations in health, education, agriculture and environmental sustainability;
- the increasing use of digital platforms and tools to encourage, facilitate, simplify and incentivise giving;
- the convergence of agencies and organisations involved in humanitarian and economic development, and a sustained move towards the localisation of aid;
- the development of more effective and accessible philanthropic networks, enabling a community of philanthropists to gain access to more relevant data, learn from others' experiences and collaborate more effectively.

Individually and collectively, these are all encouraging developments that augur well for the future of strategic philanthropy across the world. Most were becoming clear well before the onset of the COVID-19 pandemic, but several of the interviewees featured in this book agree that the pandemic has accelerated these trends, particularly in relation to the use of digital technologies. At the same time, there are some stubborn gaps and barriers to the more rapid expansion of strategic philanthropy in the high-growth regions of the Middle East, Africa and Asia.

Philanthropy and giving in these regions have deep historical roots and are strongly shaped by religious beliefs and family ties. In these cultural contexts, charitable giving is often very generous but remains discreet. It is typically individualised, often cash-based, focused on immediate community needs and dominated by traditional, faith-based giving. Government involvement in the sector focuses more on restricting certain giving practices. Tax incentives for giving are limited, and outdated regulations create barriers that can make it difficult for non-profit organisations to structure themselves efficiently and effectively, if at all. Among other things, this relatively scanty philanthropic infrastructure has not encouraged the building of relationships or trust, which in turn means the sharing of information and data among philanthropic peers is very limited. None of these barriers are insurmountable, but they are also unlikely to disappear overnight, and we must therefore be cognisant about their existence and their effects.

The good news is that a groundswell appears to be building. For example, many far-sighted businesses in these high-growth markets are increasingly coming to terms with and embracing the concept of social responsibility as a business imperative. This is a welcome development. To thrive, businesses need skilled talent, predictable supply chains, stable input costs and affordable insurance, among other things. These ingredients for success cannot exist where social and environmental resilience is threatened. In the face of multiple crises, there is therefore a strong incentive for business leaders and philanthropists to strategically pool their resources and capabilities both with one another, and with governments, to multiply and maximise their impact.

We cannot afford to waste this moment. With the world facing ever more complex challenges, we have an obligation to ensure that we maximise social and environmental returns on the increasingly large social investments that are being made in high-growth markets. This means building better infrastructure to support these investments: more programmes and institutions dedicated to enhancing the regulatory frameworks under which philanthropy and social investing are practised; working with localised data that reflects the realities on the ground; and creating stronger governance models to organise philanthropic work and make it easier for various stakeholders to pool resources with a long-term view on impact. This is the business of philanthropy.

A word about the organisation of this book. The world was in the grip of the COVID-19 pandemic when the first set of these conversations took place. Economic and social disruptions were beginning to take hold, and we could not yet envisage the full impact that the pandemic and our response to it would have on our societies and economies. Philanthropy and science were working hard – albeit not always in tandem – but a vaccine was not yet readily available, and the outlook was cloudy. It will therefore come as no surprise that the initial interviews that were conducted for this project focused on the global economic and humanitarian consequences of the pandemic, and the essential role that philanthropy must play in resolving both short-term global challenges and longer-term opportunities for building back better. Many speak of the intertwining global crises of climate change, pandemic disruption, political instability and inequality, and the potential implications of what many are calling a 'polycrisis'. While the immediacy of the COVID-19 pandemic has receded since work on this book commenced, other crises have become more urgent. War, social instability, economic stress, climate change and the possibility of future global health crises are all threatening the lives and livelihoods of billions of people. The immediacy and interconnectedness of these threats amplify the need for greater collaboration and coordination among governments, businesses and philanthropic leaders to address them.

That is where this book begins. The following two chapters describe the opportunities and challenges posed by the growth of wealth and philanthropy globally as well as by the 'polycrisis'. These analyses provide the backdrop for the inspirational work of the individual philanthropists and social innovators whose perspectives appear on the pages that follow.

The personal backgrounds and philanthropic journeys of the individuals featured in this book are diverse and different. However, many of them were independently aligned on several recurring themes: the role of business in meeting social as well as economic goals; the opportunity to blend capital and risk; the power of collaboration through structured philanthropy; the impact of innovation and digital technologies as philanthropic tools; and the importance of data, learning and measurement. Following their lead, the interviews in this book have been arranged in chapters under short introductions to each of these topics. The interviews, which were conducted as oral conversations for the most part, have been edited and condensed for greater clarity without altering the meaning and context of each conversation.

TWO

THE FUTURE OF GLOBAL PHILANTHROPY

A preponderance of the philanthropists and business leaders interviewed in this book live in high-growth regions within Africa and Asia, where there are enormous opportunities for the advancement of strategic philanthropy. The future of global philanthropy is in these regions where wealth is accumulating rapidly, and a younger population is exploding with new ideas for applying the tools of strategic philanthropy to global problems.

Wealth is being created at an unprecedented rate in many so-called emerging markets within the Middle East, Africa and Southeast Asia. Countries in West and East Asia such as the United Arab Emirates, Saudi Arabia, India, Malaysia, Singapore, Indonesia, Vietnam, Thailand, South Korea and the Philippines are growing at a particularly fast pace.[1] These markets are naturally broad – the forces that shape growth patterns vary from one country to the next. Nevertheless, and despite slowdowns created by the global pandemic, numerous economies in these regions continue to grow more rapidly than so-called advanced economies.

Estimates vary but suggest that anywhere between US$70 trillion and US$90 trillion will be transferred globally over the

"Estimates vary but suggest that anywhere between US$70 trillion and US$90 trillion will be transferred globally over the coming decades to members of Gen X and millennials. In growth markets alone it is estimated that US$26 trillion will be transferred across generations within the coming 20 years, while three-quarters of the world's GDP consumption is expected to shift to the Global South. Together, these trends are likely to result in significantly larger pools of philanthropic capital in and from these regions of the world."

coming decades to members of Gen X and millennials.[2] In growth markets alone it is estimated that US$26 trillion will be transferred across generations within the coming 20 years, while three-quarters of the world's GDP consumption is expected to shift to the Global South.[3] Together, these trends are likely to result in significantly larger pools of philanthropic capital in and from these regions of the world.

Institutional philanthropy in the form of foundations is playing a progressively important role in emerging markets. Finance for development is increasingly being supplied by a growing number of domestic foundations within these countries, according to a 2021 report from the OECD.[4] A study from the Harvard Kennedy School of Government in 2018 situated over 13,000 philanthropic foundations in Asia and found that over 75% of these were established within the preceding two decades, a significantly higher percentage than the global average.[5]

Business giving through corporate foundations or through corporate social responsibility programmes is also on the rise. Many businesses in emerging economies are family-run, and the personal philanthropy of business owners is often managed through the business. Many of these business owners are motivated to give back to their local communities. State regulation can also play a part. In India, for example, the government made a change to the Companies Act in 2014, under which larger companies must give 2% of their net profits to charity. As a result, corporate social responsibility investments have on average grown by 15% annually in the past seven years.[6]

The Islamic faith and related practices are an important influencer in charitable giving, particularly across parts of the Middle East, North Africa and Asia. Every year, between US$400 billion and US$1 trillion[7] is deployed in *zakat* (compulsory almsgiving) and *sadaqah* (voluntary donations) in and from Muslim communities.[8] These vast sums are typically given by individuals as charity and are not structured to influence systemic changes over the long term. *Zakat*, one of the five pillars of Islam, is embraced as a religious obligation to give to the poor, and this strongly influences giving culture overall. Indonesia, for example, is the world's most populous Muslim-majority country, with 231 million Muslims. In large part due to *zakat* and *sadaqah*, Indonesia was ranked by the Charities Aid Foundation in 2022 as the world's most generous country for the fifth year in a row.[9]

Over the past century, in many emerging economies of the Middle East, Africa and Asia, businesses have traditionally been established and pursued by men. Increasingly, however, women are playing key roles as entrepreneurs and business leaders. This also translates into institutionalised philanthropy as more women assume the philanthropic responsibilities of their families or create their own philanthropies. Women are benefiting from increased access to professional education and are taking more prominent roles in facilitating education, entrepreneurship and skills training for young people in their societies. The vast majority of wealthy women are donors, and they tend to donate more than men as a proportion of their net wealth. In many cases, wealthy women give more to organisations benefiting women and girls.[10] They are also leading many of the peer groups and philanthropic networks that are developing quickly across these regions.

> "Women are playing key roles as entrepreneurs and business leaders."

Another distinct feature of future philanthropy in growth regions will be their youth populations. Asia and Africa together represent over 80% of the world's youth. In sub-Saharan Africa today, 70% of the population is under the age of 30, and by 2030 young Africans are expected to constitute 42% of global youth.[11] Fifty-five per cent of the population in the Middle East today is under the age of 30. Next-generation donors are demanding more hands-on and evidence-based approaches to giving, and higher standards of accountability and transparency. These expectations are already changing the practice of philanthropy worldwide.

As more philanthropy is practised in the coming years, the availability of a strong infrastructure and conducive systems for strategic giving will be especially critical. Access to capital is not the main impediment to the growth of this sector in the burgeoning regions of Asia, the Middle East and Africa. It is the coordinated and strategic deployment of this growing pool of philanthropic capital that must be optimised. Philanthropic infrastructure is therefore a crucial component to be strengthened.

Across Asia, there are signs of an accelerating movement towards alliances and networks to promote philanthropy. The United Arab Emirates, with its advanced convening capabilities and geographic advantages, is developing as a hub that connects North and South, East and West, philanthropic networks and organisations. Singapore is increasingly recognised as a hub for philanthropy in East Asia. A pan-Asian regional social investor network, AVPN, has been operating in Singapore since 2011. The Asia Philanthropy Circle was established in Singapore in 2015 to bring together Asian philanthropists. And in 2023, the Asia Philanthropy Alliance – headquartered in Singapore – was established by Temasek Trust, including over 80 members and partners from across the world. The Arab Foundations Forum based in Cairo has served the Middle East region since 2006, while the African Philanthropy Forum serves Africa from its bases in Nigeria and South Africa. The Africa Philanthropy Network has been promoting a culture of giving since it was established in 2009 with a base in Dar es Salaam. These networks were all established over the past two decades, and while they are growing there remains significant opportunity to reinforce their capacities and reach. New local philanthropy networks and academic centres will undoubtedly be added as these regions continue to grow in wealth, and as major donors look for opportunities to learn and collaborate.

In summary, the need and the opportunity for strategic philanthropy are growing. The rising generation of young philanthropists increasingly have the means and the motives to apply their resources to make change not only in their own regions but globally. Their sense of urgency is shared by corporations and family businesses in emerging economies that are assuming new roles in social responsibility and social investment. This is a point made repeatedly by the philanthropists and thought leaders featured in this book.

The following interviews provide an overview of the global context and challenges that philanthropists face. These women and men have considerable experience and broad perspectives. Commenting on the post-pandemic world while the pandemic still raged, they underlined the importance of future multi-stakeholder collaboration on complex problems such as climate change, as well as continued work towards the Sustainable Development Goals (SDGs) of the United Nations. They also highlighted the importance of creating entrepreneurial opportunities for a generation of young people who require access to education, skills, technology and funding to reach their full potential.

Baroness Valerie Amos

Master, University College, Oxford University

Baroness Valerie Amos became Master of University College, Oxford University in September 2020, the first woman in that role. She was appointed a Labour Party life peer in 1997 and was the first black woman to serve in a British cabinet as Secretary of State for International Development. She went on to become Leader of the House of Lords. Her career has spanned local and national government in the UK as well as global leadership. She has consistently sustained an interest in, and commitment to, issues of equality and social justice.

Baroness Amos served as UK High Commissioner to Australia, and between 1994 and 1998 worked extensively in South Africa. She was Under-Secretary-General for Humanitarian Affairs at the United Nations from 2010 to 2015. From 2015 to 2020 she was the Director of the School of Oriental and African Studies, University of London.

Her work in the voluntary and charity sector and in nongovernmental organisations has gone hand in hand with her policy and political work. In addition to being a patron of the Amos Bursary, Baroness Amos sits on the board of the Mastercard Foundation, the UN Foundation and the Institute for Government.

Badr Jafar: Baroness Amos, you bring a unique and rich perspective, informed by your time in government, with the United Nations, and more recently in the academic sector. What impact do you think that geographic and generational shifts in the distribution of philanthropy will have on the global economy and society in the coming decades?

Baroness Amos: One of the things that struck me is that during a global pandemic philanthropy increased rather than decreased, even at a time where we have seen a major economic impact on various countries, and certainly on individuals and their communities. I think this is a huge opportunity in a few different ways.

In the past, there wasn't necessarily a strategic approach to philanthropy in some parts of the world. For example, on the African continent philanthropic efforts were, in many instances, investments in family interests. Over time, this changed significantly, with a more targeted and business-like approach focused on thinking through exactly what the philanthropist would like to achieve with their investment. As we've seen the consolidation of wealth in emerging markets, there is the potential to make a significant difference on social issues in those countries.

There's an ongoing debate about the way that private philanthropy could distort a national economy or, more generally, the global economy. In emerging economies, even with rapid growth, the investment needed in various sectors like education is not necessarily going to happen at the scale or the scope that will make a difference in those countries. Philanthropic investments can make a huge difference, but an important question going forward is how they are married with the priorities of the country itself, and the needs of that country's citizens.

Badr Jafar: What do you think the lasting impacts of the pandemic will be on the social sector?

Baroness Amos: This is a moment which could be hugely transformational, in both a positive and a negative way. In the United Kingdom, I see the impact that having a vaccine and improved testing will have on our world, but I also see the negative impact of the pandemic in terms of the UK's economy and unemployment rates, the impact on people socially, their ability to look after their families, and the longer-term economic impact of the government's financial support for individuals and communities.

There's a potential innovative impact in terms of how we educate, how we train, how we treat, how we use technology. We've seen significant changes that would have taken years to make without the pandemic. I would like to see how we can apply innovation and new technologies to the social sectors, and how we might use philanthropy to kick start and even transform some of the discussion.

Badr Jafar: For young people who are considering careers in the sector or philanthropists who are starting out on their philanthropic journeys, what should they be aware of in terms of risks and opportunities for engagement?

Baroness Amos: To those exploring ways to grasp positive opportunities, I encourage looking into areas where we can make significant leaps. I also urge potential philanthropists to think about some of the more pressing social challenges, such as food security. Agriculture is a huge challenge in many emerging economies, particularly in sub-Saharan Africa and in the Middle East.

How can innovation transform the agricultural sector? We face challenges around food security, agriculture and energy going forward. Due to drastic climate change, environmental sustainability is also a major issue. In emerging markets I think there are some huge opportunities for change in how to shift economies away from oil dependence.

Badr Jafar: Do you think that the youth of today will change the way that philanthropy is practised in the future?

Baroness Amos: I think our young people are interested in what kind of societies they are going to inherit. Look at the two big activist movements around environmental sustainability and climate change, and around Black Lives Matter, which are rooted in issues of equality, justice and inclusion. If we don't take our young people with us, if we don't integrate or align their concerns about wider issues with concerns about rights, equality and inclusion, then we will end up with more fragmented societies. Our young people are leading the way. They are telling us that they want to live in a world which is different, which is connected, not only through technology, but through a values prism.

Badr Jafar: Cooperation and collaboration, or the lack of it, can make a difference between stability and chaos. You have plenty of experience across all sectors. What makes for a truly successful collaboration between businesses, governments, academia, and philanthropic institutions and actors?

Baroness Amos: Crisis forces collaboration. For example, the COVID-19 crisis forced speed in the development of the vaccine, with very close work between academia and the private sector, pharmaceutical organisations, at Oxford, Imperial College and elsewhere. This points to the importance of collaboration. The global nature of the crises that we face means that they cannot be contained within borders. The costs of lack of action are significant. No one government can do this on its own. This also points to the importance of our multilateral system. The multilateral system requires speedy reform. How we do that is still something that we haven't grasped, given the individual interests of the countries that make up that system. But collaboration and partnership can't just be inter-governmental. This must work across different sectors of society as well.

"The global nature of the crises that we face means that they cannot be contained within borders. The costs of lack of action are significant. No one government can do this on its own."

I think that there are great opportunities, but there are many potential downsides. We will need huge amounts of financing. Again, that is going to require collaboration because countries cannot do it on their own. Our multilateral organisations are funded mainly through governments, but also through philanthropy. This will also force more collaboration.

Badr Jafar: I'd like to ask you about the changing role of education, and the disruptive trends that are challenging educational institutions around the world to adapt. How do you see education pivoting to accommodate new societal expectations? What role does philanthropy play in ensuring that this transition doesn't leave anybody behind, especially in regions of the world that have traditionally been under-served by the education sector?

Baroness Amos: Education must shift and indeed has shifted. At Oxford, within a few days after the pandemic lockdown began, we pivoted and moved much of what we were doing online. Many of our academics stepped up to the plate. We continue to see growth and development and the expansion of ideas in terms of what traditional educational institutions have done and can do. The educational system is a continuum, from primary education through to higher education, with a focus not just on the academic elements, but also on training and development. What the pandemic showed us is that we need to be able to help people to reskill very quickly.

We must take the opportunity to think about a wider education arc, and how within that arc we can have elite excellence in terms of higher education, but also bolster and put in place the resources for policy development, training, and skills development in a very different way. We should think about how we can deliver what we've talked about for a long time, which is the resourcing of education to enable every child across the world to be able to fulfil their potential. This is a massive global ambition. We know that where governments in emerging economies can resource education, it makes a difference to them nationally but also their position in a global context.

I think emerging economies could leapfrog past developed countries. I see the example of the UAE. This is a country in the Gulf that is massively wealthy, but with a relatively small population, and it can exercise soft power because of an investment in education and training. This is something which many countries in the Middle East can teach the rest of us.

Badr Jafar: How concerned are you about the degradation of trust that we're seeing in institutions today, especially when the scale and nature of the challenges that we need to address around the world are only getting more complex? What can we do to reverse this trend?

Baroness Amos: I'm extremely worried about this breakdown in trust. As I said before, many of our institutions need to be reformed. I am in favour of reform, reflecting the changes in our wider society, but located within a set of fundamental principles and values.

My worry is that as people have less and less confidence, particularly in the political institutions, they will begin to think that we don't need these institutions at all. History shows us that we need institutional underpinning to make significant societal changes. So, we need to begin to restore trust. This has got to be a slow process of rebuilding. The rule of law remains extremely important. People need to see the difference that institutions make in their lives, and they need to have a mechanism that enables them to have an influence on those institutions.

There is much questioning and querying of democracy and democratic institutions, how they can deliver for people on the ground, and how people can be invested in the kinds of changes that we want to see. There's no easy answer to this. But it requires a lot of hard work. And it will take time to rebuild. It's relatively easy to tear down but it's much harder to build back.

Badr Jafar: So, we move away from a transactional approach to trying to create trust, and invest in the long-term nature of building trust through institutions?

Baroness Amos: Yes. One of the things that I remember from my time at the United Nations and working on humanitarian financing issues was the lack of trust and the lack of understanding between different parts of the world as to how this could be done. People hung on to a model through the lens of the West as if this was the best and only way to do things. It didn't recognise the benefits and the advantages of ways in which this was done in other parts of the world. One of the things I'm proud of is that we were able to begin bridge-building between countries in different regions across the world. The more that we can embrace those differences, learn the lessons from each other and think about how we can move forward, the better it will be.

"The more that we can embrace those differences, learn the lessons from each other and think about how we can move forward, the better it will be."

Bill Gates

Co-Chair, Bill & Melinda Gates Foundation

Bill Gates is a technologist, business leader and philanthropist. As co-chair of the Bill & Melinda Gates Foundation along with co-chair Melinda French Gates and the foundation's Board of Trustees, Gates shapes and approves the foundation's strategies, advocates for the foundation's issues and helps set the organisation's overall direction. The co-chairs work together with grantees and partners to further the foundation's commitment to fighting the world's greatest inequities.

Bill Gates co-founded Microsoft Corporation in 1975 with Paul Allen and led the company to become the worldwide leader in business and personal software and services. In 2008, he transitioned to focus full-time on the foundation's work. He is also the founder of Breakthrough Energy, which addresses climate change by supporting the next generation of entrepreneurs and clean technologies, and TerraPower, a nuclear innovation company.

In 2010, Bill Gates, Melinda French Gates and Warren Buffett founded the Giving Pledge, an effort to encourage the world's wealthiest families and individuals to publicly commit more than half of their wealth to philanthropic causes and charitable organisations during their lifetime or in their will.

Gates was the first philanthropist interviewed for *The Business of Philanthropy*, and the discussion in September 2020 was clearly influenced by the overwhelming challenges presented by the global COVID-19 pandemic. Nevertheless, he was optimistic about the role and potential contribution of philanthropy to resolving and moving past the health crisis.

Badr Jafar: Looking beyond the COVID-19 pandemic, are you witnessing a rise in philanthropic activity within and from emerging markets, particularly in Asia, the Middle East and Africa? And if so, what do you think is or could be different about the nature and role of philanthropy in these regions?

Bill Gates: Generous giving is not new to these markets. Whether it's India, Indonesia or Nigeria, there are wealthy and very smart people who see great needs in their societies. The philanthropists I meet in emerging markets are eager to help increase opportunity for young people in areas like education, health and entrepreneurship. Many of these innovative philanthropists are first- or second-generation wealth builders. So, they're able to take the latest approaches to leapfrog and improve on practices, and set examples that governments and other philanthropists will benefit from.

> "The philanthropists I meet in emerging markets are eager to help increase opportunity for young people in areas like education, health and entrepreneurship. Many of these innovative philanthropists are first- or second-generation wealth builders. So, they're able to take the latest approaches to leapfrog and improve on practices, and set examples that governments and other philanthropists will benefit from."

Badr Jafar: Are you excited about the potential for rapid growth of online or retail giving globally, including in the US? What trends are you seeing in the space?

Bill Gates: It's early, but I do see a lot of potential. Online giving has increased over the years as digital platforms have made it easier for everyone, not just the wealthy, to give to important causes. Badr, you have worked on a platform called HasanaH, focused on the Islamic community globally. In the US, there are several platforms focused on giving, such as GiveDirectly, GoFundMe and DonorsChoose, the latter of which is focused on education and classroom supplies. Larger platforms are also getting involved. At our foundation, we've been supporting everyday giving initiatives for several years. Despite all the challenges of 2020 to 2021, there was an extraordinary amount of money raised online in a short period of time. People are generous. They want to help, particularly when they see immediate needs. It's important to think about how this retail giving complements longer-term philanthropy because it will continue to grow.

Badr Jafar: What do you think are the best ways to engage and collaborate with the next generation of strategic philanthropists, particularly the rapidly increasing number of donors from the emerging markets?

Bill Gates: I've had an opportunity to see the development of a younger generation of givers, both within the Giving Pledge Community and through the children and grandchildren of pledgers. Many of these young people feel they don't need to wait until they retire to start giving. They see today's challenges and want to start tackling them immediately. So that's very encouraging. Many of the younger philanthropists are particularly interested in impact, sustainability and equity. They also are very collaborative, and we need more of that in philanthropy. Some may be hesitant to take risks in their giving, but by working together, they can take on the tough problems. I know I was worried about risk-taking after Warren Buffett made the incredible decision to donate the bulk of his fortune to our foundation. Melinda and I wanted to be the best stewards of his resources that we possibly could be, but Warren advised us that we shouldn't be conservative. He told us to take risks and swing for the fences.

> "Many of the younger philanthropists are particularly interested in impact, sustainability and equity. They also are very collaborative, and we need more of that in philanthropy. Some may be hesitant to take risks in their giving, but by working together, they can take on the tough problems."

Professor Klaus Schwab

Founder and Executive Chairman, World Economic Forum

Professor Klaus Schwab founded the World Economic Forum in 1971, and it has become the world's foremost platform for public–private cooperation. Under his leadership, the Forum has acted as a catalyst for numerous collaborations and international initiatives in improving the state of the world by engaging leaders of society to shape global, regional and industry agendas.

In 1998, with his wife Hilde, Schwab created the Schwab Foundation for Social Entrepreneurship, which seeks to identify, recognise and disseminate initiatives in social entrepreneurship that have significantly improved people's lives and have the potential to be replicated on a global scale. The foundation supports a network of over 350 social entrepreneurs around the world.

In 2004, he established a new foundation: the Forum of Young Global Leaders (for leaders under 40). In 2011, he created the Global Shapers Community (for potential leaders between the ages of 20 and 30). The purpose of the two foundations is to integrate young people as a strong voice for the future into global decision-making processes and to encourage their engagement in concrete projects that address social problems.

He is the author of several books, including *The Fourth Industrial Revolution* (2016), a worldwide bestseller translated into 30 languages, and *Stakeholder Capitalism* (2021).

Badr Jafar: Effective collaboration between individuals and organisations from across sectors, including the social sector, has never been more important. Will the pandemic have a lasting impact on how people think about the imperative for multi-stakeholder collaboration?

Klaus Schwab: The ongoing impact of the pandemic can be compared to the situation we had after World War II. Many

> "The big challenges in the world cannot be addressed by business alone, by government alone, by civil society alone or by philanthropy alone. We need to unite in common efforts to make the world more resilient, more inclusive and more sustainable."

governments are still in fighting mode. That said, we must look beyond the current situation, and start designing the post-pandemic era. The pandemic has accelerated developments like the use of technologies of the Fourth Industrial Revolution. It has also surfaced numerous deficiencies which we had in the system well before it hit, most particularly a lack of inclusion and a lack of sustainability. So, the beginning of 2021 is an ideal moment to sit back and to design our future beyond the pandemic. We must do it collaboratively. The big challenges in the world cannot be addressed by business alone, by government alone, by civil society alone or by philanthropy alone. We need to unite in common efforts to make the world more resilient, more inclusive and more sustainable.

Badr Jafar: What can we do to engage philanthropic capital as a partner, alongside business and government, in addressing our world's challenges, including the Sustainable Development Goals?

Klaus Schwab: To achieve the SDGs, we cannot rely on public money. Governments will be very challenged in the post-pandemic era. We will need private money. Here is where philanthropic institutions and donors should enter the picture. But we will also need a new type of philanthropy. I wrote an article for *Foreign Affairs* five years or so ago, where I was critical about philanthropy providing money but not really being engaged. Today, philanthropy should be in some way united with social entrepreneurship, which means the people who provide the money also provide their leadership capabilities and their passion. I am optimistic and enthusiastic about the role philanthropic organisations can play, particularly if they are associated with young people who have asked themselves what their legacy should be and feel that they should contribute to society, by giving money and by exercising a high degree of social entrepreneurship, which means engaging beyond providing the financial means.

Badr Jafar: The fastest-growing economies in the world last year were all in emerging markets, and a lot of new wealth is being generated in parts of Africa, the Middle East and developing Asia, with trillions of dollars and assets expected to be passed on from one generation to the next within the coming decade. What impact do you think that these geographic and generational shifts could have on the global economy and society over the coming decade?

"I am optimistic and enthusiastic about the role philanthropic organisations can play, particularly if they are associated with young people who have asked themselves what their legacy should be and feel that they should contribute to society, by giving money and by exercising a high degree of social entrepreneurship, which means engaging beyond providing the financial means."

Klaus Schwab: The year 2020 was a watershed, because for the first time the GDP of Asia was higher compared with the GDP of the rest of the world, showing how much the geopolitical and geo-economic situation has changed. Emerging countries will have a major role to play. We at the World Economic Forum have been engaged for many years in the Middle East and in India. We have always believed that we cannot afford a world where people or countries are left behind. This catching up is a consequence of the force of young people acting as entrepreneurs, building new enterprises and jumping immediately into the age of the Fourth Industrial Revolution. The Fourth Industrial Revolution is a much more dynamic, service-based economy. It provides talented young people with unprecedented ways to jump-start a new way of doing business.

Badr Jafar: What is your view on how the youth of today, including the generation of socially conscious consumers and investors that you are referring to, could change the way that the world thinks about business practice and philanthropic practice?

Klaus Schwab: In 1971, I articulated the concept of stakeholder capitalism. It is not the government but the individual entrepreneur who drives the economy. And entrepreneurs must do so in the service of all stakeholders, not just the short-term expectations of the shareholders. It took many years to prove the validity of this concept because we have seen a fast-growing world, where short-term shareholder capitalism played a very important role. We are now at a sea change. We have seen it with the adoption of stakeholder principles, like those I presented in 1973, by the US Business Roundtable. Stakeholder capitalism is not just a passing phase or theory, because the fundamentals have changed. Customers, young people and employees don't want to be associated as investors, as customers or as employees with a company that is not doing good for society. There is a much greater social awareness today, and companies who do not practise stakeholder capitalism are on the wrong side of history.

Badr Jafar: In 2015, you drew the world's attention to the impending consequences of the Fourth Industrial Revolution. Five years on, do you believe that, on balance, technology is being properly harnessed for the social good of the world?

Klaus Schwab: With our Centre for the Fourth Industrial Revolution (C4IR) and our network with locations around the world, we try to make sure that those technologies are human-centred and serve humankind.

The pandemic accelerated the development of the technologies of the Fourth Industrial Revolution. The particularly successful countries in fighting the virus used their tracing capability, which is a digital capability. The COVID-19 mRNA vaccine is based on a new approach, which has never been tested or tried before, but which could be an entry into a new era of treatment, not only of viruses, but other diseases. Once the pandemic has passed, I think our preoccupation will be very much with the potential of the Fourth Industrial Revolution. In the old world, it was mainly the cost and to a certain extent the quality, which determined the success of a company. In the new world, it will be innovative capability. We will have much more of a race among companies and among countries to be number one or to be in danger of losing out.

The pandemic has shown what can be done with digital means, but we are just at the beginning. I think philanthropic institutions should devote energy and financial capabilities to developing new ways of education. We have done some research at the World Economic Forum in this area. And what we found is about half of the present workforce will need reskilling or upskilling of some kind during the next ten years to avoid being made redundant.

Badr Jafar: How do you elevate diverse voices in the discussions convened by the World Economic Forum, and ensure that these conversations lead to getting things done?

Klaus Schwab: The key here is encapsulated in two words: 'tools' and 'trust'. At the World Economic Forum, we always try to find tools. That is the reason why we have an enormous network of experts that support us. We are living in a world of diversity, including different values. We must come to common solutions, and this can only be done by dialogue, which in turn creates trust.

We do this in three phases. First, we define the issue. We listen to see how everybody interprets a specific issue, and where there may be a common denominator. This leads us to the second phase, which is to find solutions. We do not jump immediately into one solution, but evaluate all possible solutions and, particularly in an interconnected world, try to think of unintended consequences. Then there is a last phase, which is to implement the most appropriate solution through joint action.

Today everybody is speaking about the necessity to measure impact. Sometimes, and this is particularly true for the World Economic Forum, the impact is to create the initiative to act. Implementation is left to the business community or to the government community, sometimes in joint action. It can be very difficult to measure what the real impact is.

We can work only because we are a multi-stakeholder organisation. We are not a government with the power to implement action, but we can provide solutions. I take the pandemic as an example. We warned the world for many years that a pandemic may be in the making. We are proud that we created some ideas and some organisations like GAVI, the Vaccine Alliance, which plays a major role in the distribution of vaccines, because they have the networks in place. The Coalition for Epidemic Preparedness Innovations (CEPI) was created in 2016 in Davos as a mechanism to finance the development of vaccines, and has done valuable work in co-financing some of the vaccines which are now coming on the market. I could enumerate many more such examples where the Forum acted like a midwife, helping to deliver solutions.

Darren Walker

President, Ford Foundation

Darren Walker is President of the Ford Foundation, a US$16 billion international social justice philanthropic organisation. Under his leadership, the Ford Foundation became the first non-profit in US history to issue a US$1 billion designated social bond in US capital markets for proceeds to strengthen and stabilise non-profit organisations in the wake of COVID-19.

Before joining the Ford Foundation, Walker was Vice President at the Rockefeller Foundation, overseeing global and domestic programmes. In the 1990s, he was COO of the Abyssinian Development Corporation, Harlem's largest community development organisation. Walker co-founded both the US

Impact Investing Alliance and the Presidents' Council on Disability Inclusion in Philanthropy. He serves on many boards, including the National Gallery of Art, Carnegie Hall, the High Line, the Smithsonian National Museum of African American History & Culture, the Committee to Protect Journalists, Ralph Lauren, Bloomberg Inc. and PepsiCo.

Educated exclusively in public schools, Walker was a member of the first Head Start class in 1965 and received BA, BS and JD degrees from the University of Texas at Austin. He has been included on numerous leadership lists including *Time*'s annual 100 Most Influential People, *Rolling Stone*'s 25 People Shaping the Future and the *Wall Street Journal*'s 2020 Philanthropy Innovator of the Year. He is the recipient of 16 honorary degrees, including Harvard University's W.E.B. Du Bois Medal. In 2022, he was awarded France's highest cultural honour, Chevalier des Arts et des Lettres, for leadership in the arts. In 2023, he was also appointed by Her Majesty Queen Elizabeth II to the Order of the British Empire for services to UK–US relations.

Badr Jafar: Darren, for eight years now you've been responsible for managing more than half a billion dollars in annual giving by the Ford Foundation, which is one of the largest foundations in the US. Can you tell us about the Ford Foundation and its philosophy and priorities?

Darren Walker: The Ford Foundation was founded by Henry Ford and his son Edsel Ford in 1936. Henry Ford II established a mission of the Ford Foundation to strengthen democracy, and democratic practice and institutions around the world. Today, we have a focus on inequality because we believe that inequality is harmful to democracy and that in countries where there is growing inequality there is growing hopelessness. Hope is the oxygen of democracy. Societies where there is more hope and optimism are societies where democracy can thrive and flourish. So today, we are focusing on inequality in all its forms.

I am a proponent of Andrew Carnegie's idea in his historic gospel of wealth, where he talked about generosity and charity.

But I am also inspired by the words of Dr Martin Luther King Jr, who, in 1968, said: 'Philanthropy is commendable, but it should not allow the philanthropist to overlook the economic injustice which makes philanthropy necessary.' What Dr King was saying was that yes, we must be charitable, but we must also pursue justice and dignity for every person. To do that we have to look at the systems and structures that produce inequality and make them fairer, make them systems where opportunity abounds, and that bias, prejudice and discrimination are not a barrier to people realising their aspirations and their dreams. So, we are fighting for that, supporting organisations working in the various arenas of the arts, technology and society, tackling issues of racial, ethnic and gender justice, civic engagement and the public square. These are our priority programmes.

Badr Jafar: Can you imagine a day when the foundation's support would not be necessary in a world that is free from inequalities?

Darren Walker: I do look forward to a day when there isn't a need for the Ford Foundation, but democracy is always a contested experience in a society, and so we can never take it for granted. The work of philanthropy focused on democracy is likely to be necessary and needed for many, many generations to come.

Badr Jafar: You've referred to collaboration as a strategy helping to advance the foundation's mission. Examples of true collaboration between foundations and between donors are often hard to come by, especially in parts of the world where the institutionalisation of philanthropy is less prevalent, and for cultural reasons people see philanthropy as more of a personal or individual affair. How are attitudes to collaborative philanthropy in the US evolving over time?

Darren Walker: There's no doubt that philanthropists are collaborating more because we realise that the complexity of the world requires our collective resources. There is no problem the Ford Foundation is working on that we alone can solve. The Gates Foundation alone cannot solve the challenges it is working on, even though it's the largest foundation in the world. So, we must collaborate. When we come together for the greater good, we must put our individual egos and logos aside, and allow the ideas to drive discussions about how we invest. I think that humility is required to engage in some of the big problems we're dealing with in the world today.

> "Philanthropists are collaborating more because we realise that the complexity of the world requires our collective resources."

Badr Jafar: You've launched the BUILD programme, through which the Ford Foundation pledged a billion dollars in unrestricted funding to support non-profits in developing their own infrastructure. How do you measure the impact of this contribution? Do you see a general trend from the donor community towards a greater acceptance of funding infrastructure?

Darren Walker: Investing in infrastructure is not sexy and exciting, but it's the work that must be done. It's the necessary input that provides the platforms for higher-performing and more effective philanthropy. It makes it possible for philanthropists who want to listen and learn about the best practices. I think that infrastructure is critical, and yes, it is possible to measure. There are key performance indicators for unrestricted grants. In those organisations that are making improvement, whether it be in their governance, their fundraising, their outreach or their ability to convene, there are several ways to look at progress and to measure impact. I'm a believer that we have got to invest in the infrastructure that makes it possible to develop and amplify philanthropy.

> "I'm a believer that we have got to invest in the infrastructure that makes it possible to develop and amplify philanthropy."

Badr Jafar: Some of the Ford Foundation's programmes focus on climate change, civic engagement, and gender, racial and ethnic injustice in emerging markets. From your experience working in countries like Egypt, South Africa and Indonesia, have you noticed a change in the nature and prevalence of philanthropy in these places?

Darren Walker: Absolutely, some of the most exciting nascent philanthropy is happening in these regions. For the first time, we are seeing wealth aggregated at a level where people can begin to invest in non-profits and civil society; we're also seeing policy start to encourage philanthropy. We are seeing the growth of civil society in those regions, and we're seeing philanthropists beginning to understand what giving back really means in their context. I think there is a greater awareness, there's a greater engagement, there is more philanthropic community building through programmes like the Centre for Strategic Philanthropy at Cambridge University to build a sense of shared responsibility among those who have prospered during these past few years and to engage them in the conversation of what they can do to improve their communities and their regions.

Badr Jafar: In response to the pandemic, the Ford Foundation raised a billion dollars by issuing Triple-A-rated social bonds, which enabled the foundation to double its payments to grantees. Do you see new financial instruments such as social bonds becoming an integral part of foundation toolkits? Do you see an increasing role for venture philanthropy? How do you see that pool of capital working alongside traditional philanthropic capital?

Darren Walker: There's no doubt that the social bond that we issued resonated first with the markets. It was oversubscribed by six times. It was priced very attractively as a 50-year bond. Several foundations have joined; we're now at eight or ten foundations who have issued bonds. Many more are looking at it. The alignment of venture capital and venture philanthropy with traditional grant-making is happening in real time. We're seeing endowments, investment offices and family offices begin to look at the double bottom line investing that ensures the investor receives both the financial return and the social return. Among younger investors, the children and grandchildren and those new entrepreneurs who have created their own wealth, we are absolutely seeing a concern about the ways in which their investments are used to advance a better planet and to ensure that there is greater opportunity for women. This new venture philanthropy can really impact both the markets and society more broadly.

Badr Jafar: What advice can you give to young philanthropists seeking to disrupt the status quo with new models of giving, including those seeking a much deeper connection with the impact of their giving?

Darren Walker: Mistakes have been made over the years, particularly in places like Africa, India, South Asia and other regions. We, in the US and Europe, designed initiatives that had very little input from people in those regions. I think what the next generation of philanthropists understands is the need to be proximate to the problems and the people, to listen, to bring into the design process the thinking and lived experience of people so that we don't overweight the experts with PhDs at the expense of not listening to people who are closest to the problem.

We're seeing this new generation of philanthropists who are very eager to hear, listen and internalise what they hear, and in turn understand that impact doesn't happen in a one- or two-year grant cycle. They are interested in big, challenging problems like climate change. These are monumental challenges, but I'm excited because I see so many people committing themselves and their philanthropy to solving these problems.

> "We're seeing this new generation of philanthropists who are very eager to hear, listen and internalise what they hear."

Tony O. Elumelu

Founder, Tony Elumelu Foundation

In 2010, Tony Elumelu created the Tony Elumelu Foundation, which has disbursed over US$100 million to 20,000 young African entrepreneurs across all 54 African countries, who have gone on to create over 400,000 jobs and generate an additional US$2.5 billion in revenue. The foundation's mission is inspired by Elumelu's economic philosophy of Africapitalism, which positions the private sector as the key enabler of economic and social wealth creation in Africa.

Elumelu is an African investor, philanthropist and Africapitalist. He is the founder and chairman of Heirs Holdings, an African proprietary investment company, with interests in power, oil and gas, financial services, hospitality, real estate and healthcare. He is the chairman of pan-African financial services group United Bank for Africa (UBA), which operates in 20 countries across Africa, the United Kingdom, France and the UAE, and is the only African bank with a commercial deposit-taking presence in the United States. UBA provides corporate, commercial, SME and consumer banking services to more than 40 million customers globally. He also chairs Nigeria's largest quoted conglomerate, Transcorp, whose subsidiaries include Transcorp Power, one of the leading producers of electricity in Nigeria, and Transcorp Hotels Plc, Nigeria's foremost hospitality brand.

Badr Jafar: How do you reconcile the relationship between entrepreneurship and philanthropy in your own work? To what extent do you apply traditional entrepreneurial principles to the design and implementation of your philanthropic initiatives?

Tony Elumelu: My wife and I founded the Tony Elumelu Foundation in 2010, born out of the desire and the need to catalyse entrepreneurship across Africa, to fundamentally eradicate poverty and to empower people. I have come to realise, as do my colleagues at the foundation, that the best thing you can do for mankind is to teach people how to become fishermen and not just be consumers of fish. That is at the centre of our entrepreneurship programme at the Tony Elumelu Foundation. We have a radically different view of philanthropy in Africa.

Growing up in Africa, we have seen the negative effects of poverty. The extremism we see in the world today is attributable to joblessness and poverty. My colleagues and I thought, What can we do to contribute our share in alleviating poverty in the 21st century? What can we do to refocus the conversation and shine a light on what we consider critical in lifting our people out of poverty and creating jobs? That is why we adopted the philosophy of democratising entrepreneurship across the continent and why we launched the foundation. Over time, we want to create more Tony Elumelus and more Zuckerbergs out of Africa, and it's working.

This is a new approach. Before now, the approach has been more like charity, giving money to people to help feed themselves. We think that it is more important to change the approach, and that is why what we are doing is to catalyse entrepreneurship, and a new form of giving and philanthropy on the continent. Our commitment to supporting a thousand African entrepreneurs every year is working. In addition, we have been able to engage partner development institutions to support more. Today, we work with the UNDP [United Nations Development Programme], with the African Development Bank, with the International Red Cross and with the European Union, among others, to help increase the scale and impact of this new approach, of giving people non-refundable seed capital and, more importantly, training them how to run businesses, like an MBA in three months. We're beginning to see positive outcomes of this initiative. It's a new way of giving. We're proud to say that the Tony Elumelu Foundation is Africa-funded and helping to alleviate poverty on the continent.

Badr Jafar: You are the leading proponent of a concept you introduced known as 'Africapitalism', which is focused on the role of the private sector in helping to create economic and social wealth on the African continent. In your view, is the African private sector doing enough to address social challenges? And what are the keys to getting more business stakeholders on board with this concept?

Tony Elumelu: The philosophy of Africapitalism comes from a realisation that the private sector that engages in Africa has a role to play in the development of the continent. We must not sit on our hands and wait for governments alone, or development partners, to make this happen. It's a call on everyone to invest sensibly, long-term, in key sectors of the economy that create prosperity and social good for everyone. Telling people, if you want to invest on the continent, invest in businesses that create value from within.

For example, in our group we invest in the power sector because we know what access to electricity can do for the continent. So, we're calling on others to do the same. They are beginning to respond. We are beginning to see the interest and participation of African business leaders in investing wisely in economic activities on the continent. By doing so everyone is contributing their share in creating jobs, in supporting people in the business ecosystem and the value chain. We have realised it is enlightened self-interest, to make sure that poverty is eradicated and that word is spread as much as possible. This will support our own businesses and will create new markets.

My charge to the African private sector is, as you do well, make sure you carry your community, people and ecosystem along so that progressively we all contribute to developing the continent. We're beginning to see private-sector leaders not just happy to develop the economy by their investments but also beginning to commit resources in a strategic fashion to create more entrepreneurs. We have seen a few of them come to us and say, How can we support what the Tony Elumelu Foundation is doing? We like the idea of promoting entrepreneurship on the continent.

Some commit themselves directly or, through their staff, they commit to mentoring some of these young Africans, because it is not just about capital, young entrepreneurs need training, mentoring, exposure, business support and patronage.

So, we are beginning to see an integrated ecosystem. We are beginning to see African private-sector leaders changing their approach. And it is a new kind of philanthropy which is catalytic, empowering people to do more for themselves, because that is how we can eradicate poverty, create jobs and make Africa rise.

> "It is a new kind of philanthropy which is catalytic, empowering people to do more for themselves, because that is how we can eradicate poverty, create jobs and make Africa rise."

I think Africa and the Middle East share similar characteristics. The private sector has a role to play in Africa and the Middle East in making sure that we drive the economic development of our continent. What I am beginning to observe is that the global development partners are waiting to see people show interest, and they support them. I announced a €20 million partnership with the EU to support about 2,400 young African women in entrepreneurship through the Tony Elumelu Foundation. The International Red Cross supports about 1,000. UNDP and the foundation have a partnership to empower 100,000 youths in Africa, particularly from the Sahel region, because extremism, as I said earlier, is a derivative of poverty. The young people feel left out of the major economic opportunities around. So, we want to reintegrate them. I am happy African private-sector leaders are stepping forward, and that the development partners across the world are also showing interest in this area.

This is how all of us, working together, can help to develop Africa in a sustainable and truly transformative and lasting manner into the 21st century.

Badr Jafar: Do you think that the pandemic is likely to have a lasting impact on how people will think about the role of private philanthropy in responding to global challenges?

Tony Elumelu: I think the pandemic presents an opportunity for us to reset as individuals, as countries and as economies. In Nigeria, in March 2020, when it all started, through our institutions, we committed US$14 million by way of financial assistance to the Nigerian government and to governments where we do business in 20 African countries. This is private-sector involvement in helping to provide solutions to the poor. More importantly, in Nigeria, we created CA-COVID, the Corporate Alliance for COVID-19, which consists of top Nigerian private-sector leaders. CA-COVID has helped with many issues: obtaining testing kits; food security; building isolation centres; and so many other things. It is a realisation now that there should be partnership between government and the private sector with a common goal for the betterment of society, a realisation that economic development is critical. Economic development and poverty alleviation is critical for us to say that we've achieved wellbeing for our people.

I see more collaboration, and the private sector is also realising that we cannot keep relying on or waiting for governments to lead. That, again, validates my philosophy of Africapitalism, that we all must step forward and play a role. In fact, COVID-19 has reminded us all to focus on humanity and to deal with the issue of unilateralism. When this thing started in China, some people called it the 'China flu'. Today it is affecting all of us. It is a call for serious reflection; it is a call for us to reset. I think that is happening and the private sector is working on the issue of vaccine availability to make sure that the vaccine gets to every part of the globe in record time so that everyone is safe. There is no issue of self-centredness. Any infection in any part of the world can be transmitted to everyone in the world. It goes to buttress what I have always said: that poverty is a threat to all of us everywhere. And so, we will begin to realise that we need to live and work together.

Badr Jafar: What issues do you think that strategic philanthropists and the next generation of philanthropists and impact entrepreneurs should be focusing their energies on in the years to come?

Tony Elumelu: First, we need to prioritise entrepreneurship, especially among the young ones. And second, we all need to advocate for a better operating environment. If you practise entrepreneurship, through seed capital, training and access to bigger capital, you need to create the right platform for them, like we did through TEFConnect, which is a digital platform that brings over a million young African entrepreneurs together to

> "If you practise entrepreneurship, through seed capital, training and access to bigger capital, you need to create the right platform for them."

create an ecosystem that helps them to discover, to sell, to interact and to meet future partners and collaborators. We also need to create the enabling business environment that allows this entrepreneur to succeed, because if they don't succeed, we all would have wasted our time.

My call on philanthropists globally, and especially in Africa, and to development partners who want to genuinely help Africa to develop and become self-reliant, is to prioritise entrepreneurship among our young ones, because the future belongs to them. We need to give them economic hope and opportunities so that they shun extremism and migration and focus on the opportunity they see among themselves. If we do that, and create the right environment for them to succeed, then the world will be a better place for all of us.

Badr Jafar: Your foundation already works closely with a few international partners, including the UNDP and the African Development Bank. What is the best way for individuals and organisations to collaborate with your foundation? What is your outlook for collaboration in general between philanthropists to boost impact? Do you think this is an increasing trend?

Tony Elumelu: I think it is increasing. People are beginning to realise that it's not just about self alone. It is more about impact, scale and the number of people we are able to touch. There are many models today. We look at Warren Buffett providing money for the Gates Foundation to help propagate and support them in what they are doing. Similar things should happen in this part of the world. I am beginning to see a new crop of private sector leaders now who are informed and educated, who look at the big picture and who believe in collaboration and partnership. I see us doing more but there is room for us all to do a lot more.

We want to economically empower young men and women. We want to make sure that women are prioritised more than they've been before. We want to make sure that joblessness is ended and that people have economic hope. How they have it, whether through the Tony Elumelu Foundation or not, is irrelevant. Today on the TEFConnect platform, we train over 1.5 million people. You have a business idea and you want to be trained, come on the platform, and we're happy to train you. What is important to us is that we impact humanity at scale. That is the only assured path to poverty alleviation and eradication of joblessness on our continent.

THREE
PHILANTHROPY AND THE POLYCRISIS

Global philanthropy today is profoundly affected by the urgency of the overlapping systemic global crises we now face – what many are calling a 'polycrisis'. This can be described as any combination of three or more interacting systemic risks with the potential to cause a cascading, runaway failure of Earth's natural and social systems that irreversibly and catastrophically degrades humanity's prospects.[1]

These systemic crises have their origin in environmental, social, economic and technological contexts. Environmental pressures are exemplified by the extreme heat, wildfires and floods across the world, along with longer-term concerns about the impact of climate change on the ice at the poles, on biodiversity, on agriculture, water and the oceans. Social pressures arise from war, conflict, migration, humanitarian catastrophes, inequality and racism. Economic pressures are typified by inflation, global debt overhangs, unsustainable growth and inequality of opportunity across the world. And technological pressures come from the uncontrolled development of artificial intelligence, cyber terrorism and big data threats to privacy, among other things. These pressures, experienced simultaneously, create enormous complexity and uncertainty about the future.

What can philanthropy do when it is confronted with these situations of overlapping crises? The challenge for leaders in all sectors is to figure out how to achieve sustainability of planetary resources while upholding equity and access to opportunity for all. They must do so collaboratively because the crises they face are so complex. These collaborative models are not common-place. In many regions of the world, major trust gaps exist between governments and the social sector or civil society more broadly. In the wake of the COVID-19 pandemic, however, we witnessed numerous encouraging examples of much more delib-erate cooperation between sectors. Many societies, particularly within emerging economies, are still managing the after-effects of the pandemic, including economic disruptions. Cross-sectoral collaboration and partnerships are ever more important. Philan-thropy cannot act alone but must look to governments at all levels, and to corporate and civil society leaders, to act effectively on these cross-border and cross-domain crises.

In late 2020, while the COVID-19 pandemic was still expand-ing across the world, I spoke with the leaders of major multilat-eral development institutions such as the International Monetary Fund, as well as the leaders of global humanitarian organisations like the International Red Cross and the International Rescue Committee, to get their views on the complex and intercon-nected challenges of climate change, economic disruption, humanitarian catastrophes and growing inequality, accelerated in many cases by the pandemic. I asked each of them about the opportunities that they see in the global system to recover and build a better future. I asked them to tell me where they saw possibilities for cooperation between their organisations and philanthropic donors, and what advice they might give to promote that collaboration. They were all optimistic that human will, ingenuity and generosity could be brought to bear to over-come the multiple crises that we face. They spoke of the pandem-ic's lessons about the need to build more resilience in our societies. They were unanimous in their belief that philanthropy, particularly in emerging economies and regions, would play a significant role in the recovery by bringing to the table its unique assets of risk tolerance, innovation and speed of action.

Kristalina Georgieva*

Managing Director, International Monetary Fund

Kristalina Georgieva has served as Managing Director of the International Monetary Fund since 1 October 2019, and oversees US$1 trillion in lending capacity and a staff of over 2,700 professionals from more than 150 countries. Born and raised in Bulgaria, she is the first managing director to hail from an emerging market economy, a key focus area for the IMF.

Before joining the IMF, she was CEO of the World Bank from January 2017 to September 2019, during which time she also served as Interim President of the World Bank Group for three months. Georgieva joined the World Bank as an environmental economist in 1993. After serving for 17 years in many senior positions, she was appointed Vice President and Corporate Secretary in 2008. In this role, she served as the interlocutor between the World Bank Group's senior management, its board of directors and its shareholder countries.

Previously, Georgieva helped shape the agenda of the European Union while serving as European Commission Vice President for Budget and Human Resources. Before that, she was Commissioner for International Cooperation, Humanitarian Aid and Crisis Response, managing one of the world's largest humanitarian aid budgets.

Georgieva has served on many international panels, including as co-chair of the Global Commission on Adaptation, and as co-chair of the United Nations Secretary-General's High-Level

---

* Transcript based on an interview from 2020. © International Monetary Fund. Reused with permission. The views expressed here are those of the author and should not be attributed to any other organisation or entity.

Panel on Humanitarian Financing. She has authored or co-authored over 100 publications on environmental and economic policy.

Badr Jafar: The fastest-growing economies in the world are in emerging markets, and trillions of dollars of new wealth is being generated within these economies, including across parts of Africa, the Middle East and developing Asia. How is the growth of these emerging markets impacting the nature and scale of your work at the IMF? What broader social and economic effects could this have?

Kristalina Georgieva: Let me start with the very good news of the past decades. We have seen dynamism in emerging markets and developing economies, shortening their distance from advanced economies and their growth in terms of income per capita, opportunities for people's standard of living and life expectancy. We have benefited globally from the push these economies have given to growth. It translates into a massive reduction in poverty, the creation of new opportunities for innovation and for bringing the diversity of experience from these countries for their own populations so the whole world can benefit. We have seen leapfrogging on a massive scale. Just to take one example, in many countries in the developing world, such as Kenya, the step into digital transactions jumped over the traditional brick-and-mortar banking system to the point that they now have more digital accounts than people.

When we look at the moment we live in, and the future and how that is reflected in the work of the IMF, we get to the not-so-good news. This trend of convergence has been severely impacted by COVID-19 and the economic crisis it triggered. Advanced economies are doing whatever it takes to protect their economies and protect their people. They have injected 20% of GDP into fiscal and monetary policy stimulus. In emerging markets, it is three times less. We are very concerned that poverty is going up, as well as inequality of income and of opportunity. Gender inequality is trending in the wrong direction. Scarring conditions in emerging markets could be significant unless we act.

This brings me to the IMF. We have seen an increase in the space occupied by emerging markets at the organisation, which is also very visible in the policy issues we are engaged in. The IMF is there for all members. Let's remember that we played an important role in the euro area crisis. But we are concentrating mostly on supporting emerging markets and developing economies to adopt strong macroeconomic policy frameworks, to clear space for private-sector-led growth, and to improve living standards.

The pandemic taught us a very simple lesson. Economies that invested in building strong fundamentals withstood the shock much better, just as people with strong immune systems withstand the virus better. In other words, our investment in emerging markets policies pays off when action is taken appropriately. Looking to the future, the IMF will continue to strongly support emerging markets with policy advice and with financing, and by engaging so that they learn from each other faster. In this crisis, we have provided over US$100 billion in support for emerging markets and developing economies. My hope is that we will come out on the other side with more dynamic, more competitive, greener and fairer economies, and that emerging markets will leapfrog into a better future for their people.

Badr Jafar: You co-chaired the UN Secretary-General's High-Level Panel on Humanitarian Financing, which was formed to address the urgent need to improve both the quantity and quality of humanitarian aid. Has COVID-19 set us back in our efforts to meet the humanitarian funding gap as well as the UN Sustainable Development Goals by 2030? What do you think the long-term implications of the pandemic are likely to be?

Kristalina Georgieva: The pandemic created a crisis like no other, and it is the most vulnerable people who are most dramatically hit. What we see is that despite a significant increase of almost 50% in humanitarian financing from 2015 until today, the gap between needs and funding has grown almost by that much as well. Why this setback? Because we failed to shrink the needs before the pandemic.

But it doesn't mean we have to stay there. We observe two positive trends. One, in the 2016 report of the High-Level Panel on Humanitarian Financing, 'Too Important to Fail', we recommended bridging the divide between humanitarian and development work. And we see this happening quite effectively, both at the conceptual and institutional collaboration levels – but, most importantly, in the field. And two, we see sources of financing, including philanthropic contributions, growing quite significantly. What we are not yet seeing is recognition that we are living in a more shock-prone world and that we ought to build resilience to shocks to come. This means resilient people who are educated, healthy and who have social protection should the shock occur. We must build a resilient planet, and we must turn the page on how we think of our ecosystems that support life on Earth.

> "We must build a resilient planet, and we must turn the page on how we think of our ecosystems that support life on Earth."

We must continue to build the resilience of our financial systems and of our economies. That requires commitment and leadership. So, my call is for us all as one community of people to recognise that the main recommendation of our 2016 report – 'Shrink the Needs' – can only happen with this determination for resilience. Otherwise, people will suffer, and the SDGs will remain, for many, just a dream. That ought not to be the case. Every crisis is also a tremendous opportunity for change. I think the very best we can do in this crisis is to embrace this opportunity.

Badr Jafar: When most people think about the IMF, they think about loans. They tend to be soft loans with concessionary interest rates, but they're still loans. To what extent would

you like to see more corporate or philanthropic intervention in helping to build the resilience you've been talking about?

Kristalina Georgieva: The IMF is the world's first responder in times of financial distress. In the pandemic crisis, for example, we came forcefully with financial lifelines for countries that had no access to financial markets. Because of the massive injection of liquidity, most emerging markets were able to return and borrow at fairly low rates. But not all. Emerging markets, with weak fundamentals or high debt levels, and low-income countries had no place to go.

The IMF for these countries is the most important, fast-disbursing, reliable source of support. We have provided support to 83 countries, and for 78 of them that was emergency financing, coming within days of requests: hundreds of millions of dollars in two or three weeks. Sometimes over a billion would be disbursed. I heard from many leaders in these countries that if we hadn't been there, it would have been collapse for their economies, virtually a matter of life and death. I'm proud to say the staff of the IMF stepped up to these challenges. We did what was necessary.

We do not provide grants. But we do have one exception, it is to help our poorest members in a moment of dramatic crisis with debt relief. So, they don't have to pay us when their economies are in deep trouble because of exogenous shocks – not because of a fault of their own, but other shocks whether a hurricane or a pandemic. Right now, we provide this debt relief to 29 of our members, our poorest members. And that translates into US$500 million available to them to spend on their doctors and nurses and their most vulnerable people.

Badr Jafar: Does the IMF regularly engage in blended financing or look to partner in other ways with private philanthropists? What outlook do you see in general for cross-sectoral collaboration in the space?

Kristalina Georgieva: When we work with others, it is not in blended financing; we don't do that. The World Bank does it; the

IMF doesn't. The way we work with others is by working with countries on a credible economic and social development plan that facilitates private-sector trust in the policies of the country and therefore boosts investments from the private sector. And it allows other partners, bilateral donors, multilateral organisations and philanthropists to put money behind this plan because they trust that once it has the IMF stamp of approval, it means the country is on the right track. I come from an emerging market economy. I know the difference between bad policies and the cost they impose, and good policies and the opportunities they provide. This is what the IMF does; it creates opportunities for countries.

Badr Jafar: Over the past few years, there seems to have been mainstream awakening to rethink the role of business in a more holistic fashion. What else should business leaders be doing to help to address some of our world's greatest challenges, whether on their own or in collaboration with others?

Kristalina Georgieva: The private sector is doing a very important job by creating opportunities for growth, employment and improvements in living standards. Doing so helps countries do better. But it can do so much more. Let me give you my three thoughts about where the private sector could act.

One, the private sector has a huge role to play in embracing environmental and social sustainability and good governance. Many leaders in the private sector have recognised that they cannot have financial success if societies are failing, and I wholeheartedly endorse that recognition. What I am hoping to see in the coming years is the private sector stewarding multi-stakeholder platforms for their own growth. Some of it is happening, but not enough, not fast enough, nor far enough. Second, I dream of a private sector that recognises that during rapid change, some benefit much more than others. In this crisis, who are the big beneficiaries? Digital companies, tech companies, and people like you and me, who can work remotely as well as the highly educated are doing well. Who is doing poorly? Low-skilled workers, women, young people, the list goes on. How can we take to heart the responsibility to prevent what is so worrying, a K-shaped recovery? One part doing great, and another one falling off a cliff. How can we get the upper end of the K to take responsibility to prevent the lower side from slipping down? This is a hugely important matter. It is also a fiscal issue. How can we have taxation that is more progressive, recognising that unless we do so we are going to damage the social fabric on which the success of the private sector ultimately depends?

My third hope for the private sector is to recognise what is going to be coming down the road: higher debts and higher deficits. In many developing economies, that burden is going to be so heavy that some form of debt reprofiling and, in some cases, debt restructuring will be necessary. And the private sector should think of it as mutual benefit. Act early so we have a chance to prevent the problem from becoming an obstacle to growth. So, three things: embrace environmental and social sustainability, and good governance; recognise that we need more sharing for a fair society; and specifically, we must recognise that we are faced with the problem of debt. We can only solve these issues by working together, and the private sector has a role to play.

Badr Jafar: You represent a very large institution that's been a key pillar of the global system for the past 75 years. To what extent can we solve the world's problems in an environment where people seem to be losing their faith in institutions? And what can be done to reverse some of these trends?

Kristalina Georgieva: There is no way to solve these problems on our own. We are in this together. The pandemic clearly demonstrated that we are as strong as our weakest link. We are on a long ascent, climbing and connected by a single rope. And there is no way but to be united faced with the challenges ahead of us – climate change being the most dramatic, and inequality as well.

"There is no way to solve these problems on our own. We are in this together."

Let's also remember that because we built cooperation, we are not in a great depression today. If you look at history, we built the ability to act in a synchronised manner. Because we have the IMF, we have the G20; we have different fora for central bank governors or finance ministers to come together, and action was swift. Instead of massive bankruptcies, and catastrophic unemployment, we are going through a tough time, but we are not seeing an economic collapse. There is no depression. So, we should value what we have, but recognise that over the past decades we have seen inequalities growing. We have seen a bit of complacency about the cost of globalisation for some segments of our society. Yes, the benefits are obvious, but they're not shared by everyone. And unless we zero in on solving these problems, those who feel disfranchised and who face a lack of opportunities – thus seeing no hope for their future – will easily fall prey to populism, to polarisation within societies. We cannot allow this to happen to our children. We must be honest about the problems we have, such as inequality, growth that is unsustainable, divergence across countries, and then muster the will to work together to solve these problems. We have no choice but to do that if we are to succeed.

Badr Jafar: No conversation these days can be considered complete without referring to our youth. What general advice or guidance might you provide to those young people considering careers in the social sector?

Kristalina Georgieva: Do your best to help others. I have had many opportunities to do interesting things in my life, but being commissioner for humanitarian aid, having a front-row seat to observe the most dramatic, devastating situations on this planet, witnessing people suffering through no fault of their own, and being able to help; these are the very best experiences of my life and have made me a better person. It is often said, but nevertheless true: giving is receiving, the greatest gift you can give to yourself.

Filippo Grandi

UN High Commissioner for Refugees

Filippo Grandi is the 11th United Nations High Commissioner for Refugees. He was first elected by the UN General Assembly in January 2016 for a five-year term. The General Assembly has re-elected him to a second term to serve until December 2025.

As United Nations High Commissioner for Refugees (UNHCR), he heads the UN Refugee Agency leading the international response to refugee crises around the world, working with governments to ensure that refugees have access to protection and support, and helping find solutions to displacement and statelessness.

Before being elected High Commissioner, Grandi was engaged in international cooperation for over 30 years, focusing on refugee and humanitarian work. He served as Commissioner-General of the UN Relief and Works Agency for Palestine Refugees, UNRWA, from 2010 to 2014, after having been Deputy Commissioner-General since 2005.

Prior to that, Grandi served as Deputy Special Representative of the UN Secretary-General in Afghanistan, following a long career first with NGOs and later with UNHCR in Africa, Asia, the Middle East and at the organisation's Geneva headquarters.

Badr Jafar: Can you give us a sense of the current state of the humanitarian sector in terms of global needs and shortfalls in funding as well as the impact of COVID-19 on the sector and the world's most vulnerable?

Filippo Grandi: Clearly, we're not meeting all the basic needs that we in the humanitarian community assess every year. There are many humanitarian crises. My organisation deals with refugees, with displaced people and with stateless people. But there are other humanitarian problems, hunger, issues affecting children and problems generated by the climate emergency.

Unfortunately, with conflicts that never get resolved, and with the multiplication of global problems like climate change, poverty, inequality and a huge global pandemic, the spiralling of needs is not matched by an equal amount of resources pledged. Let's make no mistake, the humanitarian community mobilises billions every year and this has been growing steadily from governments and the public sector, which still provide most of the funding. However, most of the humanitarian work is not funded through quotas like peacekeeping or the political work of the UN, it is funded through voluntary commitments. States can decide one year to give us money, and the next year not to. To meet the deficit, we have seen growing contributions from other sources, including private philanthropy.

Let me give you an example, translating it in UNHCR terms. We have a yearly budget. The totality of needs for 80 million refugees and displaced people, and up to 10 million stateless people, is between US$8 and US$9 billion. We collect about half of that, between 50% and 60%, when we're lucky. Of that, about 12% to 13% is from individuals, companies, foundations, non-government sources, essentially private philanthropy in a very broad sense. This year, for the first time we will reach half a billion dollars in this type of contribution. It is still small compared with the public contributions, but when I was a much younger official in the UNHCR 15 or 20 years ago we were lucky if we collected US$20 million from private sources. So, it has really multiplied. This is very positive, but much more needs to be done to meet the totality of needs.

Badr Jafar: I'm perplexed that the funding gap exists in the first place. Many hundreds of billions, if not trillions of dollars in philanthropic capital are disbursed every year, in addition to the large amounts of government aid, and increasingly from a socially conscious business community. But we're still unable to come up with the few billion dollars to plug the gap to help the world's most vulnerable. So, what's going on?

Filippo Grandi: I must add to your concern. UNHCR funding results on average are on the high side compared with other organisations and compared with the totality of needs. It is difficult to meet these large targets, but at the same time we are only talking about a tiny percentage of the world's resources, as the total GDP of the world is in the tens of trillions. More can certainly be done. But I do appreciate that there is a certain fatigue, partly because these crises do not get resolved with money. Money serves the immediate needs or consequences of conflict or climate change, but we must address the root causes. And there we are failing, which is not encouraging. Philanthropy needs to see a way forward. My appeal to philanthropists is to help us in that direction.

To answer your question, I want to say something that for me is fundamental, and which I have really understood much better recently. In the past, we humanitarians would go to philanthropic donors to ask for a charitable gesture of money. This is normal and it's very generous. Solidarity is still the foundation of humanitarian work. But many philanthropic partners don't stop at giving. They want to be partners in making progress, making interventions more sustainable and moving towards solutions.

> "Many philanthropic partners don't stop at giving. They want to be partners in making progress, making interventions more sustainable and moving towards solutions."

We've made incredible progress, especially in the private sector, with a few partners who say, 'Okay, we'll give you US$10 million. But let's work together towards a better business model. Or, let's choose what investments to make, so that we can also reassure our stakeholders that the money is not simply a donation, but contributes to solving problems and gives an opportunity to the beneficiaries to move towards a solution.'

I would never want to criticise pure charity. I think it has a fundamentally important value. But we know now that we need to create real partnerships between public organisations and the private sector. There's so much that philanthropists can do to help us improve the way we work.

Badr Jafar: The fastest-growing economies of the world are in emerging markets. A new generation of strategic philanthropists is beginning to emerge across Africa, the Middle East and developing Asia. The nature of humanitarian crises has also changed significantly in the past few decades. How can organisations like the UNHCR help this rising community of philanthropists navigate these complexities, especially when many might be reticent to engage in situations of conflict or where they may not see more immediate resolutions?

Filippo Grandi: There is no conflict between altruism and strategic partnership. They're both part of the same cooperation. I can give you many examples. Let's take the Rohingya refugee crisis when Rohingya refugees from Myanmar fled to Bangladesh, especially in 2017, and now almost a million people are in a very poor area of Bangladesh dependent on humanitarian assistance. I remember visiting just after the exodus. It was terrible to see the trauma, the pain, the suffering and the difficult conditions. Who were the first responders? The local community, with a bit of money, who felt compassion for these people coming from the other side of the borders and who helped them. This happens in so many humanitarian crises where the first philanthropy is from community to community.

We are trying in many places to evolve that into sensitising the local business community. In all these countries, there is a thriving business community that can do a lot to help. I'll give you another anecdote. The Venezuela crisis is a big humanitarian problem, with many Venezuelans fleeing to neighbouring countries. I went to Brazil and organised a meeting with the important business community in São Paulo to help them to understand the global mechanisms of philanthropy. When I spoke to them, the business leaders were more interested in knowing how they could help Venezuelans in Brazil. They wanted to employ them or donate money to help them either directly or through NGOs. Then, I understood that the ideal starting point is working with local business communities, in situations that they understand with more immediacy and perhaps even better than us, and for which they have opportunities to help, and not just with money. Employing people is as valuable as giving money, because you give them a more sustainable form of support.

So, can we be ambitious and bring the private sector, the philanthropists in emerging economies, to the global scene? I think the answer is yes. I started from the community level, then moved to business communities interested in local humanitarian issues and helped them step up to a global level. We see this in Gulf countries clearly where the outlook is more global than in other places. And we see it elsewhere. I remember a trip to South Africa and meeting representatives from the business community in Johannesburg, and they told me, you tell us how it works, the humanitarian dynamics, we tell you what to do in Africa, we know it better than you. It was so true. They had such great ideas. This marriage between global and local is where there is a great space and future potential for philanthropy in emerging economies.

> "This marriage between global and local is where there is a great space and future potential for philanthropy in emerging economies."

Badr Jafar: One of the key trends being encouraged within philanthropy is pursuing collaborative models that achieve a multiplier effect on impact. How would you rate the current state of collaboration within the humanitarian sector? Is there such a thing as healthy competition when it comes to this sort of work?

Filippo Grandi: There is no doubt. For the private sector, for businesses, fulfilling an element of social responsibility is a positive badge that improves their image while doing a good thing. I think that this is very healthy. I am pragmatic in this matter. We know business has to work in a competitive market. If acting in a socially responsible way allows them to look better than another company, why not? I will certainly go to the other company and tell them about it to stimulate healthy competition.

We need, of course, to remain ethical. We are always conducting due diligence on companies to make sure that their practices do not contravene the fundamental ethics of humanitarian work. But given those parameters, I think competition is good. And how do I rate that partnership? Partnership is the key word, working together as opposed to simply giving. We need to explore even further what businesses can do in this area. There are so many areas and fields in which we work together already, and technology is a great accelerator for knowledge sharing. For example, we have a great project with Vodafone in several African countries to improve connectivity in remote schools that host refugees. It's very successful and we're expanding. We also collaborating with IKEA in Ethiopia on a community development project where refugees and local people work together on sustainable energy, economic self-reliance and agriculture, as well as on education and health. The government has noticed it and is using it as a model for other areas because the IKEA Foundation came not only with money, but with a different business model, which translated from the private sector into the public sector. We listened to proposals from businesses or individual philanthropists because we are open to suggestions and know we don't have all the answers. We've adopted them and we've made great progress. Now, in Asia, we work with companies to boost employment for refugees, working with companies that agree to employ a small quota of refugees. It is these kinds of new approaches that are crucial to philanthropic progress.

Achim Steiner

Administrator, United Nations Development Programme (UNDP)

Achim Steiner became UNDP Administrator in June 2017 and was reconfirmed by the United Nations General Assembly for a second term to serve until June 2025. The UNDP has a presence in 177 countries, and is primarily focused on the eradication of poverty, supporting human development and advancing the UN Sustainable Development Goals. Steiner is also the vice-chair of the UN Sustainable Development Group, which unites 40 entities of the UN system that work to support sustainable development.

Steiner has served across the United Nations system, looking at global challenges from both a humanitarian and a development perspective. He led the United Nations Environment Programme from 2006 to 2016, helping governments invest in clean technologies and renewable energy. He was also Director-General of the United Nations Office at Nairobi.

Prior to joining UNDP, he was Director of the Oxford Martin School (a research institute which cuts across disciplines to find solutions to the world's most urgent challenges) and Professorial Fellow of Balliol College, University of Oxford.

Over nearly three decades, Steiner has been a global leader on sustainable development, climate resilience and international cooperation. He has worked tirelessly to champion sustainability, economic growth and equality for the vulnerable.

Badr Jafar: I'd like to start by asking you from where you currently stand, how far back does the social and economic disruption caused around the world by the pandemic put us in our efforts to meet the UN Sustainable Development Goals by 2030?

Achim Steiner: The simple answer to your question is, it's a major setback, potentially of generational proportions, because it is not only a downturn in our economies, but also literally eroding social capital. The recovery from the pandemic's effects has been partial, incomplete and unequal. In 2023, rich countries are experiencing record-high levels of human development while half of the world's poorest countries remain below their pre-pandemic level of progress as measured by our Human Development Index [HDI]. As a result, inequality in the HDI between the countries at the top and the countries at the bottom is widening after two decades of progress in closing divides. In addition, we're facing an increase in feelings of distress and insecurity across the world, stoking polarisation within and across countries. When polarisation festers, it becomes harder to mobilise collective action to address shared global problems – like a pandemic. So, from that point of view, we are facing a major setback. But out of every downturn comes a moment and an opportunity to recover, to rebuild. I think the great challenge will be how we are able to shape that recovery process from here onwards.

Badr Jafar: What do you think are the longer-term implications of the pandemic? Will we be able to reset our priorities vis-à-vis societal development and environmental resilience?

Achim Steiner: In the current situation, we have seen people talking and referring to a future that is going to be different, building forward better. These are many different narratives that are playing out in societies across the world. They point to the fact that what COVID-19 has done is to reveal a great deal of what is not right. The so-called underlying conditions are vulnerability and lack of resilience, but also inequality and unsustainability. These conditions are clearly moving into the centre of our attention. We're just beginning to see how this will drive change. Trillions are going to be invested in managing and stabilising the crisis, and they will have an impact.

I would say to some who state that the Sustainable Development Goals are no longer achievable in the current crisis that maybe the opposite is true. We will see people, communities and societies prioritise differently, invest in different futures and therefore create extraordinary opportunity. By 2030, we may find ourselves close to realising the targets we set for ourselves in the 2015 Paris Climate Agreement. Look at the Green Deal in Europe, look at Canada, look at China, look at many countries that are trying to mobilise significant investments in a transformative agenda. It's difficult to predict, but the one prediction that is clear is that things will be different out of this crisis, and in many respects things could be better.

Badr Jafar: How do you see the role of private philanthropic capital in helping to address the world's long-term social and economic and environmental challenges? What are the keys to creating successful collaborations between philanthropy and international NGOs engaged in development and humanitarian work?

Achim Steiner: In this unprecedented crisis, philanthropy has been enormously important not only in the volume of finance that it has provided, but also in its agility, its ability to connect to communities, to pioneers, to innovation. I want to particularly pick up on the last two, because clearly, in a crisis of this magnitude, we have all turned back to the state and public budgets to achieve the kind of scale in stabilising the situation that is needed. But at the same time, in moving forward, what we need is a great deal of innovation and rethinking. I think philanthropy always has the advantage that it can be far more targeted and far more agile. It can take more risks, it can also connect to non-mainstream actors whose ideas, technologies and business platforms could be tomorrow's economy. Therein lies the first opportunity.

"Philanthropy has been enormously important not only in the volume of finance that it has provided, but also in its agility, its ability to connect to communities, to pioneers, to innovation."

We have a humanitarian moment in looking after the people who are most vulnerable in our communities, and there we see philanthropy doing an enormous amount of good. But I would argue equally that strategic philanthropy needs to look at the future of development, and then extrapolate back to what we can invest in now, to make this new set of futures possible. In 2018, the UNDP established accelerator labs in 60 countries as a deliberate injection of skill sets into our organisation and to better study innovation in the countries in which we work, exploring ways to support governments and entrepreneurs, as well as scaling up start-ups.

There is an opportunity for collaboration between philanthropic investors, and institutions such as UNDP, or public institutions in the country that have the capacity to take things to scale, and to link to public policy. Philanthropy often struggles in taking the ingenuity of what they have experimented with into a broader public policy arena. At the end of the day, public policy can prevent or accelerate innovation. It is at that interface that I see a particularly interesting arena for us as UNDP, working in 170 countries, connecting to that sea of philanthropy and philanthropic investments in innovation, and new possibilities. I would hope that we will see a great deal more of that interface, not least because together we can also mobilise the private sector more effectively.

Since my arrival in UNDP, I've invested a significant amount of energy in trying to understand how we can help to attract more private capital into the public good outcomes that the SDGs represent. We have developed SDG impact guidance and norms for bonds and equities. We are beginning to see financial markets investing in that kind of hybrid future investment proposition that for far too long had not worked well.

Badr Jafar: On the topic of that interface, and engagement of private sector, are you witnessing an increase in the use of blended finance in economic development projects?

Achim Steiner: We have seen a broadening of the outlook of where investments are likely to grow in the financial markets, such as new investment markets and new technologies. Take climate change, for instance. In terms of renewable energy, technology and infrastructure, it's a US$300 billion economy that started 10 to 15 years ago from virtually nowhere. We are seeing the whole automotive sector transforming itself, not in a generation, but in a period of just a decade and a half. Electric mobility is beginning to become a driver in terms of technology innovation, but also of the markets. Energy, mobility, agriculture and land use are the major drivers of a rapidly shifting set of imperatives to act differently, but also opportunities to invest.

We are seeing massive possibilities. For instance, countries are now raising public bonds on the financial markets. Mexico raised over €860 million in Europe for an SDG bond that UNDP also accompanied, and it was oversubscribed three or four times. So, the financial markets clearly see an opportunity from an investment perspective. The risks of not investing in transformation are also becoming ever more present. The costs are transcending narrow sectors. National economies, and the major corporations in the financial markets, are clearly sensing that there is a need to invest in a different future pathway.

"National economies, and the major corporations in the financial markets, are clearly sensing that there is a need to invest in a different future pathway."

We have fiscal policy, we have subsidies, but we also have regulations for markets, we can incentivise, we can reward investments in the future, and make the true costs of hanging on to legacy economies and technologies more expensive. That is what we have done for the better part of the past 100 years. It's what has driven innovation, new markets and economic growth for decades. I think this is a moment in which we will see a great deal more of that. And it is where UNDP really focuses its attention, when it advises governments, helps them to analyse where very constrained fiscal space can still be leveraged with private sector funding at national level.

Badr Jafar: A few years ago, you co-chaired the UN's Task Force on Digital Financing of Sustainable Development Goals. What did you identify as opportunities to deploy best in class technology to enhance financing mechanisms around the global goals? How can we use tech to better engage the community of givers?

Achim Steiner: Just postulate that digitalisation will change virtually everything in our economic and personal lives, but also in creating new opportunities and new markets. I led, together with Maria Ramos, the former CEO of Absa Bank from South Africa, the taskforce on digital financial technologies and the SDGs. It was an eye-opener. We had an extraordinary group of taskforce members from the frontiers of the technology sector, the finance sector and the public regulatory sector, who took a deep look at what was unfolding already and the implications for the future. The report *People's Money: Harnessing Digitalization to Finance a Sustainable Future* is available on the web for those who want to look deeper. Connecting people is one thing that digital does in an extraordinary way. You're able to connect somebody who is giving with somebody who is receiving and do so transparently. You're allowing people to aggregate. For instance, in Bangladesh, we believe that millions of micro investors or savers, literally with just US$10, US$20 or US$30, can join now. And governments can borrow in the domestic financial market rather than having to go outside the country for mega national infrastructure projects. This used to be very expensive and very difficult to do.

We see it happening in more and more countries. Kenya has opened the ability of citizens to buy into public bonds and, therefore, you have millions of people who can come together. Perhaps the most powerful and vital part of fintech, as it is evolving, is going to centre around not the technology-led advancement but the human creativity that we are seeing emerge. Inclusion is going to be critical. Certainly, fintech in the early years has been phenomenal. We have hundreds of millions of people today who can participate for the first time in our financial system. They were excluded in the past by virtue of having no passport or having no address, no credit rating or record, and therefore unable to open an account. Today, we have ubiquitous examples of people borrowing through their smartphone in the morning, money to buy produce, to then take to market, sell and repay the loan by the evening. It is an extraordinary opportunity.

I think we will also see much more engaged public investment discussions. People can have an idea of how their pension funds are being invested and how their savings are being invested, because much of the past 30 to 40 years has seen an extraordinary disintermediation between those who own the money and those who invest it. Pensions and savings and virtually all the money in the world belong to people, not the institutions that manage it for us. And yet people were essentially left out of that decision-making realm. They were takers, rather than shapers of their investment decisions. That's not to say that we will not need professional advice. But transparency in the market, the opportunity to choose different things that you can invest in, the increasing enthusiasm for seeing your money earn a return while also doing something good with it, is growing exponentially. Every financial institution confirms that. So fintech and digitalisation are going to change not only the world of finance but will fundamentally reshape the future of development.

Now we need to figure out how to incentivise, regulate and engage the public, so that this is a financial ecosystem where people are able to participate by having access to digital connectivity, and be empowered to be decision-makers about their money. That is going to be a very interesting process. In the larger context of development, finance is going to change significantly, and it is why in UNDP we have invested over the past few years in understanding the future of digital and the way that it will shape the future of development.

David Miliband

President and CEO, International Rescue Committee

David Miliband became President of the International Rescue Committee (IRC) in 2013. Founded in 1933, the IRC now has humanitarian relief operations in more than 40 war-affected countries, and refugee resettlement and assistance programmes in over 20 United States cities.

Under Miliband's leadership, the IRC has expanded its ability to rapidly respond to humanitarian crises and meet the needs of an unprecedented number of people uprooted by conflict, war and disaster. The organisation is implementing an ambitious global strategy to bring clear outcomes, strong evidence and systematic research to the humanitarian programmes through collaborative partnerships with the public and private sectors.

From 2007 to 2010, Miliband was the 74th Secretary of State for Foreign Affairs of the United Kingdom, driving advancements in human rights and representing the UK throughout the world. In 2006, as Secretary of State for the Environment, he pioneered the world's first legally binding emissions reduction requirements. He was Member of Parliament for South Shields from 2001 to 2013.

Miliband's first book, *Rescue: Refugees and the Political Crisis of Our Time*, was published in 2017.

Badr Jafar: What trends or forces are driving the demands on the IRC? I've heard you argue that the global refugee challenge is manageable and not unsolvable. What are some of the practical things that philanthropists or people not directly engaged in the sector can be doing to help solve it?

David Miliband: Just to give people a sense of the IRC, we have 200 field sites, with 13,000 employees and 17,000 volunteers in about 35 countries, and about 800 staff in 25 offices in the United States, who are dedicated to refugee resettlement and supporting asylum seekers.

This is an important conversation. There are two parts to your question. One is about trends, and one is about the role of philanthropy. The trends that we see are three- or fourfold. First, there's the COVID-19 emergency itself, which in direct health terms has been less of a killer than we expected. The fact that 80% of cases in Africa, for example, are asymptomatic, defies the prediction that I would have made if we'd been having this conversation six months ago, that densely populated areas with poor water and sanitation would see COVID-19 running rife with a trail of destruction in its wake. There has been death and destruction, much of it not well recorded, but it's not been on the scale that I expected. So that's the first trend.

Second, there are the non-COVID-19 health impacts, and the trend there is an interruption of supply chains for immunisations, people fearful of going to the health centres and a diminution of healthcare of a sizeable kind.

The third trend is the economic and social collateral damage of COVID-19 and its lockdowns, and that is very serious indeed, as 265 million people are expected to face life-threatening hunger this year. At a time when fewer people have been reaching our clinics, more people are facing the most acute economic needs, and famine is being predicted in three countries: Nigeria, South Sudan and Somalia.

Underpinning these relatively short-term impacts of COVID-19, there's the wider picture, which is that the world is becoming more integrated, but nations are becoming more nationalist. You're seeing a disjunction between an increasingly important global commons and increasingly important interdependence globally, but a deglobalisation politically. We see, in many of the places we work, a crisis of diplomacy. Syria is suffering a crisis of diplomacy; Yemen is suffering a crisis of diplomacy. There is diplomacy in Afghanistan, but it seems to be driven more by politics than by the conditions on the ground. That fear that our interconnected world is being mismanaged by disconnected politics is a meta trend that people in business and in philanthropy need to be concerned about. Certainly, people in the NGO sector are on the receiving end of it.

The role of philanthropy isn't to substitute for government, but to lead government when government isn't leading. I always say to people, philanthropy is our risk capital because governments aren't willing to take risks. Philanthropy is our 'out of the headlines' capital; because governments are often drawn to headlines, philanthropists need to be drawn by principle. Philanthropy is our 'special needs' capital for groups who are underserved by conventional donors. The hardest to reach in the countries that aren't fashionable, or are outside the reach of

"The role of philanthropy isn't to substitute for government, but to lead government when government isn't leading."

> "My very strong belief is that philanthropists, NGOs and the private sector need to offer leadership when government isn't, and then try to drag governments along by showing that there are solutions."

governments, are where I think philanthropy has an important role. My very strong belief is that philanthropists, NGOs and the private sector need to offer leadership when government isn't, and then try to drag governments along by showing that there are solutions. The International Rescue Committee is an NGO that focuses on solutions, not just on suffering. That's where philanthropy has a critical role to play.

Badr Jafar: There's a major shift underway in the global economy and you can see it on the ground in many parts of Africa, the Middle East and developing Asia. I'm talking about the rapid growth of the world's emerging economies, and the associated creation of wealth in these markets. What impact do you think that the rise of these fast-growing economies could have on our ability to fund humanitarian relief operations and to develop coordinated local solutions to complex local challenges?

David Miliband: The first starting point is to recognise that when it comes to humanitarian aid, 80 or 90% comes from conventional Western donors. They are decreasingly willing to bear the whole burden. The second starting point is that part of wealth creation in emerging markets comes from connection to the global economy. My message is a simple one. Those who are doing well out of the growth in emerging markets are going to have to face up to the responsibilities of the connected world if they want to continue to enjoy its blessings. We're beginning to see that, which is encouraging.

Let me give two parts of where I think it's going to have impact. One is that if we're working in northeast Nigeria, for example, it's powerful to have not just local staff, but local philanthropy supporting us. There is credibility, there is legitimacy, there is sustainability and there is knowledge that comes from local capital. If we're working in the Middle East, with all the dangers of being seen on one side or the other, we're a neutral organisation. Humanitarian work is independent. The principles of humanitarian action are about independence, neutrality and impartiality. When you go local, the danger is that you become partisan. It's very important to get the benefits of localisation without the partisanship of localisation. That needs to be a self-denying ordinance when you're funding humanitarian work in your own backyard.

The second thing is that I hope philanthropists in emerging markets are going to correct the failings of Western philanthropy; and not just copy it. There are some great things about Western philanthropy but too often it's short-term, boutique and with a premium on novelty rather than a premium on scale; a reinvention of the wheel rather than taking the wheel to more places. There's room for philanthropy and relationships of organisations like mine with philanthropists in the emerging markets to show that there are better ways of doing things. That's certainly what we would like to see.

"There are some great things about Western philanthropy but too often it's short-term, boutique and with a premium on novelty rather than a premium on scale; a reinvention of the wheel rather than taking the wheel to more places."

Badr Jafar: Are you seeing an uptick in the use of blended finance, or other innovative approaches to financing projects in the work that you're doing? How can we better enable the pooling of resources between donors from different sectors and from different parts of the world?

David Miliband: The short answer is no; we're not seeing blended finance. Humanitarian aid is often seen as too compli- cated and too dangerous for research studies, outcome targets and impact evaluations. We reject that completely. We are the International Rescue Committee; we are the largest impact evaluation agency in the humanitarian sector and we reject the idea that just because it's a matter of life and death, you can't measure it. Quite the opposite; because it's a matter of life and death, you *should* measure it, and you need to make the dollars or the euros or the pounds, and in the future maybe the renminbi, go further.

The truth, though, is that we are seeing growing emergencies, and a race to catch up, and that's not a good scenario for complicated blended finance. Longer-term finance would be an innovation for us. We have 450 government grants of a year in length. Even when we renew there is bureaucracy. So, if philanthropic capital comes in and says, 'Look, we're interested in three to five years, because we know this problem is not going away,' that would be innovation. If there is finance that is linked to outcomes rather than linked to inputs, that would be innovation.

Blending immediately means committees and complication. There's a danger that we get caught up in our own complexity. I would urge that we think about outcomes, that we think about timescales, that we think about innovation, and then we can think about partners. There's one caveat or rider. It would be great to think that philanthropists and donors in emerging markets and elsewhere come together and rather than trying to invent the wheel, support proven plans that we've developed or proven innovations that we want to roll out.

Badr Jafar: We seem to be dealing today with high levels of polarisation, disinformation and a lack of trust in institutions. Do we stand a chance at solving the world's acute problems in such an environment?

David Miliband: Well, the answer is, it's up to us. Rather than predicting whether we're going to succeed or fail in the next 30 or 50 years, I think it's up to us to make sure that we make as much progress as possible. There are dark clouds, but there are more resources than ever to make a difference, and I think that's what we should focus on. We need humility about the scale of the problem. The managing of an interdependent world of eight billion people is a challenge on a scale that's probably never been known.

If you see some of the changes that have been made in some countries in the space of one or two generations, that would have seemed like a dream, utopia or a revolution, something out of a novel. My maxim is that the resources are there to manage these problems. If they're human-made problems such as climate change, war or poverty, they are amenable to human solutions. It's our fault if we don't do it. So, we've got to get on with it. President Kennedy said, just because a problem is big, that's not a reason to delay, it's a reason to get started.

> "If they're human-made problems such as climate change, war or poverty, they are amenable to human solutions."

Badr Jafar: One of your strategic priorities at the IRC since 2013 has been to build and deepen partnerships with a growing network of public- and private-sector organisations. How would you encourage philanthropists in the emerging markets to build effective long-term, and not just transactional partnerships, with organisations such as the IRC?

David Miliband: The key thing I've learned is to think 360 degrees, not just the 90 degrees that is the signing of the cheque. Think about the exchange of ideas, about co-creation and about the exchange of expertise. There will be partners who want to write a cheque, but maybe they've also got a law department that wants to do some pro bono work, or they've got an advertising department that wants to help, or they've got a group of young employees who want to spend a day shadowing an aid worker. There are ways of developing a partnership. We can never pretend that the bottom line of a company is the same as the bottom line of an NGO, but we can recognise that there are some shared elements at the bottom line or shared contributors to the bottom line, employee development being one of them. It's important to think in the round about partnership so that there's a real relationship and not just a transaction.

Peter Maurer

President, Basel Institute on Governance and former President, ICRC

Peter Maurer served as President of the International Committee of the Red Cross (ICRC) from 2012 to 2022 (at the time of this interview he was still in the post). Founded in 1863, the ICRC carries out critical humanitarian work in over 90 countries through its 18,000-strong, dedicated staff. Maurer's priorities for his presidency included strengthening humanitarian diplomacy, engaging states and other actors for the respect of international humanitarian law, and improving the humanitarian response through innovation and new partnerships. After retiring as President of the ICRC, he became chair of the board of the Basel Institute on Governance.

Previously, Maurer served in the Swiss diplomatic service in various positions in Bern and Pretoria before being transferred to New York in 1996 as deputy permanent observer at the Swiss mission to the United Nations. In 2000, he was appointed ambassador and head of the human security division in the political directorate of the Swiss Department of Foreign Affairs in Bern.

In 2004, Maurer was appointed ambassador and permanent representative of Switzerland to the United Nations in New York. In June 2009, the UN General Assembly elected him chairman of the Fifth Committee, in charge of administrative and budgetary affairs. In addition, he was elected chairman of the Burundi configuration of the UN Peacebuilding Commission. In January 2010, he was appointed Secretary of State for Foreign Affairs in Bern.

Badr Jafar: Could you describe the current humanitarian financing situation around the world? It's generally known that we are falling short of the funds that we need to address all the immediate crises that we are facing. Can you put that into some perspective, including the impact of COVID-19,

since the World Bank estimates that a further 115 million people could face poverty by the end of next year due to the pandemic?

Peter Maurer: It's an interesting question to try to frame the landscape of needs that we are encountering. There are very different perspectives that you can take. If we look at classical humanitarian work, all our converging calculations, be they at the Red Cross or at the UN, are indicating that we are certainly falling short by a couple of billion US dollars, even for emergency operations related to COVID-19. We could argue that the shortfall is somewhere between US$4 billion and $US8 billion, even for the short-term emergency work which should be done to prevent the worst and to keep 100 million additional people moving from precarious wealth into poverty. If I take a larger perspective, if we look at shortfalls of capital to achieve the SDGs, there are many estimates. But I think the international financial institutions identify a figure of US$2.5 trillion that would be needed annually to achieve the SDGs over the next ten years.

Whether you're thinking short-term humanitarianism, or long-term sustainable development and resilience building, these figures look very large at first sight. If I put that into perspective, private capital in financial institutions is worth US$250 trillion. So, US$2.5 trillion doesn't look like an unsurmountable challenge to the international community. If I look at the US$5 billion needed for emergency funding, that doesn't look like a big issue, knowing the budgets of wealthy states, organisations and people. In the present landscape of needs the financial means are there, but they don't find their way to filling this huge gap in short-term as well as medium- and long-term consolidation.

We must also relativise the gap. There are serious absorption capacities when we go into the very fragile context of where the biggest needs are. The ICRC is working in 25 to 30 contexts that we consider to be high fragility, in which poverty, conflict, climate change, COVID-19 or the economic consequences of COVID-19 have caused a massive breakdown. These 25 to 30 contexts are at the origin of 80% of irregular migration worldwide. They are at the core of the security concerns worldwide not only for those countries themselves, but also for affected neighbours. Lebanon is one example, being located next to the Syrian conflict, which has so predominantly influenced our view of humanitarian work over the past decade. I believe that organisations like mine can act as a translator between potential capital and the needs on the ground.

Badr Jafar: The nature of humanitarian crises, as you mentioned, has changed significantly in the past few decades with a clear trend towards human conflict as a root cause. What trends and forces have been driving the demands on the ICRC these past few years? How do you see that changing over the next few years?

Peter Maurer: When I look at the places in which we see the biggest needs and the worst developments, I can put this under the heading of complex emergency. What makes a situation complex is violence and conflict. When I talk about violence, it's also the fragmentation of power, which is striking, and which is so complex to manage. The predominant feature of violence in fragile contexts is not two sides fighting with each other. Most of the conflicts have more than 10, 15 or 20 parties. The drivers of violence are exclusion, injustice and political conflict between and within societies. The average presence of the ICRC now in our 20 largest operations is more than 30 years. These don't look like short-term emergencies.

On top of violence, with all its intrinsic dynamics, we see climate change as a powerful accelerator and as a factor which complexifies the situation. I just visited the Sahel, and when you are there, you see that the changing rainfall patterns bring about violence and conflict because there are scarcer surfaces for productive agricultural and cultural activities.

We also see rapidly changing weather patterns, with either too much or too little rainfall, much more frequently. I visited Niger and Burkina Faso, and the predominant issue during my visit was flooding. Who would expect that floods are the key issue in Sahel? So, we have climate change and environmental degradation as a key factor. We have structural poverty, which we haven't managed to overcome over the past decade, despite all the MDGs and SDGs. And we have serious governance and institutional issues in many fragile countries.

This complex situation, which is then topped by COVID-19 and its primary and secondary economic and social impacts, makes for an explosive mix, which cannot be addressed by humanitarian actors only. You can throw tons of money at these problems, but you won't be able to solve them if you don't have a more sophisticated and differentiated approach to these complexities, from support to training, capacity building to institution building, creating inclusive societies and orienting your work towards stronger resilience. More complex interaction between organisations is needed to deal with those issues.

Badr Jafar: Are you witnessing an increase in the use of blended finance or other innovative approaches to financing humanitarian projects in your work at the ICRC? Can we enable or encourage more pooling of resources between donors from different sectors and different parts of the world?

Peter Maurer: Blended finance is something we strongly advocate for. On the one hand, we have emergencies which need emergency money to help people survive. But then you need to allow for pathways to help people get back to more independent lives. And this calls for blended finance. Once people are displaced, uprooted and marginalised through violence, conflict, climate change or anything else, they need to be brought, step by step, back into more productive activity. Most of the time, the first step can't be the market. They will be marginalised again if you subject them to the logic of the market. Blended finance comes with the promise that you can have a differentiated approach according to needs and you can design a pathway into more autonomous and independent lives for people. That's really

"Blended finance comes with the promise that you can have a differentiated approach according to needs and you can design a pathway into more autonomous and independent lives for people."

where the ICRC has a role to play. While I would advocate for states to finance more generously towards our emergency work, I don't think that we can have emergency finance for 30 years in a row. We need to design pathways out of it. And blended finance, which ties into emergency finance in the first phase, is probably the best template that we have at the present time to design those pathways. We work hard with the World Bank, with regional development banks, with development institutions from states, with philanthropy and with different actors in this area to see how we can intelligently align ourselves so that we can use different instruments, including financial ones, for these very complex situations.

Badr Jafar: How good is collaboration within the humanitarian sector by different sector actors? How has the nature of the interface that you referred to between humanitarian and development intervention changed over the years?

Peter Maurer: I think there is a strong willingness and awareness about collaboration. But there are also the challenges and complexities of aligning our different tools in a way that makes sense. My biggest preoccupation today is that in the most fragile contexts of the world, which we are most challenged to stabilise, we don't see hundreds of actors present. Very often development actors are absent in these situations. That's the reason why, as a frontline humanitarian organisation, in many of those contexts where development actors with their ramifications and conditions cannot yet be present, we must step in and offer some other forms of finance.

We decided at the ICRC to look at those areas in which we have measurability of activities, which gives a certain promise of economic logic even to the most fragile context and which would allow us to use those tools. But contrary to the general expectation, while the worlds of humanitarian organisations and development organisations seem to be well populated, we don't find these actors in the most difficult contexts. We find them in capitals of what we would consider at ICRC relatively stable countries. In South Sudan, in the eastern Ukraine, in rural Afghanistan, in southern Somalia, in many places in Sahel and in Lake Chad, we don't see these actors contributing to stabilising fragile contexts. So, sometimes the lack of presence is what drives us as a humanitarian organisation to develop tools, hoping that we can bring more climate funds and more development funds towards those situations. One of the big issues is risk. I think if we don't get our head around having more organisations, people, capital and taking some risks, then we will have difficulty stabilising these contexts.

Badr Jafar: A new generation of strategic philanthropists is beginning to emerge across parts of Africa, the Middle East and developing Asia. How would you recommend that they engage or work with organisations such as the ICRC in addressing humanitarian crises in aid of the most vulnerable of the world?

Peter Maurer: I hope that strategic philanthropists from emerging markets will bring a spirit of better understanding to the complexities of these very fragile contexts. In their lifetimes, they have experienced how their own countries have emerged from often difficult, marginalised, poor contexts into booming economies, which have brought them wealth. An advantage of strategic philanthropists from emerging markets coming to the work that we are doing is that they come with a sounder and more in-depth understanding of the complexity we are dealing with. What we hope to offer to those philanthropists is an engagement platform which separates emergency money, which I still believe should be largely financed by public power and states, from a pipeline of projects and activities which are designed to be what I call the pathway out of dependency, and towards autonomy. This may be attractive for those philanthropists who see that at the end of the day, strategically, we have to fix the most fragile and the poorest, and bring them out of dependency and deprivation.

The ICRC, with its frontline experience, its knowledge and its understanding of the logistics on the ground, is an organisation that tries to offer strategic philanthropists, platforms, projects and programmes of engagement with a longer-term perspective. For example, the projects that we are developing for water systems in urban contexts, from Goma to Maiduguri to Sahel, are interesting for strategic philanthropy. We are a key actor for disabled peoples worldwide because of our work in conflict and war, and we hope that strategic philanthropy can also engage in building health systems and building systems for the physically challenged in these contexts.

> "We can offer engagement platforms for strategic philanthropists, which will look attractive because increasingly we are looking at delivering impact to investors – blended finance possibilities that try to build a value chain from philanthropy to market graduation."

We can offer engagement platforms for strategic philanthropists, which will look attractive because increasingly we are looking at delivering impact to investors – blended finance possibilities that try to build a value chain from philanthropy to market graduation. That's where I hope that humanitarian organisations like mine can offer attractive solutions, in cooperation with the World Bank, with financial institutions, with the UN and with our partners in humanitarian development, climate change and other areas.

FOUR

RESPONSIBLE BUSINESS AND PHILANTHROPY: INVESTING IN COMMUNITY

In emerging markets, entrepreneurs and family businesses dominate the economy. Many are first-generation business owners and they often bring their entrepreneurial approach to philanthropy, with giving back being intertwined with their own success. They want to empower others, particularly the young and disadvantaged, to follow similar paths of success, and, as a result, we often see first-generation business owners creating new non-profit or philanthropic organisations that focus on building access to skills training and opportunity for aspiring young entrepreneurs. Others will bring an entrepreneurial approach to nurturing social capital. This may mean supporting a social enterprise or charity with a mission to reduce poverty, advance education or improve health, utilising the assets and tools of business such as marketing, sponsorship and technology. As they grow their business activities, these owners may choose to create a corporate foundation to manage their philanthropic activities in conjunction with the business itself.

There are many models for business engagement in philanthropy. It could begin as charitable giving to communities and grow to become more strategic and with broader social development aims.

To illustrate the various ways in which business and philanthropy have had an impact in emerging regions of Africa, the Middle East and Asia, I interviewed several business leaders about their own philanthropic journeys. I asked them what motivated them to engage in their communities and how they went about it.

Yue-Sai Kan is an extraordinary business leader who has had success in building her businesses in China and in the United States. She spoke to me about her cosmetics and beauty business, and how she has used it to support and encourage women's empowerment in China, as well as pursuing her individual involvement in promoting philanthropy in China and cross-cultural exchange between China and the West.

An important business leader from the Middle East, Fadi Ghandour, explained his philosophy of corporate entrepreneurship responsibility, an approach that has entrepreneurial business actively supporting new and young entrepreneurs in their communities, in a win–win for both – creating jobs and opportunity, bringing people together, helping the whole community prosper. In this philosophy, business and philanthropy are intimately connected, not in separate worlds.

Another key business leader from the region, Fady Jameel, spoke about the dual strategies of his family business, investing directly in community and building a vibrant arts culture in the UAE and Saudi Arabia, while at the same time redirecting some of his business investments specifically into fighting climate change by investing in green technologies and green businesses.

I talked to Kathleen Chew, a prominent business leader and member of her Malaysian family business YTL Group. She spoke about her corporate foundation and the ways in which she has deployed the skills and expertise within the business to serve and direct the programming of the foundation to improve educational systems in Malaysia.

His Excellency Abdul Aziz Al Ghurair, a leading UAE businessman and philanthropist, spoke to me about the need for the business sector to invest in the wellbeing of society, which in his case is investing heavily in education in the Arab world. He spoke eloquently about the importance of businesses not only engaging in philanthropy, but also communicating their philanthropic goals and collaborating with each other and with governments to have the greatest possible impact.

Finally, Lord Karan Bilimoria, a British entrepreneur with Indian roots, is another example of a philanthropist who combines his entrepreneurial instincts with his business interests to generate highly successful fundraising strategies and new philanthropic ventures and investments in the UK and across South Asia. This is strategic business philanthropy in action.

Yue-Sai Kan

Founder, Yue-Sai Kan One World Foundation (formerly China Beauty Charity Fund)

Yue-Sai Kan is a television host and producer, entrepreneur, author and humanitarian.

A New Yorker since 1972, she founded Yue-Sai Kan Productions, which produced the long-running television series *Looking East*, the first of its kind to introduce Asian cultures and customs to an American audience. In 1986, the television series *One World*, produced and hosted by Kan, aired on China's national television network CCTV, with a weekly viewership of 300 million. Her many other TV credits include the ABC documentary *China Walls and Bridges*, which earned her an Emmy Award, *Journey through a Changing China, Yue-Sai's World* and *Yue-Sai's World Expo*.

In 1992, Kan created the Yue-Sai cosmetics brand, which grew into China's leading cosmetics company. More than 90% of the Chinese population today recognises the brand, which was purchased by L'Oréal in 2004.

Since 2011, Kan has chaired the China Beauty Charity Fund, which has raised millions of dollars to fund cleft lip and palate surgeries, provided free medical supplies to underserved regions in China, and awarded scholarships to students at the Beijing Film Academy, the Shanghai Theatre Academy and Chinese students at the Fashion Institute of Technology in New York.

Badr Jafar: Much of what you've done in your life is around beauty: you started a cosmetics empire; you own the Miss Universe China franchise; and you started a foundation called the China Beauty Charity Fund. Why beauty?

Yue-Sai Kan: Many people think that beauty is frivolous, but it doesn't have to be. In Chinese, the word *Zhen Shan Mei* means three things: *Zhen* means truth; *Shan* means kindness; and *Mei* means physical inner beauty. So, beauty does not have to be superficial. I created a cosmetics company in 1990 in China. In those days, no one used cosmetics in China. The way we promoted cosmetics to Chinese women was not about cosmetics themselves but that cosmetics can allow us to change into whatever we want to be. If you can change the way you look, you can be what you are, but you can also be more than what you are.

The cosmetics company not only made Chinese women feel empowered, more importantly it was also used for charity work. We showed women that we were a role model of a company that was using profit to do meaningful philanthropic work. Later, I bought the Miss Universe China franchise, and people said it was frivolous. No, it's not frivolous at all. We used the final contest as a charity event, which became extremely successful. I say to the contestants, you have received beauty as a gift, now you must use it to do good. So, they are role models for other Chinese women. I wanted young Chinese women to learn to do charity work as well. This was extremely innovative in China.

Through my China Beauty Charity Fund, we created a green programme for the fashion industry in China. The most polluting business in the world is fashion, and China produces more garments than anywhere else. So, pollution is a very real problem in China. I created a class for Chinese executives of fashion companies to come to America to learn about green production. From A to Z, we taught them how to create a green industry in the fashion world. We also put this online, so hundreds and hundreds of Chinese fashion companies can benefit from it. I think fashion is power; we can do a lot of things with it.

Badr Jafar: Let's talk about cultural diplomacy. You've produced hundreds of TV programmes that explain the world to China and vice versa and now you are the co-chair of China Institute in New York. What is the mandate of China Institute and what constitutes success for this initiative?

Yue-Sai Kan: Those TV shows that you mention were an important vehicle for cultural exchange, especially when the country was very closed. I consider those TV shows, which I wasn't paid for, as cultural philanthropy, to begin the process of opening avenues for dialogue between China and the rest of the world.

The China Institute in New York has been around for almost 100 years and it is the only home of Chinese culture that I know of in New York City. The aim of both the institute and myself is to preserve and promote the culture of China, which is more than 5,000 years old. We already promote it with music, dance, art, a museum, lectures and language classes for all ages. Recently, we created a development fund to build out the ground floor. This will open a total of 5,000 square feet celebrating Chinese food, films, fashion and anything else we want. We can host events and weddings, and it will be the first time a Chinese organisation has a front to the street. It is an opportunity for all people, Chinese or not, to learn about the culture and achieve our mission of preserving it.

Badr Jafar: According to the well-established Hurun Report, 61% of the world's top self-made female billionaires are Chinese. In what ways do you think this community of increasingly affluent women can affect philanthropy in China, but also around the world?

Yue-Sai Kan: In 1990, when I founded my cosmetics company, I was the only Chinese woman who started a business during that time. But many things have changed since then. When Chairman Mao said women uphold half the sky, it gave Chinese women the freedom to do everything. They are equal in that sense to men. In China, women don't have any problem buying a property in their own name, starting a business in their name or borrowing money in their name.

The sky is the limit as far as Chinese women are concerned in terms of business. We have many wealthy women today in China. But of the 100 top philanthropists in China, only ten are women.

I do want to mention some interesting Chinese women philanthropists. They are local philanthropists; they don't do much outside of China and all of them focus on similar causes: women and children; education; health; and poverty reduction. The wealthiest woman is Yang Huiyan; her money, US$34 billion, was given to her by her father, a property developer. The second woman is Wu Yajun. She's nicknamed the 'Real Estate Queen'. She is probably the wealthiest self-made woman in the world, worth US$18 billion. The third one is Zhong Huijuan, who is CEO of her own pharmaceutical company. She is known to be the first woman to have founded a charity in China, in 2005. Her charity is numbered 001, and since then she has helped about two million women in China. The last one is Zhang Yin. She is nicknamed the 'Garbage Queen' because she imports millions of tons of garbage, turns it into packaging materials and sells it to Coca-Cola, Nike and other companies. She owns the largest paper-recycling company in the world.

I know four Chinese billionaire women who do philanthropic business outside of China. Chrissy Luo founded the Shanda Group. She is worth US$1.5 billion, and she and her husband donated US$115 million to Caltech for neuroscience research and another US$80 million for the Shanghai Huashan Hospital for research, mainly on Alzheimer's disease. Dr Priscilla Chen, the wife of Mark Zuckerberg, runs their charity and concentrates on education, particularly online learning. Zhang Xin is a co-founder of Soho China, a huge real estate company, and she started as a factory worker and went to Cambridge. Later, she and her husband gave US$100 million to create scholarships for poor students to go to international colleges. Lastly Clara Wu Tsai, who co-founded the Joe and Clara Tsai Foundation, has pledged US$220 million to research into how to improve human fitness.

Badr Jafar: Would you say that there is an increasing institutionalisation of philanthropy within China, not just for the larger donations, but also more on the retail philanthropy level? Is it being more institutionalised and structured or is it still deployed in more traditional fashion?

Yue-Sai Kan: In China, philanthropy is controlled by the government. If you want to have a charity foundation, you must work hard to apply to register a charity. Three decades ago, there was absolutely no money in China. Like everything else in China, charity has grown so rapidly I can't keep up with it. But let me try to say something about the history of philanthropy in China.

> "Like everything else in China, charity has grown so rapidly I can't keep up with it."

In Communist China, the Chinese government is supposed to take care of you – housing, food, medicine, everything from cradle to grave. I remember when I first started doing charity in China and gave away money, people were embarrassed to take it. They said, 'This is the government's job. Are you joking that you are giving away money?' In 1995, for the UN's Women's Conference in Beijing, I donated the first year of my Yue-Sai cosmetics money through the Chinese Women's Federation, which was the host. The government said that I must pay tax for the donation.

Then things began to change; the government started giving tax deductions for donations and it is interesting how fast things have moved on. Charity is a new word in China. Even as recently as 2015, China was one of the least generous nations in the world, ranking 144. It was not in the tradition of Chinese people to give money to the public. It was given to their own family and to children. The Chinese have never been known to be that generous. Creating a foundation is very difficult in China.

However, in 2021 alone, seven billionaires donated more than US$6 billion. You ask me why? The Chinese government enacted a new Charity Law in 2016. It gives people an easier way to register a public benefit company and it also gives a better and broader framework for charity. In 2015, the China Global Philanthropy Institute was founded, to teach people how to do philanthropy. Bill Gates and Ray Dalio were the two Americans who helped to fund this. Anyone who wants to learn about philanthropy can go to this school and take courses. This year [2021], the government launched a programme called Common Prosperity. This is an effort to narrow the gap between the very wealthy and the poor. The two biggest tech companies in China immediately responded. Alibaba donated US$15 billion, the equivalent of one-fifth of current assets, to help that programme. Tencent made a net profit of US$14 billion in the first half of this year and donated US$15 billion in four months to this Common Prosperity Initiative. These are only two examples. During COVID-19, almost US$6.5 million was gathered from all walks of life to help to combat COVID-19.

As you know, China is very big on e-commerce. Live streaming sales are now the hottest sales model in China. During this period, many Chinese celebrities are going on e-commerce sites, and they will sell products from farms, to help the farmers. They teach the farmers how to use e-commerce to sell their products. That helps the poor in rural areas. Every year in China now we have an event called 9/9 Charity Day. It was started by Tencent in 2015 for WeChat users to give through the platform over nine days in September. This year, a whopping 69 million people participated, and over US$600 million was raised. This is just amazing; what a huge difference from those days when the Chinese

"I'm really excited about the philanthropy sector in China; I've witnessed the growth first-hand and I think the future is magnificent."

government was embarrassed to receive donations. About 12 years ago, I could not sell a charity ticket for more than US$25. Two years ago, my charity event sold tickets at US$5,000 in less than two weeks, and 500 tickets were sold. I'm really excited about the philanthropy sector in China; I've witnessed the growth first-hand and I think the future is magnificent.

Badr Jafar: Within the context of what you just shared with us, what are the youth's attitudes to philanthropy compared with their parents within China?

Yue-Sai Kan: The young people in China are much more willing to do charity than the older generations, who found it difficult to part with their money. The young have heard the word 'charity' often, and they are participating in many more charity-related activities. As I said, the future of philanthropy in China is extremely bright.

Fadi Ghandour

Executive Chair, Wamda Group

Fadi Ghandour is the Chairman of Wamda Group, a platform that invests, nurtures and builds entrepreneurship ecosystems across the Middle East and North Africa. He is also the founder of Aramex, a global logistics company. He spent the first 30 years of his career as CEO of Aramex, building it into a leading emerging market logistics company, which employs over 15,000 people in over 250 offices in 90 countries. He took the company public twice, first on Nasdaq, making it the first company from the Arab world to do so, then on the Dubai Financial Market. He continues to be active on the Aramex board.

Ghandour has been involved with founding, investing and launching tens of companies and non-profits, ranging from digital tech, hospitality, fitness and wellness to security. Passionate about impact and social entrepreneurship, he founded and chairs Ruwwad for Development, a private-sector-led community empowerment platform that helps marginalised communities in Jordan, Lebanon, Palestine and Egypt, through activism, civic engagement, education and financial inclusion. He also co-founded and continues to support Al-Riyadi, one of the leading not-for-profit sports clubs in Jordan.

Badr Jafar: Fadi, I'm interested to hear your perspectives on the intersection between business and philanthropy, and how we can strengthen that nexus in the Middle East. Can you start by telling us about Ruwwad, its journey to date and what you've learned along the way that you wish you knew at the outset?

Fadi Ghandour: Ruwwad is at the heart of strategic philanthropy. We are celebrating our 15th year with our community. Ruwwad is about what I would call the dual marginalisation of certain communities, those who are already marginalised and those in the private sector or the entrepreneurial community. If we in the business community don't participate in the development process of the countries we live in or of the communities we touch, then we have self-marginalised. We've put ourselves outside of participating in the development of our communities and abdicated a role that is essential for us. This story of 'the business of business is only business' doesn't work anymore. There is a social responsibility for business, not only in the PR sense of social responsibility. We live in communities, we affect them, they affect us. We cannot deny that, and we cannot say your only social responsibility is to pay taxes or adhere to rules and regulations.

The core idea of Ruwwad is bringing the private sector to the marginalised communities to work with them, so that we are all part of a community's development. We work with youth on character building. We establish community centres in every marginalised area we choose. We say to the youth if you want to go to university and get your degree, fine, but you're going to come to this community centre, and over the weekends you're going to give us four hours of volunteer work to solve the community's problems yourselves. We want them to ask themselves: Can we fix our own problems? Do we have enough knowledge to do that? Do we have the capabilities as youth? We want them to feel that the initiative is owned by them, builds character effectively and gives them something that universities don't. This is funded purely by the private sector. It is about community mobilisation for the youth by the youth at the end of the day.

Badr Jafar: Seven years ago, you made a persuasive call for something you called corporate entrepreneurship responsibility, which was basically a call for private-sector organisations to support the development of entrepreneurship ecosystems in their own backyard. Do you think that businesses in the Middle East are doing enough to help address the region's social and economic challenges? What have you found to be the most effective ways to get more local businesses and business leaders engaged in advancing societal needs more directly?

Fadi Ghandour: This question is very important. The idea of corporate entrepreneurship responsibility is to kill the concept of CSR [corporate social responsibility]. We need to kill it because it is a PR story, so that the private sector can feel good about itself. When a business places its CSR programmes in its advertising and marketing departments, that's when you know that it's not serious.

The idea of corporate entrepreneurship responsibility gets back to the question of how the private sector understands the importance and responsibility of doing things in the community. In the private sector, we are entrepreneurs, we know how to employ, we have networks, we can lobby governments and we can do many things for emerging entrepreneurs. I'm saying to the private sector, 'Okay, you want to do stuff, do it with entrepreneurs, this is what you know how to do. Let's not beat around the bush and find projects, let's work with entrepreneurs, because it is at the heart of the businesses that you do. Do you have people who can mentor entrepreneurs? Do you want to invest in entrepreneurs?' It's sticking to the core of what the private sector does and telling them to do more for entrepreneurship.

There is a problem of unemployment in our region and globally. Youth are graduating by the millions and are not able to find jobs. The best way to create jobs is to create more companies, and you create more companies by creating entrepreneurs. The private sector has the responsibility to take its capabilities, its knowledge and its networks to help these entrepreneurs establish their businesses. Do we do a lot of it here in the region? We're doing much more than when I started my business 30 years ago. But is it enough? No. This is at the core of having secure, stable communities. We need to step up. You can make money by supporting entrepreneurs. If we want to benefit from it and do good at the same time, let's do that. But step up and take whatever capabilities you have, and put them in the service of creating new jobs, companies and opportunities for the youth.

Badr Jafar: There's one type of entrepreneurship that's neglected in this part of the world. We have a thriving community of micro and small businesses, which are the backbone of our economy. These are owned and led by entrepreneurs, who've already proven that they know how to build and run successful companies. I think a big part of our ongoing effort as a community must be to support these owners to scale up their operations, because these businesses run by very capable entrepreneurs stand a better chance of creating new productive jobs, at least in the short and the medium term.

Moving to philanthropy, how would you describe the state of philanthropy in the Middle East in general? What have you found to be the most distinctive characteristics of philanthropy in the region?

Fadi Ghandour: I'm no expert on this subject, but my observation is that there is less strategic philanthropy, although there's a lot of giving. My question is how to make this giving more strategic, because when you do it strategically, you're thinking carefully about the long-term impact. The critical question is how to get societies to stand on their feet and not be in need. That's what strategic philanthropy is about. It's the old cliché of do you give them the fish or help them learn how to fish? At the end of the day, wellbeing is about a society being proud, self-empowered and owning its destiny.

The region needs more strategic philanthropy. We need to spread the word, foster learning and education, and have that discussion with the people who want to give. How do you get them to think about it from a strategic perspective so that they impact society? There is not much dialogue across sectors. Development is not only up to governments, or social entrepreneurs, or civil society, or NGOs or global impact organisations, it's also up to the private sector. How do we get everyone together to address this issue? In our region we don't have much of that. Private philanthropy is haphazard, occasional and knee-jerk reactive. Our laws and regulations are restrictive for political reasons. Let's have that discussion and bring in the people of goodwill to find ways to do this together. There are good intentions out there to help governments solve the challenges of society, so that we can all shoulder the responsibility.

Badr Jafar: The fastest-growing economies are in emerging markets. Although they might not have a long history of institutional philanthropy, most of these countries have deep-rooted traditions of giving. What impact do you think that this could have on the nature and practice of strategic philanthropy? How can we ensure that this new generation of philanthropists have access to the tools and knowledge that they'll need to maximise their impact?

Fadi Ghandour: I can't even calculate the wealth that is being generated today in emerging markets, the new wealth that's been generated in the past 15 years, because of the digitisation of economies and the creation of new businesses.

Badr Jafar: The projection is US$5 trillion across the emerging markets, transitioning to the next generation within the next 15 to 20 years.

Fadi Ghandour: It's fantastic. And these entrepreneurs are different, they're socially aware, they are much younger, they grew up in a different time and they are seeing the challenges. There are role models, such as Bill Gates with his Giving Pledge initiative. People can see what he is doing with his foundation, and he wants to give it all away probably in his lifetime. He thinks about how he wants to impact the world.

In a variation of that model, all these young new entrepreneurs who have generated wealth that they don't know what to do with, need dialogue. You will be able to solve many problems of the world, because entrepreneurs not only give away money, they have ideas, they are innovative, they are more agile and more structurally built to solve problems and match that with their wealth. This is a new style of social impact organisation. Perhaps we need to call them an entrepreneurial impact organisation that solves many of the problems that we have from education to the environment, etc. All these problems cannot be solved and will not be solved by governments alone.

> "Entrepreneurs not only give away money, they have ideas, they are innovative, they are more agile, and more structurally built to solve problems and match that with their wealth."

Badr Jafar: To what extent do you believe that one can apply traditional entrepreneurial principles to the evaluation and scaling up of philanthropic initiatives and/or organisations?

Fadi Ghandour: I'm a believer that entrepreneurial principles apply across the board. But there are variations. The discussion about these philanthropic initiatives always involves the question of sustainability. We need to have a serious discussion about the definition of sustainability. Some people say, if you're not generating internal income, you're not sustainable, so don't do it. I'm not sure I'm an adherent of that concept. I say, 'Let's define what impact is, let's define our mission, and what we really want to do, and let's see how we can get that funding going, so that the impact matters.' At the end of the day, it is not about financial sustainability alone in the traditional sense, it is about the impact that you want to have. An accelerator will help. You can define how you're going to move forward in doing certain things with each project by itself in that accelerator. So, if the project is about educating people such as the poorest of the poor, and you can't generate income out of that in the traditional sense, there are people that will provide ongoing funds from a foundation, so that impact can happen.

Some of these projects end, because if you solve the problem, you can say, 'I've achieved my mission, and I want to do something else.' I think accelerators are essential, because that's how we show these young people who have ideas that there are people there to nurture and help them, by asking, Is this doable? What impact does it have? And what returns are we thinking about? Financial returns or societal returns? How do we understand things together? So that whatever we do, it is impacting society wellbeing.

Badr Jafar: Can you share lessons that you've learned from your own experiences in philanthropy, and what advice might you give to those who are embarking on their own philanthropic journeys, or considering becoming more active?

Fadi Ghandour: Work in marginalised communities makes a difference to lives. It is working for the long term; this is not about instant gratification, this is about long-term, hard work. You will be opposed; people will question your intentions. When I went to the first community of Ruwwad, they thought I was running for election. They asked, 'Who are you? Why are you coming here? Where is your money from?' I don't blame them for being sceptical about strangers with money. When we started

"Strategic philanthropy works, and it should be at the core of the thinking and philosophy of anybody in the private sector who needs to do more in the society that he or she lives in."

the work, when we started showing people in these marginalised communities that we were serious they were completely on board. Strategic philanthropy works, and it should be at the core of the thinking and philosophy of anybody in the private sector who needs to do more in the society that he or she lives in. That's my biggest lesson. It works but it takes time. The first time I felt that Ruwwad was working was ten years after we launched it. In talking to the community, then I understood that it's working, we need to do more of it, we need to go deeper.

Fady Jameel

Vice Chairman, Community Jameel

Fady Jameel is the Vice Chairman of Community Jameel, an independent, global organisation advancing science and learning for communities to thrive. In this role, his interests include the work of the Abdul Latif Jameel Poverty Action Lab (J-PAL) – whose co-founders won the 2019 Nobel Prize in Economics – in strengthening data and rigorous evidence in the ESG (environmental, social and governance) space, and determining the impact of emissions trading schemes on improving air pollution, a major contributor to mortality rates.

Jameel is the Deputy President and Vice Chairman, International, Abdul Latif Jameel, a family-owned diversified business, founded in 1945 by the late Abdul Latif Jameel. He heads the international operations of the Abdul Latif Jameel network of businesses and is a board member.

He is also founder and chairman of Art Jameel, which supports artists and creative communities, including at its two institutions, Hayy Jameel in Jeddah, and the Jameel Arts Centre in Dubai.

Badr Jafar: Can you tell us about Community Jameel, including its basic philosophy and what it's most focused on today? I think it's a fascinating example of a family and a family business taking a truly innovative approach to strategic and corporate philanthropy.

Fady Jameel: In a nutshell, our philosophy is supporting a culture of evidence-based policy and building a research ecosystem. Everything we do is based on that philosophy of evidence. Whether we're working with institutions, working with universities or tackling a certain issue, we take a very scientific approach. This is the way we like to do things; this is what we find the most productive in all our endeavours and businesses.

> "In a nutshell, our philosophy is supporting a culture of evidence-based policy and building a research ecosystem."

Badr Jafar: You founded Art Jameel. Why did you choose to put your energies into art and culture specifically?

Fady Jameel: Art Jameel started with supporting other organisations or museums, either setting up an endowment for them or by grants or working very closely with them in the region and abroad. Only recently, we decided to set up our own Centre for the Arts, and that started in Dubai two years ago. We have a centre opening in Jeddah, which is a little different than the one in Dubai. Dubai was really a government grant for the land, which was very generous from the Dubai government and His Highness Sheikh Mohammed bin Rashid Al Maktoum. We wanted to have our own programming and our own organisation in that region. Of course, Dubai is very developed compared with other parts of the world. Jeddah Art Centre will open next year. It will be a series of art galleries, studios, an independent cinema, a comedy club, as well as a community centre. So, it's really a hub for creativity, and it's called Hayy Jameel, after the Arabic word for neighbourhood. We're very excited about that.

Badr Jafar: What advice would you give to aspiring philanthropists from emerging markets who are also interested in supporting initiatives in this area?

Fady Jameel: What I would recommend for others is not to make the mistakes that we did. I think it's very important to set up a trust or an endowment, however small, to start with. It's important to institutionalise that for the future. Families want things to last for a long time. Longevity is important. Maybe it's difficult to set up a foundation in the Middle East, but you can set up an endowment, and build on it so you have that continuity. Apart from that, if you don't want to set up an endowment or a trust, you can support the local art scene. It's important to have this art scene as part of an economy, to allow youth to display their works or talk about their work in various mediums. It's very important for the creative economy and beyond.

Badr Jafar: You have decided to focus on the arts more broadly as one of your key themes in Community Jameel. When you look at history, true innovation happened at the intersection of humanities and sciences. If we're not taking humanities and arts seriously and seeing art as fundamental as opposed to just ornamental, then we're not going to have a chance of building true innovation and knowledge economies.

Fady Jameel: Absolutely. You're seeing the public sector in the region reinforcing and investing in that sector. You need to complete the circle; the private sector needs to play its part in various ways or else it becomes a little slow. Once everybody is on board, then you can see a change, a richness in culture that is important for everybody.

Badr Jafar: What are some of the consistent principles that guide your philanthropic work across the different areas that you and your family are engaged in? Are there some golden rules that govern your approach to philanthropy, or the approach of Community Jameel?

Fady Jameel: We are re-evaluating what's important for us today, whether we're combating, for example, food-borne pathogens, or whether we're addressing inequalities for women, or whether we're working with poverty alleviation. We're starting to realise that we should consider climate and carbon emissions, especially in our region, which will be affected the most; I can't stress that enough. Whether we work with philanthropy, or whether we work in business, we must map out that challenge. Climate change is coming, so if you want to survive and flourish in business, you must take that into consideration. It's extremely important. We must pivot towards climate goals and issues. Investors, clients and sovereign wealth funds are demanding this from public companies. So, this will change, and many countries are taking the lead. I think we are taking the lead to some extent, but again the private sector should take it as a priority. You can have a carbon consideration in your businesses and in your funds and make market returns. This is where you can have business and philanthropy work together. That's very viable.

> "Climate change is coming, so if you want to survive and flourish in business, you must take that into consideration."

Badr Jafar: Do you believe that one can apply business investment and entrepreneurial principles to philanthropic work and vice versa? What lessons can business learn from the philanthropic sector, especially as more and more businesses are looking to redefine their raison d'être through a social lens?

Fady Jameel: Philanthropic work today, whether it's in policy or in scalable evidence, is focused on the effects of climate change and how to mitigate them. And that gets transferred to everything you do in the business world, whether it's in the automotive business like us, or in the renewables business, or cement or oil and gas, it affects everything we do.

I urge people to look at the policies of organisations, with the evidence that's there, and see the possibilities of what can be done. There are many big private families in Europe, in the US and in Southeast Asia that are doing this. We should be the ones taking most advantage of it, because we are the ones who are going to be affected by it. There's going to be a revolution in the way we do agriculture and the yields from agriculture in the future. Water affordability is another aspect that we look at very seriously. There's an opportunity there. So, looking at the new technologies, and at these fields through a different lens, can yield a lot of opportunity.

Badr Jafar: Do you think that the business community in the Middle East and North Africa in general is doing enough to address the region's social and economic challenges? How can we make it easier for businesses, governments and private philanthropists to work together in partnership? Much is being discussed around the importance of blended finance. What role does philanthropic capital have to de-risk some private business investments in social causes?

Fady Jameel: If you're talking about blended finance to help bring infrastructure or projects to the region, yes, there are government departments that are very serious about these issues, for example in Saudi Arabia, Morocco or in the UAE. Many banks are also serious about these issues. In the private sector there's some sprouts of hope. Some are indifferent, it's business as usual for them, but that's a risk. The risk is not what you do but what you don't do. I'll give you an example. I've been working on a project in Kenya for water desalination for two years, and that's partly blended finance, and a blended distribution. The pricing you do for industry is very different than the pricing you do for homes, and that sort of thing. But we work with banks and institutions that help and encourage that sort of investment. In Egypt, another example, at least for our own operations, is water, and how important that sector will be or is. There is huge opportunity. Yes, there is a lot of risk. How to mitigate that risk is quite difficult if you're talking about currency risk or country risk. But you have a huge advantage if you are in this region, and relatively speaking you understand the culture and you understand the market. The business can be quite enticing, to be honest, so I encourage people to look at this on a project-by-project basis. We are looking into projects like this, and we are seeing a huge benefit both socially and business-wise.

Badr Jafar: I would agree with you that the trend is in the right direction. There is still a large community that feels that there is a trade-off between purpose and profit, or between positive social impact and serving the shareholder. But the region simply will not be able to address our challenges, many of which are systemic, without the active role of business engaging alongside philanthropic capital and government capital to address those challenges.

Fady Jameel: One thing I'd like to add is, in terms of philanthropy, if you have a philanthropic division, you should go into the green sector. There's a lot of business that can be done in the green sector. This is happening in the region. Green technology and green industry across the board are gaining a lot of momentum. We have to catch up, as private businesses and families, because it's instrumental in the next 20 to 30 years for survival. I'm trying to encourage other families to join.

Badr Jafar: Will the pandemic change any of the work that you do at Community Jameel in terms of priority areas? More generally, how do you see COVID-19 impacting the role that philanthropy plays in our region and more broadly?

Fady Jameel: It's not wrong to say that we are in the age of pandemics. This has been very tough on businesses and on people across the world. It's unlike anything we've ever experienced before. What we are doing now is that we have a lab at Imperial College that works with pandemics. It was started four or five months before the pandemic began. That work was more about mapping pandemics across the world, so we have increased our commitment to that. It obviously has changed how things work in the Middle East, how we meet and how we buy and sell products. It's going to be a way of life for some time, and it might not return to how it was. But we must be ready now.

Kathleen Chew
Group Legal Counsel, YTL Group

Kathleen Chew is a lawyer and executive based in Malaysia. She was a partner in the law firm Abdul Aziz Ong & Co. in Kuala Lumpur before she became a legal advisor for YTL Corporation Berhad, which has international operations in eight countries. She serves as Group Legal Counsel and is part of the Senior Management Team at YTL. She has been involved in major acquisitions undertaken by the YTL Group across all business segments of the company and its subsidiaries. In her charitable work, she serves as Programme Director of the YTL Foundation, which seeks to contribute to better societies by providing educational and leadership opportunities for Malaysian communities to help them reach their full potential.

Chew sits on the boards of various Malaysian and UK charities, such as the Asia Philanthropy Circle in Singapore and Acumen Fund in New York. She is also chair of Hospis Malaysia and of Alpha Malaysia, a Christian organisation.

Chew is an active social entrepreneur and the founder of Mad Squared, a media services agency dedicated to serving clients in the non-profit sector, and Mangosteen Organics, a bath and body brand that commits 100% of its profits to improving the lives of women and children in Southeast Asia.

Badr Jafar: Can you give a brief history of the YTL Foundation and its mission? How connected is the foundation with the day-to-day work of the YTL Group and its employees?

Kathleen Chew: We started with a deep interest in education. My late father-in-law was the founder of YTL. From an early age he funded those who needed school fees to get through the school year. He fundamentally believed that education was a way to change lives. He did not have a formal university education. He grew up during World War II, during the Japanese occupation, and had to work for a living with his father. Education was a very precious commodity to him, and he made sure that all his children were educated in British universities. We have a very strong link to the UK, and we have businesses in the UK as well.

In 1997, we decided that instead of more informal giving, we would formalise it into a foundation and put structure around it. Our mission was to provide educational opportunities to young individuals so that they could fulfil their potential. We started giving scholarships, as we had done before, but this time we were looking for young people who showed great potential. We tried to place them in the best universities possible. We have supported many scholars in Cambridge, and in different UK universities, as well as in Malaysia.

As we did this work, we started trying to develop the leadership potential of the young people that we were nurturing. We saw the opportunity to go broader within the schools. We looked at trying to empower schools with technology. With the advent of edutech, we thought, let's see how we can help schools move from the traditional chalk and talk into something more interesting for the kids. For the past ten years, we have invested in helping schools upskill the teachers and give them facilities to use technology in class.

When we started this, it became apparent that school leadership was important, because a weak school leader meant that the school couldn't progress very fast. So, we worked to bring in a school leadership programme. We incubated the organisation Pemimpin GSL, and we are proud that they are now independent with other sponsors and funders. Finally, we recently started the Malaysia Acumen Academy. Acumen runs a wonderful leadership programme. I met Jacqueline Novogratz [founder of Acumen], and we said that the next step for young people that we are nurturing was to develop moral leadership. This is what we do today.

The foundation is obviously very interconnected with the business. I am a legal advisor or a general counsel for the group, but I also run the foundation. It has its own staff so they can concentrate on their own programmes. We have an independent board of trustees, but we try to leverage the assets of the YTL Group wherever we can. We think that this creates a synergy that makes us effective.

We try to bring the YTL staff on board, volunteering or just keeping them informed of the programmes that we run. I think our human resources in the group can be a catalyst for philanthropy. As an example, when the pandemic started, Malaysia went into lockdown, and we reacted quite quickly. There wasn't much time to prepare. Schools were not prepared at all for lockdown, they were just shut down. Because we worked so closely with schools and with parents, the immediate concern at the foundation was how parents were going to cope with trying to help their children at home, especially the ones from lower-income groups. It was obvious to us, being in technology, that helping the schools with technology would be the answer. Everybody is safe at home, we ran the classes and children learned at home. But how many people had enough data, even had a device at home in this country? And even if we could provide them with this, what about learning materials? The schools tried their best, but some were not prepared. So, teachers couldn't reach their children.

Within the group we have a telecommunications business, and we have an edutech company. We asked, 'How can we all sit down and find a solution that solves this problem? They need data, devices, learning resources.' The telco said, 'We'll give out SIM cards, we'll preload them with data.' They helped us source the devices at the best price possible, because during lockdown it was not easy to get devices. So, they used their contacts. We were looking at international shipments to try to get the devices here. And FrogAsia, our edutech company, has a learning platform so they could create lessons on the platform and then we brought in our network partners, like Teach for Malaysia. We work with universities because of our scholarship programme, so we brought them in, and they created content.

The whole idea was that this content was directed at parents not at teachers. We taught parents, and we also mapped it to the national curriculum so that parents would know whatever they needed to do with their children at home to help them when they started formal school again. This was a crazy experience because everything was locked down. Normally we would do this type of business in a store, you get people to come and register, but we had to do everything online. We had to deal with the logistics, we had to gather people to create lessons from everywhere. It was amazing how the staff pulled together because they saw what this was about, and they had understood the mission of the foundation. Within two weeks and after many sleepless nights, we launched the programme. Up to today, we have given out more than 400,000 SIM cards with data, 100,000 phones, we have 1,272 lessons in maths, English, science and Malay uploaded on our website. I think this demonstrates the power of the business to help philanthropy.

Badr Jafar: I want to stay on this subject of corporate foundations, because I think in many parts of the developing world it's still a nascent phenomenon. Here in the Middle East, there aren't too many examples of institutionalised corporate foundations. There are more and more registered family office entities doing philanthropy, but the corporate philanthropy arms or corporate foundations are fewer. What advice would you give to other corporations or even start-ups and SMEs from across these growth markets that might be considering a dedicated foundation or a corporate philanthropic arm? What should they be thinking about to maximise impact and to avoid any possible conflict of interest between the business and the foundation itself?

Kathleen Chew: I think it's the same in Malaysia as in many parts of the developing world. Corporate philanthropy is slowly growing and gaining traction. If companies are thinking of starting a separate and dedicated philanthropic organisation, first they need to be clear on the mission. That mission should align with the corporate mission as much as possible. For us it was the value placed on education by our founder that ran though the full organisation. So, education was a natural step for us, but we were not in the education business at the time we started the foundation. The alignment of values is important, but if it can align with your businesses as well, I think that adds a lot of value.

Our UK business is a water and sewerage business. A huge part of what they do is protecting the environment, because it obviously has an impact on the water that we supply. And so, it's natural, if one was to look at environmental issues as a corporate, if that was your business then it would be fully aligned. Those synergies that I talked about and that we managed to achieve would be so much easier. Leverage your businesses and see what you can provide to your foundation. It will cost you so much less and maximise your impact. Ask yourself, What is your endgame? Be clear about the impact that you want to make. If your impact is short-term and if you're not looking for sustainable long-term impact, maybe it's not necessary to have a dedicated foundation. You could have a CSR programme. Many companies do that and then you can report on that.

> "Leverage your businesses and see what you can provide to your foundation. It will cost you so much less and maximise your impact."

But if you want to create sustainable change, then set up a foundation. Ask yourself, what is your theory of change? Get some help externally. There are many people to help you map it out so that as you progress, and as you look at programmes, you can benchmark to what you set out to achieve. When people come to you for a grant, you can ask: is that within what I'm trying to do, within my theory of change? If not, your impact will be quite diluted because you're trying to do too much. That also means you should start with maybe one programme, the one that you feel is the lowest-hanging fruit, the one that your heart is in and just invest in that. When you see the results, you can expand. I think it is important to monitor your impact. It doesn't have to be hard. Monitoring and evaluation look difficult, but you can get guidance and use some simple tools to monitor progress, evaluate what you're doing. That would maximise effectiveness.

Badr Jafar: How would you describe the state of philanthropy in Malaysia and in Southeast Asia? What trends and changes have you observed and what's driving that change?

Kathleen Chew: I think we're still at an early stage in Malaysia, but what has happened is that a lot of the GLCs, the government-linked companies, have set up foundations and they've taken a major role in driving this space. In 2015, Khazanah Nasional, the sovereign wealth fund of Malaysia, set up its corporate foundation and it has done a lot to build an ecosystem where social entrepreneurs can thrive. The impact of what they do is being felt in the community. I think many of the large, listed companies have gone on the same path, but there are still many companies who regard this as CSR, not philanthropy to create impact.

If one wants to make the most strategic and impactful decisions, it's good to have a corporate organisation to do this. I think we have around 40,000-plus companies registered in Malaysia of which only about 600 are not-for-profits. There is a big discrepancy in how formal the giving has been, with a long way still to go. Looking at Southeast Asia, in Singapore and Hong Kong, corporate philanthropy is much more developed. In Singapore in 2000, they set up the National Volunteer and Philanthropy Centre, and that's really driven change. It's been very successful in pushing the private sector to think that way. In other emerging countries, such as the Philippines and Indonesia, they have a vibrant social sector, but it's driven by the international NGOs. There are some large family foundations that do a lot of great work, but I think it will be some time before we can catalyse more companies to go down this path. The landscape is quite diverse and there is still a lot to do.

Badr Jafar: What do you think that people should understand about the nature and practice of philanthropy in

Malaysia and the wider region? Are there social, cultural or regulatory factors that might have an impact on how people think about or engage in philanthropy in the region?

Kathleen Chew: In Malaysia we are a diverse country with three major races, the Malays, the Chinese and the Indians, and in East Malaysia we have many indigenous peoples, so there are a lot of cultural nuances around giving. For the Chinese, one of the most important things is education. People invest a lot in education, primarily in Chinese-language education. That's because they feel that they have a responsibility to preserve the culture and to preserve the language even outside China. I think sometimes we Chinese Malaysians are more obsessed with doing that than the Chinese themselves. To an extent, the Indians invest in Tamil education. And then there's a lot of religious giving, because faith is an important element of life in Malaysia, and in much of Asia.

"Younger people are looking at the impact they want to make, whether in environmental or ocean conservation or education. I think the younger business leaders will look at philanthropy strategically and not just through a cultural lens."

Especially with the older generation, you'll find that these cultural elements are important. The next generation is beginning to move away from being so culturally attached to philanthropy. Younger people are looking at the impact they want to make, whether in environmental or ocean conservation or education. I think the younger business leaders will look at philanthropy strategically and not just through a cultural lens.

I belong to an organisation called the Asia Philanthropy Circle, which was started in 2015 with the mission to grow Asian philanthropy. Our members do diverse things. For example, one is championing a project to build a peace university in Rakhine State in Myanmar to bridge the gap between the Muslim Rohingyas and the Buddhists. That's a project being run out of Singapore. Philanthropists are looking around and asking, How can I make an impact in the region? We have someone addressing stunting in remote Indonesian islands.

We brought the school leadership programme that I spoke about into Malaysia and our Indonesian members have taken that and are running a similar programme in Indonesia. There is a growth of collaborative philanthropy, and APC is doing a great job in catalysing that.

Finally, you mentioned families. In Asia, families are still important, and they are looking at handing over stewardship to the next generation. Even within a corporate family business, like ours, it's the family that believes that their own members should be engaged in the philanthropy. We don't outsource it so much at YTL. The family members are deeply engaged. Of course, there are professionals who assist, but I think it is still something that families find an important part of their legacy.

Badr Jafar: I have a question on the story of Mangosteen Organics, which you founded. How did the concept come about? How did you go about launching it?

Kathleen Chew: I'm a corporate lawyer. Doing a personal care business is not intuitive to me, but I've always loved fragrances, like pomelo, which is a Southeast Asian fruit, or the fresh smells of a Thai salad or Vietnamese salad. I've been trying to find a personal care brand that has these ingredients. I couldn't find anything that was of quality. At the same time, I am on the boards of many charities and I try to help them raise funds. I wondered, How can I do something that is more sustainable? This came together and I said, Why don't I try to start a personal care company, based on Southeast Asian scents? And at the same time, generate enough profits to support some of my charities.

Part of our business in the YTL Group is hotels and resorts. I went to my brother-in-law, who runs that division, and I asked, Would you use my products, and help me promote these products? He agreed. So, we have it now in the YTL Resorts. I've been on the cusp of taking it to the consumer market, which is a different ball game altogether. It's been a difficult journey, but I've recently recruited someone with a good business mind, as well as passion for the mission. So, watch this space.

Badr Jafar: Are there lessons in this for aspiring social entrepreneurs? I was speaking to someone recently about the dangers of what they refer to as 'heropreneurship', where people get obsessed with the cause, and want to charge in and help without properly assessing the sustainability angle from a business perspective and without taking the time to understand the problem that they're trying to solve. Both of those can be detrimental to success.

Kathleen Chew: My advice to young entrepreneurs is get your business case right. Many people are driven by a mission. But at the end of the day your consumers want good products. It doesn't matter whether you're creating a product for the rich or the poor, all want something that's good. So, make sure your product is of good quality. Make sure you've got a strong business case. As I said, the business case and the product come before the mission. Once you get that in place, then try to nurture that business.

His Excellency Abdul Aziz Al Ghurair

Chairman, Mashreq Bank and Chair, Abdulla Al Ghurair Foundation

Abdul Aziz Al Ghurair is a prominent figure in the United Arab Emirates' banking and business sectors. His long tenure as CEO of Mashreq Bank, spanning 30 years, before taking on the role of chairman, highlights his significant influence and leadership within the financial industry. He is a member of the board of directors of one of the biggest and most successful business groups in the Middle East, with operations spanning more than 20 countries and business roots stretching back half a century.

Al Ghurair has held various positions both in government and business, which have had impact both regionally and internationally. His extensive experience in banking and in business has made him one of the best-known personalities in the Arab world.

He is chairman of the Abdulla Al Ghurair Foundation, chairman of the Executive Committee of Al Ghurair Investment, chairman of Dubai Chambers, vice chairman of the Higher Board of Dubai International Financial Centre (DIFC) and board member of the Emirates Foundation. He is also the chairman of Masafi Company and Oman Insurance. In 2012 he was appointed as chair of the UAE Banking Federation. He has also served as the Speaker of the UAE's Federal National Council, the country's main parliamentary body.

The Abdulla Al Ghurair Foundation was founded by his father in 2015 who committed a third of his personal wealth, AED 4.2 billion, to support generations of Emirati and Arab youth.

Badr Jafar: How would you describe the state of philanthropy in the Middle East region? What are some of the most distinctive characteristics of philanthropy in and from the region, or the UAE?

Abdul Aziz Al Ghurair: Giving is a strong part of Emirati and Arab culture. Traditionally, most organisations and individuals choose to give privately, often by helping people directly without making it public. However, times have changed, and I believe our approach to philanthropy in the region must evolve to adapt to these changes.

We should approach philanthropy in the same way we would our businesses, with clear and specific goals in mind. This includes examining our long-term goals and the impact we want to make on society, whether in education, health or the environment. I believe that by focusing our collective efforts on these strategic goals, we can achieve greater results.

> "We should approach philanthropy in the same way we would our businesses, with clear and specific goals in mind."

Badr Jafar: Your father is a respected business pioneer and philanthropist, and you share a strong sense of commitment to making a positive impact in the community and the lives

of the vulnerable. Can you share with us the process that you undertook to decide on which causes to focus, and how you chose to have the most meaningful impact as a second-generation businessman and philanthropist?

Abdul Aziz Al Ghurair: When my father established the Abdulla Al Ghurair Foundation, he dedicated a third of his personal wealth to philanthropy. The first step for us was to identify our focus area. Given the vast and diverse challenges facing the Arab region, it was crucial to choose a sector in which we could make a meaningful impact. We already believed in the power of education for long-term impact, so we worked to make education more accessible. That could mean enhancing an education system by improving educational quality or providing young Arabs with access to high-quality education opportunities – in all cases, we work to yield big benefits.

> "I pushed for transparency because I believed it was important in today's philanthropic landscape to promote clear communication. I believe it can encourage the broader business community to contribute towards similar goals, helping us create a collective impact across different sectors and minimise duplication of efforts."

The next decision was whether to publicise our efforts. My father initially wanted privacy, in line with my grandfather's and the general approach to giving. However, I pushed for transparency because I believed it was important in today's philanthropic landscape to promote clear communication. I believe it can encourage the broader business community to contribute towards similar goals, helping us create a collective impact across different sectors and minimise duplication of efforts. For instance, while we focus on education, others may focus on environmental concerns, refugees or health. These are significant issues that cannot be addressed in silos. Strategic collaboration rooted in transparency both within and outside of the private sector is crucial, with each stakeholder playing a key role. So, I encourage other business leaders in the region to share ideas and collaborate with governments for positive impact.

Badr Jafar: The socio-economic consequences of the pandemic are likely to reverberate for many years. Do you think that it will have a lasting impact on how people in the Middle East region think about the role of private philanthropy in responding to challenges, and if so, how? How important is it for businesses, governments and philanthropists to be working together to find solutions to complex challenges?

"Strategic collaboration rooted in transparency both within and outside of the private sector is crucial, with each stakeholder playing a key role."

Abdul Aziz Al Ghurair: The foundation has been working on online learning for years, even before the COVID-19 pandemic. Governments across the Arab region, however, did not embrace it, and educational institutions were hesitant to offer online courses, programmes and certifications.

When the pandemic started and countries went into lock-down, it had a huge impact on education, preventing students from attending school. We quickly realised that we needed to move online to prevent learning loss. Educational institutions had to face the challenge of accelerating their transition to online learning and implementing high-quality online learning in a short amount of time.

The pandemic was an opportunity to explore some things that were not thought possible before. It pushed everyone – the government, universities, students and parents – to recognise that quality education can be accessed from home. It helped people to understand the importance of providing high-quality online education to students throughout the Arab region and beyond.

Current trends show that most learning will take place online in the future, with only a few disciplines requiring in-person instruction. So, our governments have started acknowledging the validity and necessity of online degrees in different fields. This has further motivated us to build on our existing online learning initiatives and launch new programmes for students who previously had limited access to education, and educational institutions who are seeking to expand their online offerings.

Considering this, an increasing number of UAE universities are approaching us, seeing the value we offer and seeking our expertise in online education and capacity building. The foundation established the University Consortium for Quality Online Learning, bringing together the UAE's Ministry of Education and nine UAE universities to make high-quality, accredited online programmes available to a wider pool of students. At a regional level, to facilitate better access to high-quality online education, we have also partnered with two universities: the American University of Beirut in Lebanon; and the American University of Cairo in Egypt.

When it comes to the importance of collaboration, it is important for the private sector to work closely with strategic partners from the wider ecosystem including the public sector and private family businesses and governments to uplift our society. Equally important is the collaboration between businesses and philanthropic efforts. There are few forums in the Arab region where the business sector can come together, share ideas, leverage collective experiences and make a meaningful impact on society. As a result, we must establish these platforms and encourage more people to explore the field of philanthropy.

I was fortunate to be given the chance by my father to lead the Abdulla Al Ghurair Foundation. Initially, I thought philanthropy was something to consider later in life. However, after seeing the impact of my father's work and meeting students from across the Arab region, I have realised that you don't need to wait until you're older to engage in philanthropy. I recommend starting young, even while still in school, to cultivate a giving culture that will grow over time.

This realisation inspired me to establish my fund, the Abdul Aziz Al Ghurair Refugee Education Fund, in 2018, with the firm belief that every young person in the Arab region deserves access to high-quality education. Since its inception, the fund has exceeded its intended target of serving 20,000 young people, reaching over 74,000 of them. We accomplished this because we partnered with over 20 organisations to implement high-quality educational programmes.

Moving forward, I hope to see increased engagement between the private sector and family businesses to promote philanthropy. I also hope to see more young philanthropists in our region and encourage them to start with the resources and connections they have.

Badr Jafar: Your Excellency, in what ways do you think that our future generation of philanthropists will change the way that philanthropy is practised?

Abdul Aziz Al Ghurair: One of the challenges we face as philanthropists is a lack of coordination. To solve this, we must collaborate and share our experiences. For example, many people are doing excellent work, but we are unaware of it due to a lack of experience-sharing. By sharing our experiences, we can stay informed on each other's work, coordinate our efforts, and benefit from each other's expertise. So, we should collaborate and devote some of our time to philanthropy, because this culture of strategic giving doesn't develop overnight.

It must be practised from childhood to high school to university and beyond, and at all levels, from small communities to larger cities, and national and regional levels, where a much greater impact can be achieved. So, to ensure that philanthropy succeeds in the region, the younger generation of philanthropists can strengthen collaboration by working together and sharing their knowledge and experience.

> "To ensure that philanthropy succeeds in the region, the younger generation of philanthropists can strengthen collaboration by working together and sharing their knowledge and experience."

Lord Karan Bilimoria

Founder, Cobra Beer and Chairman, Cobra Beer Partnership Limited

Karan Bilimoria is the founder of Cobra Beer, and chairman of the Cobra Beer Partnership Limited, a joint venture with Molson Coors. A former chancellor of Thames Valley University (now the University of West London), he was the youngest university chancellor in the UK when appointed. He is one of the first two visiting entrepreneurs at the University of Cambridge. In 2005, Lord Bilimoria established the Cobra Foundation, an independent charity that provides disaster relief, health, education and community support to young people in South Asia, especially through the provision of safe water, among other causes.

In 2006, he was appointed Lord Bilimoria of Chelsea, making him the first ever Zoroastrian Parsi to sit in the House of Lords. He is an Honorary Fellow of Sidney Sussex College, Cambridge (his alma mater) and was chair of the Advisory Board of the Judge Business School, Cambridge University from 2015 to 2020 and subsequently appointed as an Honorary Ambassador. In July 2014, he was installed as the seventh chancellor of the University of Birmingham, making him the first Indian-born chancellor of a Russell Group University in Great Britain, and he is the President of the UK Council for International Student Affairs (UKCISA). Since 2017, Lord Bilimoria has been a Bynum Tudor Fellow at Kellogg College, University of Oxford. He is also an Honorary Group Captain in 601 Squadron Royal Air Force. He was President of the Confederation of British Industry (CBI) from 2020 to 2022. He is a Visiting Fellow at the University of Oxford Said Business School based at the Centre for Corporate Reputation. In 2022, he was appointed a Trustee of Policy Exchange, a non-profit educational charity. In December 2023, Lord Bilimoria was appointed as Lieutenant to His Majesty's Commission of Lieutenancy for the City of London.

Badr Jafar: Lord Bilimoria, how has the extensive cross-sectorial experience you've had influenced the way that you think about issues around social capital? Can you start by telling us about the Cobra Foundation, its basic philosophy and what it's focused on today?

Karan Bilimoria: I go back to my early days when I started Cobra Beer with £20,000 in student debt. In India, they don't say small and medium-sized enterprises, they say, micro, small and medium enterprises. We started as a micro business. There were just two of us, my business partner and I, and we built it up from there. Now we've got a global joint venture with one of the world's largest brewers, Molson Coors, head-quartered in Chicago. Even in those early days, when there were just two of us, instinctively we wanted to give back whenever we could. We would find opportunities, we would come across a charitable event taking place in an Indian restaurant that was one of our customers, and we would say, 'Look, let's help this charity, we will give you free beer to serve at this event, that will save your charity some costs, which will help you to raise funds.' In this way, charities welcomed us. It was good for us because our brand was getting some profile, and we were able to help a charity raise money and raise their own profile.

This built momentum from day one. What started to happen was we'd have auctions and raffle prizes, and one auction prize was free Cobra beer for a year. If you won that auction, you'd have a case of Cobra beer per month, delivered to your doorstep. These auctions, even in the early days, raised several hundreds of pounds, in some cases thousands of pounds, that would go straight to the charity.

That's how we started our charitable work, by giving away free beer. We do that to this day and on a very large scale. For example, every year the Lord Mayor of London has the Lord Mayor's Curry Lunch in the Guildhall, the 800-year-old building. Over 1,000 people around the city come to this event. We raise about £250,000 a year net for the Armed Forces charities on that day and Cobra provides the beer free, thousands of bottles every single year.

If you support a particular charity consistently year after year, the impact grows. If you're giving £10,000 per event per year, for example, in ten years you've supported them to the tune of £100,000. I could give you example after example. We have competitions between the House of Lords and House of Commons. The biggest one is a tug of war. And this is not the tug of war of legislation, it is a real tug of war that takes place opposite the Houses of Parliament. We raise a quarter of a million pounds net for Macmillan Cancer Support at this event every year and it is attended by 600 to 700 people. Cobra Beer provides the beer free for that event. Thousands of pounds of beer every single year, year after year. That's how we've done it. We've donated millions of pounds' worth of beer.

Then I started the Cobra Foundation. Very few companies have their own foundations in the UK. We formalised that. Field Marshal Sir John Chapple, one of my father's great friends who was the head of the British Army when my father was head of the Central Indian Army, is the president of our foundation. My father was the founding president, but he sadly passed away; the charity got its formal status the day he died. So, it's a very sentimental thing for me.

When you have this proactive attitude, you spot opportunities. A few years ago, I shared a platform with the chief executive of Belu Water. I was noticing that this water was in all the top restaurants, even in the Houses of Parliament. At the end of the presentation, I realised why it was doing so well – because it was a social enterprise. Belu Water donate 100% of their profits to WaterAid, the charity for clean water and sanitation, saving lives around the world. I asked, 'How many Indian restaurants do you supply?' The CEO said, 'None'. I said, 'Well, we supply 7,000. Why don't we do a joint branded programme?' We've done that for the past few years. We specified that the co-branded water bottles were going to South Asia, the origins of many of our restaurateurs and the origins of the Cobra Beer brand. We've been saving lives with sanitation and clean water through

WaterAid, which gets 100% of the profits from that water. Everyone else makes their profit, the restaurant makes a profit, the customer pays a normal price, the distributor makes a profit, but the profit we make we donate 100%. It's hundreds of thousands of pounds that have been raised over the past few years. There's no end to it when you have that attitude.

Badr Jafar: What advice would you give aspiring philanthropists across the emerging markets who might be thinking about setting up their own philanthropic ventures either now or in the years to come?

Karan Bilimoria: One, you need the attitude and the mindset, which I've just spoken about. If you have an entrepreneurial mindset, seeing an opportunity, and then making it happen quickly, you've got to get on with it and do it. And you've got to follow the mantra which I follow, that it's not just good enough to be the best in the world. You've got to be the best for the world.

> "It's not just good enough to be the best in the world. You've got to be the best for the world."

Badr Jafar: When people think about emerging markets, India is one of the first economies that comes to mind. India is not alone. A much broader economic shift is taking place across parts of Africa, the Middle East and Asia. What impact do you think that the rise of these economies will have over the next few decades on the practice of philanthropy and the growth of the social sector?

Karan Bilimoria: There are many ways that this has traditionally been done by NGOs operating within countries. So, you have well-known charities, whether it's Save the Children or Oxfam, or charities headquartered in the UK but operating around the world, including in countries like India. What's happening more and more is you're getting that activity starting from within the country, including from the entrepreneurs, and the successful business communities.

What I've also noticed is the power of cross-border philanthropy. I'll give you a quick example. In 1997, Tony Blair became prime minister. I remember there was an Asian awards event in London. Tony and Cherie Blair came as the chief guests to this event. At the end there was a chap called on to the stage who I had never heard of before and he got Tony Blair to launch his charity for educating widows and children in India. I thought, what a great thing to do. So, I went up to him, and I said, 'How can I help you?' I became chairman of his Advisory Council, which I am to this day, and then we started fundraising. The model was very simple. We'd raise the money in the UK and then he would go state by state in India, and get 100 widows and children educated in each state at the cost of £120 per child. We would have fundraising dinners, get people to pledge to educate one child for one year. And in this way, this charity grew. He then said, 'There are hundreds of millions of widows and children all around the world. How can we help them?' So, we got the United Nations to establish International Widows Day, which is now on 23 June every year. This has become a global movement, starting off with one person's idea based on the experience he had with his own mother being widowed in India bringing up seven children. That's an inspiring story of what can be done.

Badr Jafar: To what extent do you apply traditional entrepreneurial or business principles to the practice of philanthropy, whether that's through the Cobra Foundation, or other things that you've been involved in? Has your approach to this changed over time?

Karan Bilimoria: You can bring this entrepreneurial attitude to any charitable event and organisation that you're involved with. It helps to spot opportunities and to accelerate action very quickly. That's what really propels philanthropy.

For example, I chair the Memorial Gates in London – the war memorial that was inaugurated by Her Majesty the Queen in

2002 to commemorate the service and the sacrifice of the five million who volunteered in the First and Second World Wars, from South Asia, Africa and the Caribbean. We organise and raise money for a commemorative ceremony every year. We got an introduction to the Royal British Legion, which is the biggest charity for armed forces in the UK. They said they wanted to focus on the Commonwealth and told us, 'You're doing this every year, we want to work with you.' One of our objectives is to get the message out to schoolchildren and youth around the country and have it embedded in the curriculum so that our youngsters are inspired and learn from their history. The Royal British Legion has a huge educational programme. So, we're working collaboratively with them to help to provide the funding and the educational programme for us. That's what happens when you have that open-minded entrepreneurial approach – new opportunities for a charity that's been around since 2002. This is the thing about serendipity. One of the professors at the Cambridge Judge Business School, Mark Durand, defines serendipity as seeing what everyone else sees but thinking what no one else thinks. That's what we entrepreneurs do.

"You can bring this entrepreneurial attitude to any charitable event and organisation that you're involved with. It helps to spot opportunities, and to accelerate action very quickly. That's what really propels philanthropy."

Badr Jafar: You've worked in business, you also sit in the House of Lords, you're the chancellor of a university, you have been the president of the CBI, which brings you into contact with a whole spectrum of businesses across the UK. What do you think are the keys to facilitating successful collaborations between business, government, academia and non-profit institutions?

Karan Bilimoria: The pandemic brought to the fore how important collaboration is at every level. I've seen the government in the UK not being able to do things on its own, whether it's testing the population or trying to set up a hospital from scratch. They've only been able to do it when they've collaborated with universities or the private sector.

There's no better example than right on our own doorstep in Cambridge. AstraZeneca, a British–Swedish company headquartered in Cambridge, has collaborated with Oxford University to produce the Oxford AstraZeneca vaccine, which is a game changer around the world because it's affordable, can be distributed at normal refrigeration temperature and produced at scale. Also, the collaboration is cross-border. The Serum Institute of India, owned by my fellow Zoroastrian Parsis, the Poonawallas, are producing it in India. They said that during the pandemic they will be giving it at cost and not making a profit. Cyrus Poonawalla, and the Serum Institute of India, the biggest vaccine manufacturer in the world, are renowned for being able to produce vaccines at an affordable rate. That's why they're the biggest and they go to every corner of the world. They're going to continue to do that with this vaccine. There you are, you've got lifesaving philanthropy on a global scale, with a huge pharmaceutical giant – AstraZeneca – and the biggest vaccine manufacturer in the world in India: cross-country, cross-border, and with academia and industry all working together.

FIVE
PHILANTHROPY AND THE CLIMATE CHALLENGE

Much has been said about the crucial role that government and business must play in the fight against climate change but much less attention has been paid to the increasingly important role that philanthropy can and should play in this effort. Well over a billion dollars in philanthropic capital is deployed by foundations and individuals around the world every single year yet only a fraction of this philanthropic capital is allocated to climate-related causes. According to recent analysis by the ClimateWorks Foundation, philanthropic giving by individuals and foundations focused on climate change mitigation makes up less than 2% of global giving. Another reality is that only a small fraction of that climate philanthropy went to supporting communities across the Global South, many of which are on the front lines of this challenge. Encouragingly, however, the same study showed a broadening appetite among philanthropists for funding more *diverse* approaches to climate change mitigation, even if the total amount of climate-focused philanthropy remains relatively low.

This is an important trend, because it is not only the *quantity* of philanthropic capital that makes it a potentially transformative resource in the global response to climate change. Philanthropic capital also has several distinctive characteristics that make it a powerful tool for pushing the boundaries of what is possible and achieving urgently required scale. Among other things, philanthropic funding is often more flexible, risk tolerant and patient than other forms of capital. When strategically deployed at an early stage, de-risking follow-on investments, it can generate a multiplier effect by unlocking even larger pools of government and business capital.

Philanthropy can be particularly valuable in the deployment of nature-based climate interventions – including reforestation, restoring mangroves and protecting biodiversity – that may not offer an immediate financial return and have historically struggled to compete for business and government funding. The reality is that nature and climate goals are inseparable, with research finding that natural climate solutions could yield one-third of the emissions reductions required to achieve a 1.5-degrees limit pathway. These reductions won't come cheaply, however. To address biodiversity loss and land degradation alone, it is estimated that nature-positive investments of US$8 trillion are needed between now and 2050. Philanthropists could play a pivotal role in filling this gap.

Achieving an equitable climate and nature transition by 2050 is going to require an 'all hands on deck' response from every part of the global community. For many government stakeholders, that will mean raising ambitions and making good on commitments that they and their predecessors have already made. For many business leaders, that will mean making the leap from pledges and declarations to tangible action and implementation. For many of the world's philanthropists, that will mean coming off the sidelines and throwing more of their considerable weight and unique attributes behind global efforts to address climate change.

In the same way that we can no longer decouple the human development agenda from the climate and nature agenda, we can also no longer afford to keep governments, businesses and philanthropists operating in isolation. They must work together and in parallel, collaborating where they can while playing to their respective strengths. When we get this right, blending capabilities and capital from across these different sectors, we can produce outcomes on a required scale and timeframe that not one of these individual stakeholder groups could achieve on its own.

There are abundant opportunities for business and philanthropy actors to meaningfully engage. From supporting game-changing climate 'moonshots' and breakthrough technologies, and expanding indigenous peoples' direct access to investment, to accelerating the transformation of food supply chains across the Global South; the diverse options run the gamut of climate and nature-related immediate needs and opportunities. Most importantly, they provide an accessible way for business and philanthropy leaders to engage in ways that are suited to their capabilities and competencies, including accelerating technology transfer, de-risking green investments, enhancing natural capital, boosting green SMEs and start-ups and increasing investment in resilience for vulnerable communities around the world.

In this context, I interviewed Razan Al Mubarak, a philanthropic leader from the UAE, about her efforts to accelerate more aligned global action on nature and climate, most recently at COP28 UAE. Al Mubarak is the President of the International Union for the Conservation of Nature (IUCN), the largest environmental conservation network in the world, with a remarkable cross-sectoral membership of governments, civil society organisations and individual scientists working together to preserve biodiversity and deploy nature-based solutions to counter the impacts of climate change and nature degradation.

I also spoke with HSH Prince Albert II of Monaco, who has dedicated more than three decades to philanthropy and the environment. Long before others, he worked to raise awareness of the damage being done by the changing climate, and the need for concerted global action to address and mitigate this damage. He has used collaboration, convening and recognition to leverage greater impact through his foundation. Together with another foundation, Prince Albert has convened an annual Prince's Roundtable with major philanthropists to exchange and inspire them towards common goals such as the Sustainable Development Goals. He continues to be optimistic about the innovation and creativity of so many individuals and organisations working in this space, many of whom are being recognised through his Prince's Prize for Innovative Philanthropy, which honours the most inspiring individuals and organisations participating in building a more sustainable and more equitable world.

Razan Al Mubarak

President, International Union for the Conservation of Nature (IUCN)

Razan Al Mubarak is a dedicated leader in global efforts to protect and conserve nature and to mitigate the impacts of climate change on the environment. She was elected President of the IUCN in September 2021, the second woman to hold this post in the organisation's 75-year history, and its first from West Asia. She also currently serves as UN Climate Change High-Level Champion for COP28 UAE. For more than two decades, Al Mubarak has played a vital role in the UAE, driving the nation towards a more sustainable future while spearheading progressive environmental protection, species conservation and climate action across West Asia and globally. When she was appointed Managing Director of the Environment Agency in Abu Dhabi in 2010, Al Mubarak was the youngest person to lead an Abu Dhabi government entity. She is also the founding director of the Mohamed bin Zayed Species Conservation Fund, helping to build the organisation into one of the world's largest philanthropic foundations supporting direct species conservation. She began her career in conservation in 2001, when she helped establish Emirates Nature, an NGO associated with the World Wildlife Fund. She currently chairs the board for the International Center for Biosaline Agriculture, and is a board member for numerous environmental entities and stakeholders, including Masdar, the world's largest renewable energy investor, based in

Abu Dhabi. Internationally, she is an advisory board member of the Rockefeller Foundation Economic Council on Planetary Health, the Cambridge Conservation Initiative and the Emirates Diplomatic Academy, and serves as a board member of Pantera and the Women in Sustainability, Environment and Renewable Energy initiative.

Razan is my partner in life and in philanthropy. In 2019, we joined the Giving Pledge, and we share a commitment to help catalyse systemic change within the philanthropic sector, in the hope that we can accelerate the growth of transformative partnerships and supportive networks in this space.

Badr Jafar: The IUCN is a membership organisation composed of over 1,400 NGOs and 160 countries helping to set conservation priorities worldwide. Could you start by telling us a bit more about the union, its philosophy and the things that it is most focused on today?

Razan Al Mubarak: Thank you, Badr, for having me as part of your business and philanthropy series because I really do believe in the integral role of this sector in addressing some of the most complex challenges that we collectively face. I'm going to start with a promise not to use acronyms. In the construct of climate change and biodiversity conservation, we tend to speak in acronyms. Let's dispel the noise around the first acronym that you use. What is the IUCN? IUCN stands for the International Union for Conservation of Nature. In essence, it is the largest environmental network on the planet. The philosophy of this 75-year-old organisation was to challenge the construct of multilateralism by ensuring that its members consist of both state actors and non-state actors, including civil society indigenous peoples' organisations – all on an equal footing. In addition to its 1,400 member organisations, it has more than 15,000 scientists around the world who specialise in species conservation, ecosystem and protected-area management, environmental law, wildlife trafficking and many other disciplines related to the conservation of nature.

This unique status positions the IUCN to be the sole intergovernmental environmental institution as a permanent observer to the United Nations. Why is this important? This is crucial as it represents the coming together of diverse actors, with each actor playing a specific and vital role in conserving nature. Collectively, we work hard on setting the global environmental agenda. We do this first by defining environment–nature priorities to enable states and civil societies to focus in order to enhance impact. Second, is to mobilise our very diverse backbone of more than 15,000 scientific experts to establish the tools and the standards of measurement for nature conservation so that nations and non-state actors around the world can use the most effective tools to benchmark their progress towards international biodiversity targets and goals.

Badr Jafar: At COP28 UAE, you announced the initial commitment of over a billion dollars to support nature and climate projects, including the UAE strategic investment of US$100 million with a focus on the world's largest forest basins across Latin America, Africa and Southeast Asia. You described this as a turning point where we collectively recognise the indispensable contribution of nature to our climate systems and its profound, intangible value to our communities and cultures. Could you tell us what your hopes are for a greater commitment from philanthropy to nature climate projects?

Razan Al Mubarak: COP28 was a turning point because for the first time the global community came together to agree to phase out fossil fuels in an orderly and *just* manner. Equally important was the recognition of nature as central to climate change at COP28. There was an admission and a realisation that, in fact, we cannot reach the goals of the Paris Agreement, nor can we fully leverage the UAE Consensus outcome document without integrating nature. For the first time ever, there was a global agreement among nations to end deforestation by 2030. For me, COP28 was not merely another climate change conference; it was a beacon of hope, a call to action and a renewed recognition that climate and nature cannot be addressed separately any longer.

In terms of what I hope that the community, including business and philanthropy, will do, I'm looking for several key elements. First, we need to be able to leverage and scale up nature-based solutions. I'm proud to say that the internationally accepted and recognised definition for nature-based solutions has been set by the IUCN. These are solutions that leverage the power of nature to deliver on climate mitigation and adaptation, on biodiversity conservation and restoration and most crucially to benefit people and communities. Nature-based solutions offer triple benefits and serve as powerful allies in combating climate change, potentially delivering up to 30% of our climate mitigation requirements by 2030. My hope is that we can scale up nature-based solutions.

> "Nature-based solutions offer triple benefits and serve as powerful allies in combating climate change, potentially delivering up to 30% of our climate mitigation requirements by 2030."

Additionally, we need to phase out fossil fuels and triple our renewable energy capacity by 2030. It's important that these initiatives – scaling up nature-based solutions and transitioning energy sources – do not come at the expense of nature or community. Furthermore, we must recognise that nature-based solutions are not a one-size-fits-all; they must be tailored to specific local contexts and nuances. Engaging with local communities and indigenous peoples is crucial; they are the custodians of nature and central to the success of such solutions. Without their involvement and leadership, we risk failing those we aim to serve most, making engagement at the local community level extremely important.

Badr Jafar: It was great to see, largely thanks to your engagement and involvement, nature front and centre of the action agenda at COP28. You're the Founding Director of the

Mohamed bin Zayed Species Conservation Fund, which since inception has supported more than 2,000 species conservation projects in over 160 countries, bringing many species back from the brink of extinction. How do you measure the impact of the fund over time? What does expansion look like for the fund going forward?

Razan Al Mubarak: We can measure impacts tangibly and intangibly. Tangibly, we can measure them by the number of species that were brought back from the brink of extinction, or the number of species that were rediscovered. We have 2,750 species conservation projects, each with its own measurable key performance indicators. We know how these projects are doing and how they are impacting nature and species from a tangible perspective. I believe the intangible perspective is just as powerful. This is where philanthropy has the most impact, as other investors like governments and multilateral development banks may be less equipped to measure intangible value due to the specific reporting metrics and templates they are obliged to follow. Intangible impact focuses on communities, people and the intrinsic value of species.

While we often emphasise the measurable aspects of conservation, such as metrics and economic viability, it is equally crucial to consider those elements that are difficult to quantify but are intrinsic to our existence and the natural world. Indigenous wisdom, for example, which sees tigers as central to their forest relationships and way of life, provides profound insights and innovative solutions that transcend traditional metrics.

As such, the MBZ Fund is as much about people as it is about nature and the species that are conserved. The founder, His Highness the President of the United Arab Emirates, recognised the multifaceted challenges with the species extinction conundrum. He observed that conservationists themselves, as well as the discipline of conservation, could disappear if not supported, leveraged, highlighted and cultivated. This discipline requires ongoing support because it is not only an art and a passion, but also indispensable. You cannot protect nature with funding alone, you must protect it by empowering those individuals that protect nature and whose very lives and livelihoods are intertwined with its fate.

> "You cannot protect nature with funding alone, you must protect it by empowering those individuals that protect nature and whose very lives and livelihoods are intertwined with its fate."

Badr Jafar: Do you see an opportunity for cross-sector collaboration in the area of nature conservation? Can philanthropy promote faster action by all stakeholders, including business and government, on the race to reach '30 by 30', or the conservation of at least 30% of the world's land, freshwater and marine ecosystems by 2030?

Razan Al Mubarak: You've always showed me that the real magic happens at the nexus of things and the nexus of disciplines. We talk about the existential crises of climate change, biodiversity loss, and other sustainable development challenges we must overcome. We won't be able to address them in isolation. For far too long, we've been working on these issues in isolation from each other. We have the scientists working alone, and the policymakers, the technologists, the investors and the funders – all working in isolation. Instead, we must be able to break the barriers because these solutions will require different tools, expertise and perspectives; and will require us to recognise that these issues – and all our unique perspectives – are linked. If we don't address the issue of social and economic justice, we will not address the issue of nature conservation. Recognising and breaking these barriers are extremely important. It's imperative; we cannot merely depend on connecting the dots but must truly converge these issues and address them together.

> "If we don't address the issue of social and economic justice, we will not address the issue of nature conservation."

Moreover, we need a diversity of actors to work on these complex challenges in a way that complements our respective roles and responsibilities instead of competing with one another.

That's why I'm extremely proud of what COP28 was able to accomplish. For the first time, it called for the convergence of the three Rio Conventions. The Rio Conventions are the Convention on Biodiversity, the Convention on Climate Change and the Convention on Desertification. We must address these complex issues together, and not in isolation from one another. The nexus requires collaborative efforts across expertise, interests and perspectives. These are all-of-society challenges that require all-of-society solutions.

Badr Jafar: You've said that the more women and girls that are included in efforts to tackle climate change and advance sustainable development, the faster we move towards a healthier, safer and more equitable society for all. Yet women and girls continue to suffer some of the worst consequences of climate change, and data shows they're not sufficiently included in climate and nature solutions. How can philanthropy, in your view, catalyse more collaborations with governments and businesses to address this need to bring about a more inclusive and gender-just transition?

Razan Al Mubarak: Let's get something straight. Climate change is here, global warming is happening and it's already disproportionately affecting the most vulnerable. This vulnerability is not gender neutral. Women and girls are facing the brunt of climate and biodiversity loss. With that recognition, we must also recognise that we cannot talk about a fair transition if women are left behind. In my view, we need investment and a closer look at three key areas. The first area is data. We cannot achieve a just energy transition or a more equitable world without understanding how these impact women and accounting for their contributions to climate solutions. Today, this sort of disaggregated data does not exist. We need to be able to design gender-responsive climate policies. To do so, we must have gender-disaggregated data to fully understand the impact of climate change on women and girls and the impact of their contributions to solutions. Only with a full understanding of this landscape can we better support women and girls through policies, support mechanisms and financing.

Financing is the second element. We often say that ideas and plans without finance and implementation are mere hallucinations. Therefore, it's crucial to financially support women and girls who are on the frontline of climate impacts and hold key solutions. The third element is genuine empowerment and engagement. Women and girls need to co-design and co-implement the solutions that we require to achieve a genuinely just transition.

His Serene Highness Prince Albert II of Monaco

His Serene Highness Prince Albert II became sovereign prince of Monaco in 2005. Since his ascension, he has been outspoken in the field of environmentalism, and an advocate of ocean conservation and the adoption of renewable energy sources to tackle global climate change. He founded the Prince Albert II of Monaco Foundation in 2006, dedicated to protecting the environment and promoting sustainable development at local and global levels. The foundation's three priority areas are: limiting the effects of climate change; preserving biodiversity; and managing water resources.

Prince Albert participated in five Winter Olympic Games, from Calgary in 1988 to Salt Lake City in 2002, as a member of Monaco's bobsleigh team. A member of the International Olympic Committee since 1985, he is President of the Monégasque Olympic Committee. He is Honorary President of the International Union of Modern Pentathlon and the International Athletics Foundation. He is also a member of the Honorary Board of the International Paralympic Committee.

He is also the vice chairman of the Princess Grace Foundation – USA, founded in honour of his late mother's legacy, which continues to support emerging artists.

Badr Jafar: Your Serene Highness, you founded the Prince Albert II of Monaco Foundation in 2006 to focus on causes

related to the environment and sustainability. Can you share with us why you created the foundation, a bit about its vision and future aspirations, and how you decided on its main areas of focus?

Prince Albert: Very simply, I created my foundation in 2006 out of a personal commitment. Monaco, through its diplomatic channels and through its foreign relations, was already involved in different environmental projects around the world, but I thought there was an entity that I could put together to address more urgent needs. We were already being approached by different organisations and stakeholders, with specific projects. For me, it was obvious that I needed to do something on a more personal note and to try to bring many people around these issues not only in Monaco, but in other countries as well. So that's how and why the foundation came to be.

It was in a year where I had different opportunities to witness first-hand the state of our planet and more specifically through a trip that I made to the North Pole. That was one of two polar expeditions – one in the Arctic and one in the Antarctic – that I did several years ago. After witnessing all these worrying signs, not only concerning climate change, but also the loss of biodiversity and access to water by different peoples and populations, I thought these should be the main areas of focus for the foundation. So, over 15 years, well over 500 projects and several scores of millions of euros later, we have been able to help in addressing these incredibly complex and worrying issues that concern our planet, and how we can envisage a future for it.

It's thanks to the generosity of many people, of our donors and other organisations that we've been able to partner with, that we were able to have some success on the ground and in all corners of the world. Our primary areas of focus are the Mediterranean regions because we are a Mediterranean country, but we also focus on developing nations around the world and the polar regions. We've been active on all continents and in over 60 countries. Despite the different crises that the world is facing, we are more capable now collectively with different organisations, governments and stakeholders, and civil society. If we all pull our resources together, we can have an impact on the state of our planet. It's only the beginning and it's going to take a long time and a lot of commitment and funds to be able to find the right solutions for these issues. But I am decidedly optimistic and I think we have the capabilities and the know-how. Some of the needed technologies are already here, but we need to invest more in them; certainly in the clean energy sector, to be able to provide a future for our children and grand-children. That is a tall order but we are absolutely committed to these ideals and we must try to gather as many people as we can to move forward.

Badr Jafar: What motivated the launch of the Prince's Prize for Innovative Philanthropy, Your Highness, and how important is innovation, technological or otherwise, in the social sector?

Prince Albert: In 2020, we celebrated the tenth anniversary of the Prince's Roundtable on Philanthropy. This is organised by my foundation and the Tocqueville Foundation every January. This year, we welcomed nearly 40 philanthropists from around the world who came to discuss the role of philanthropy in the context of the Sustainable Development Goals. To have an informal discussion is incredibly valuable; it enables all of us to have a better understanding of not only what everybody does, but also how we can pull resources together, how we can make our actions and our projects even more effective and to implement the change that we want to see around the world.

In 2014, we and the Tocqueville Foundation decided to launch the Prince's Prize to honour the most inspiring individuals and organisations that participate in building a more sustainable and more equitable world. I was very enthusiastic about this idea and I know that everyone else around the table shared these ideas and these values. We were able to find some incredible individuals and organisations who have made an impact, which is very encouraging and I hope that we will be able to continue in this manner. Over the years, the Prize has grown and we feel the enthusiasm around it.

There have been different types of organisations that we've been able to help, ones that are important not only in emerging countries, but also on our doorstep in Europe and in the Mediterranean regions. I think that the real issue is how to keep these programmes going, and how to implement long-term financing for these endeavours and the kinds of mechanisms that make these initiatives sustainable in the long run.

Badr Jafar: How optimistic are you that we will soon see meaningful action to address the climate crisis? What is the most useful thing that philanthropists could be doing to help address this crisis while also trying to deal with the consequences of unexpected crises, such as the pandemic?

Prince Albert: The pandemic knew no borders; it hit every country at every latitude and every community around the world in a devastating way. We must come together and act collectively without delay both with the pandemic and with climate change. What has been showcased is the inextricable link between humans and nature, and the connection between the animal world and the human world. Let's take this opportunity to take a closer look at animal health and human health. When you do this, you can see that when there is disruption of everything that affects nature and the mechanisms that regulate nature, that's where you get a dangerous situation that can lead to negative impacts on human health. Here in Monaco, we are looking at ways to encourage studies by veterinarians and experts on animal health, and how we might have a conference on the links between animal health and human health. That's one thing that can come out of this.

We must also take the opportunity to work on better addressing climate change and the loss of biodiversity through global

> "What has been showcased is the inextricable link between humans and nature, and the connection between the animal world and the human world."

collaboration. The World Conservation Congress of the International Union for Conservation of Nature is a big event every four years. Then there's the global meeting on the convention on biodiversity [originally scheduled to be held in China in October 2021, but held in December 2022 in Montreal]. We hope to set new goals for the next 10 to 20 years. And we absolutely must do that – because we haven't been able to meet the targets that were set in 2010 in Japan, to have more protected areas around the world and to protect the most vulnerable species. COP26 in Glasgow, Scotland [2021] will be incredibly important as we will try to have the signatories to the Paris Agreement fulfil their commitments. Of course, we want to welcome the United States back into the discussion, as President Biden pledged in 2021, because we absolutely need the leadership of countries such as the United States and the other major countries in the world to show us the best path forward as we continue to fight climate change in the most effective way possible.

Badr Jafar: How do you think that the nature of philanthropy has changed in the decades that you have been involved in the sector?

Prince Albert: I think philanthropy has been a good answer to the biggest social and economic challenges of our societies. Access to education, health, food, the protection of the environment, arts, culture and every area that needed assistance or needed development has been helped by philanthropy. I feel now that philanthropy is more relevant than ever and can give a real added value for the development of society at large and for the transition to a better society.

"I feel now that philanthropy is more relevant than ever and can give a real added value for the development of society at large and for the transition to a better society."

Badr Jafar: How do you think that the youth of today will change the way that philanthropy is thought about and practised in the future?

Prince Albert: I think youth is looking to philanthropic answers to many different questions. Governments or other institutions can only do so much. There will always be that need to drive things forward in a different way. The youth of today will believe in this pathway even more so in the future and we have to keep that interest alive. Over the past few years, I sense a heightened sense of collective responsibility. This is very encouraging and feeds into the appeal of philanthropy to act more directly and in a more personal way, just as I was able to do with my foundation.

Different generations understand the need for change. There are serious problems facing our planet. There's more of a desire to help and to want to commit oneself to these issues. I have faith in the younger generation that they will have not only the tools at their disposal to implement and to drive these changes, but the incentive to do it. This pandemic crisis has shown us that there's more solidarity and more people trying to help one another in most countries. Let's keep this momentum as we move out of the pandemic and transform that into a desire to move our planet to a more sustainable and healthier place.

SIX

BLENDING CAPITAL AND RISK

Strategic philanthropy is about having impact at scale and speed. But the complexities and the interconnectedness of many issues in our world today, from the climate and ecological crisis to the problems of structural poverty, inequality and lack of access to health and education, mean that philanthropists cannot do their work alone. These complexities force strategic philanthropists to work in collaboration – with each other, with the state and with business. This is true of every country, but particularly true in emerging economies where philanthropic infrastructure is fragile and related networks are underdeveloped. Philanthropists must reach out if they truly want to have impact.

One of the advantages of philanthropy is that it can take risks that businesses and governments may be reluctant to take. It can provide first-mover capital to de-risk and to stimulate innovation as well as to support and scale up new approaches. Philanthropic capital can be deployed in a blended fashion with business capital across a spectrum of investment opportunities ranging from outright grants to loans to direct investments and to social impact investments. Philanthropic capital can be used in conjunction with public investments to pilot test what will become large-scale publicly funded programmes and services. It can also be brought to bear to generate social outcomes with investments that are paid back through public funds, as the 'social impact bond' examples demonstrate.

Yet collaboration of this kind, whether in the form of blended capital or pooled funding, has its challenges. It takes determination, imagination, commitment and a willingness to take risks together. These are characteristics of many of the social entrepreneurs and non-profit leaders that I interviewed.

One of the leading thinkers in the field of impact investing and outcomes finance is Sir Ronald Cohen. I had a fascinating conversation with him about the potential for social finance to make an enormous difference to the future of our society and planet. His analysis of the conditions for successful growth in social purpose finance is complemented by the experiences on the ground of path-breaking innovators in this field such as Jacqueline Novogratz and Professor Muhammad Yunus. I spoke to each of these influential leaders about their work in using social finance with a business approach to solving social problems. Jacqueline Novogratz is a deeply thoughtful and articulate social enterprise investor who has excellent advice for would-be social entrepreneurs and philanthropic investors. Professor Yunus remains as passionate now as he was at the beginning of his long career about using the tools of finance and social business to improve our world.

Another creative investor is Haifa Faloum Al Kaylani, an economist who founded the Arab International Women's Forum in 2001 as an independent non-profit with the mission of enhancing the role of women in the social and economic development of their own communities across the Middle East. She is a social entrepreneur in her own right, with successful projects in Jordan and across the Arab world. She believes fervently in the importance of working with a wide range of partners to achieve sustainable change. Her conversation with me provides several examples of the power of philanthropic entrepreneurship and collaboration in applying blended capital to social problems.

Sir Ronald Cohen

Chairman, Global Steering Group for Impact Investment and the Portland Trust

Sir Ronald Cohen is a co-founder and director of Social Finance UK, USA and Israel, and co-founder chair of Bridges Fund Management and Big Society Capital. For nearly two decades, Cohen's pioneering initiatives in driving impact investment have catalysed several global efforts, each focused on driving private capital to serve social and environmental good.

Cohen chaired the Social Impact Investment Taskforce established under the UK's presidency of the G8 (2013–15), the Social Investment Task Force (2000–10) and the Commission on Unclaimed Assets (2005–7). In 2012, he received the Rockefeller Foundation's Innovation Award for innovation in social finance.

He founded Apex Partners in 1972, was a founder director and chairman of the British Venture Capital Association and a founder director of the European Venture Capital Association. He is the author of *IMPACT: Reshaping Capitalism to Drive Real Change*, published in 2020. His previous book, *The Second Bounce of the Ball*, was published in 2007.

Badr Jafar: Sir Ronald, I'd like to ask you about the current state of impact investment. There's a clear trend towards the adoption of the broader philosophy around the role that financial investments can play in enhancing social outcomes. However, many are still sceptical that there is no trade-off between profit and purpose. Is this trend unstoppable in your view? How long will it take for it to become mainstream, and even the norm?

Sir Ronald Cohen: The answer to your question is that we've reached the point of no return with regards to impact, and it is inevitable now, in my view. I will explain why. What started out, for me, as a journey on the path of impact investment 20 years ago, led to the realisation that if you optimise risk, return and impact as an investor, then it puts us all on the path of bringing risk, return and impact to the centre of our economies. Why? Because of the trends that led investors today to channel more than US$30 trillion of capital to environmental, social and governance investing, and which have led investors to channel what will be a trillion dollars this year to impact investment, where you measure the impact created, as well as the intention to create it. That trillion is equivalent to the whole of the venture capital pool. More than US$30 trillion represents more than a third of professionally managed assets in the whole world. We're not talking here about a flash in the pan.

One important element is missing, and that is impact transparency. You and I know that conversations around measuring impact have been going on for decades, with the environmental movement getting going first on measuring environmental impact, and the social impact side coming into real focus maybe a decade ago. Today, technology enables us to bring transparency to all the impacts of a company. That means measuring its employment impact, of course, measuring its operational impact and measuring its product impact – all these impact people and the environment. A Harvard Business School project that I've been involved with – the Impact-Weighted Accounts Initiative [IWAI] – has published the environmental damage in monetary terms created by 1,800 companies across the world. This will lead to change. For example, shareholders of Procter and Gamble voted [in October 2020] to take unsustainable forest products out of its supply chain. You can look at Procter and Gamble's numbers and see that it creates US$1.7 billion worth of environmental damage in a year, equivalent to more than 10% of its pre-tax profit. That Harvard data is beginning to include employment impact as well, the cost of diversity and so on. Soon, we will have product impact too. Within the next few months, we will be able to look at the total impact of a company and then I think it will be inevitable that governments will have to mandate this.

Badr Jafar: Will COVID-19 affect the appetite and the urgency behind the use of financial investments and instruments towards social and environmental goals alongside generating financial returns?

Sir Ronald Cohen: We can see COVID-19 accelerating the advance of impact. First, it's shaking all our habits and beliefs. It's also leading to huge questioning of both capitalism and democracy across the world. And governments are going to emerge from the COVID-19 crisis with huge national debt. We're going to see high levels of unemployment. A lot of the big businesses that have furloughed workers will not take them back because they got used to working on a slimmed-down basis. We're going to have to retrain the unemployed to get into jobs. We're going to have issues of poverty, of homelessness, and so on. The only way that governments can cope with the surge of social issues and with the huge environmental problems we're facing is to bring businesses and investors alongside to realise solutions instead of the self-defeating system we're living with now, where companies in their pursuit of profit create environmental and social damages and governments try to tax us to try to remedy them.

"The only way that governments can cope with the surge of social issues and with the huge environmental problems we're facing is to bring businesses and investors alongside to realise solutions."

Impact investment has many tools at its disposal including social and development impact bonds [SIBs and DIBs], outcomes funds, social investment banks, social bonds, and so on. These tools are going to be very important in bringing investor capital to help tackle these issues. I think governments are going to have to follow the path of our predecessors, when, after the crash of 1929, the US government [in 1933] mandated transparency on the profit of companies with auditors using generally accepted accounting principles [GAAP], which hadn't existed until then. The reason, I think, that governments are going to have to do the same thing for impact transparency is that the information from Harvard and other places begins to prove that it's price-sensitive information. You can see a correlation in the Harvard data between companies in the same sector that pollute very heavily and that pollute less. You can see a correlation between the levels of pollution and the market ratings of companies; their price earnings ratios, their value on the stock market.

Regulators are going to become aware that to maintain an orderly market, they must shift to generally accepted impact principles. So, we have technology and transparency on impact beginning to create an inevitable path now to risk – return impact optimisation. What we are going to discover – and I speak as somebody who spent his whole life in the investment business – is that optimising risk, return and impact delivers better returns than only optimising risk and return.

Badr Jafar: The fastest-growing economies in the world are in emerging markets where wealth is being generated by new generations of socially minded entrepreneurs and investors across Africa, the Middle East and developing Asia. How do we capture this opportunity in a way that ensures solutions are designed for local needs and suited to local cultures?

Sir Ronald Cohen: The great thing about impact investment is that you can address the key issues in different countries in different ways. Let me take the issue of education in emerging countries as an example. We have an effort now to bring US$1 billion to improve the education of 10 million children in the Middle East and Africa (the Education Outcomes Fund). If you were thinking traditionally, you might say, 'Let's give the money in grants either through aid or philanthropy – or help governments fund programmes by making grants to them.' But when you begin to think through an impact investment lens, you say, 'Let us get aid organisations and philanthropists and local governments to put the billion dollars into an outcomes fund that is professionally managed, and that will sign outcomes contracts with delivery organisations, non-state actors working on the public education system.' Once these contracts are signed, the delivery organisations will be able to raise investment capital, as tech entrepreneurs raise venture capital from development impact bond funds, which are now being set up by UBS, British Outcomes Partnerships and others. Let us create a new type of ecosystem where private investment money funds charitable organisations and businesses to achieve social goals and the outcomes payers (the combination of aid organisations, governments and philanthropists) pay only for results achieved.

So, the investor is taking the delivery risk, expecting to make a very attractive and correlated return of 5% to 10% for that delivery risk. I think the ability now to use impact investment in emerging countries can accelerate improvement against the many constraints on economic growth that currently exist. If you combine the use of these instruments with the transparency that investors are going to have on the performance of companies – not just in profit terms, but in terms of impact – it should drive massive amounts of capital to emerging countries.

Badr Jafar: How does the field of strategic philanthropy intersect with social investment? How can lessons and insights from one help to enhance the other? Are you excited about the often-touted concept of blended capital or blended finance, combining business capital, philanthropic capital and even government capital to help enhance social returns?

Sir Ronald Cohen: Totally! Let me give you an example that will speak to your question. Technology such as artificial intelligence is enabling us to tackle a host of social issues in ways we could not have tackled before. Ziv Aviram is a very successful Israeli entrepreneur. A few years ago, he co-founded a company to help the blind called OrCam. It involves creating a pair of spectacles with an assistive AI device on the side that whispers into the ear of the wearer the page of the book they're reading, or the bank notes in their hand, and so on. This creates huge value for the 35 million blind people in the world, and the 250 million visually impaired people. Now, if you think about technology, from the perspective of impact, you ask yourself the question, how can this technology help the largest number of people in the world?

What if you gave these spectacles to the 800 million illiterate adults in the world? What would that do for their lives and livelihoods, for their economies and for the world economy? You now have a US$1.1 billion market. What's the business model going to be for illiterate people who are at the bottom of the pile in their ability to pay? You need philanthropy to kick it off. So, you might want to raise US$200 million of philanthropic capital, to be able to distribute these spectacles to illiterate people working within companies where they might get some form of advancement for their ability to read.

You can then begin to imagine a business model where companies in the future will pay for their employees to have these spectacles and perhaps receive the payment back over time from the employee. If we're talking large numbers, we're talking a relatively low price for these spectacles. If you want to expand it to the 800 million illiterate people, perhaps financial organisations will come in to fund, through philanthropy and investment money, the purchase of these spectacles. So, the blending of impact investment and philanthropy is a major tool in tackling the big social and environmental challenges we face.

> "The blending of impact investment and philanthropy is a major tool in tackling the big social and environmental challenges we face."

Badr Jafar: It's a powerful example of how sectors could come together towards the same outcome and impact. What role do governments have beyond regulation in fostering impact investment and strategic philanthropy? What else could they be doing to encourage more of these practices?

Sir Ronald Cohen: They can be doing a lot. For one, they must tweak the duties of company directors and trustees of pension funds and charitable endowments, to take into account social and environmental considerations when making decisions about investment. That is a very important dimension now in empowering company directors and trustees to optimise risk-return impact. It's a necessary change. The second thing governments can do is begin to measure the cost of social issues, as the UK did in 2014, and make this information publicly available so that we can start to see outcomes funds come into play. This would be alongside attracting impact bond investment at scale, to tackle issues of retraining the unemployed, training youth through apprenticeships, reducing dropout rates from education, preventing pre-diabetics from becoming diabetic, taking the homeless into homes and jobs and so on.

In addition to the outcomes funding, governments can provide incentives for investors to get involved. We want to democratise this form of investment. We would like the average person to be able to invest in a social impact bond fund that addresses an issue that they're particularly passionate about. The UK government introduced incentives a few years ago. We want other countries to do the same. So, governments can help to create the enabling environment that is going to allow impact investment to get to scale. And finally, government can shift its own expenditure from purchasing services to looking at the outcomes and measuring the outcomes that are achieved. I mention all of this in my 2020 book *IMPACT: Reshaping Capitalism to Drive Real Change*. There's a whole chapter on government. If we can get government to understand that they should create this enabling environment (because it really is the next frontier for society and capitalism), then we will progress a lot faster to improve our society and our planet.

Jacqueline Novogratz

Founder and CEO, Acumen

Jacqueline Novogratz is the founder and CEO of Acumen, which turns philanthropic funds into investment capital and makes long-term investments in individuals and early-stage enterprises that are focused on addressing challenges associated with poverty through market-based solutions. Since 2001, Acumen has invested US$146 million to build 155 social enterprises across Africa, Latin America, South Asia and the United States. These companies have brought basic services like affordable education, healthcare, clean water, energy and sanitation to hundreds of millions of people. In 2015, Fast Company named Acumen one of the world's Top 10 Most Innovative Not-for-Profits.

Novogratz's work began in 1986 when she quit her job on Wall Street to co-found Rwanda's first microfinance institution, Duterimbere. The experience inspired her to write the best-seller *The Blue Sweater: Bridging the Gap between Rich and Poor.* Before founding Acumen, she founded and directed The Philanthropy Workshop and The Next Generation Leadership programmes at the Rockefeller Foundation.

Badr Jafar: You've managed to combine both entrepreneurialism and altruism in the work that you do with Acumen, especially in the 'Patient Capital' approach to investing that Acumen is so widely associated with. Could you begin by explaining how you go about assessing whether a particular social enterprise is the right fit for Acumen?

Jacqueline Novogratz: While we are an investment vehicle first and foremost, when we're identifying a social enterprise we go back to our basic principle, which is standing with the poor. Our first screen is whether this enterprise is one that will specifically impact the lives of low-income people. Second, we look at the entrepreneur. Does she have the vision and the execution skills to scale up a company that can reach hundreds of thousands if not millions of low-income people and provide profitability and returns to the investors in the long term? We have come to realise that Thomas Edison's adage that 'vision without execution is hallucination' holds very true.

Third and most importantly, we assess the character of the entrepreneur. If you are truly going to build a company where both markets and governments have failed low-income people, you need to have a new set of leadership skills: listening; what we would call the moral imagination; the humility to recognise the world that you are in while still holding to a vision that you will be building; the ability to partner across lines of difference sometimes with entities you might consider your adversary; and, probably most important, the grit and resilience to do this work, not for a few years, but for many years.

If the enterprise has those three – standing with the poor, the right vision and execution, and an entrepreneur with character – and satisfies the due diligence that looks like that of any other private equity firm, we decide to go with it.

Badr Jafar: In your experience at Acumen and elsewhere, how much variation is there in the ways in which individuals and organisations think about and practise philanthropy or social entrepreneurship in different parts of the world? Are there any iron-clad principles for generating impact that you think should be universal?

Jacqueline Novogratz: Whether there's a religious impetus for giving or there is more of a societal impetus, at the heart, there is the same human yearning to do good, to recognise that from whom much is given, much is indeed expected. What excites me about this moment in history is that you're seeing two consistent trends across every culture in which we work. First, that wealthy individuals are getting weary of traditional approaches, top-down approaches to charity that too often create dependency, and they're looking for opportunities to build dignity, allowing people choice and opportunity through mechanisms that are, in fact, financially sustainable.

"Wealthy individuals are getting weary of traditional approaches, top-down approaches to charity that too often create dependency, and they're looking for opportunities to build dignity, allowing people choice and opportunity through mechanisms that are, in fact, financially sustainable."

Second, the trend towards social entrepreneurship. In every culture in which Acumen works, I see people using the tools of business to solve tough social problems, and then finding the right kinds of capital to animate those businesses or non-profits in ways that succeed in solving problems.

Badr Jafar: To what extent can you apply a traditional investment mindset to the evaluation of non-profit or even charitable initiatives and organisations and the scaling up of their operations. What's transferable about that process and what's not?

Jacqueline Novogratz: In many ways, Badr, it's why I started Acumen in the first place. A lot is transferable. The more I do this work, the more I am sure that it is not the organisational structure – whether non-profit or for-profit – that is important, rather that it is the right organisational structure for the problem that you are trying to solve, and that it is done in ways that are sustainable.

Using an investment mindset is powerful. First, good investors know that the most important factor on which to bet is the people. So, bet on character. Second, bring a long-term rigour and discipline to the work that's being done. In business, it's easy, because you have profit as your metric. It gets a bit trickier in the social sector. Yet increasingly, we're seeing metrics that do allow us to measure what we value, not just what we can count, and Acumen's work on lean data has been a real bonus for that. Third, there's an honesty in investment about failure, and cutting losses, as well as about seeing opportunities for collaboration, consolidation and mergers. We don't see that enough in the social sector.

Those would be the three areas where I see enormous transference from traditional investing into social enterprise and non-profit. Where I think we could do better is that too often philanthropists think that they're taking an investment approach, but in fact when it comes to their philanthropy they're short-term in their thinking. While they want to bet on the person, they also want to determine the programmes in which they will invest rather than giving unrestricted capital to the entrepreneur, so that she can build an organisation that can deliver real results.

Because of the power dynamics that often exist in philanthropy, it's hard for social entrepreneurs to talk about failure. You'll hear people almost avoiding the word 'failure' like the plague, saying, 'Well, we're still doing a great job, and we're learning from all of this.' That reduces the real conversations. It reduces trust and prevents the kind of long-term relationship where the philanthropist can be like an investor and help accompany the enterprise, using not just their financial resources, but their social capital, or access to other entities or other philanthropists. If we could shift in those directions, I think we'd have a much more productive sector.

The world is very different today from when you and I were born – we truly are interdependent. And in this new chapter, we need to redefine our social contract. Both business and civil society are essential to that social contract, as is government. The focus on equality, the focus on the poor and building community is something the world critically needs right now. Businesses too often overlook the poor and overlook our responsibilities to the environment, and there's a recognition of that now. If we're truly going to reimagine not only capitalism but what it means to live in society with each other, then we must speak about the different roles and the ways that business and the charitable sector can do more in concert than either sector can do on its own.

"If we're truly going to reimagine not only capitalism but what it means to live in society with each other, then we must speak about the different roles and the ways that business and the charitable sector can do more in concert than either sector can do on its own."

Badr Jafar: I'd like to go back to something you mentioned around what makes a successful social enterprise but more than the enterprise, the individual. That goes to skills. For at least two decades, you've been involved in different ways

in training and mentoring philanthropists, social entrepreneurs and the next generation of social sector leaders. What do you think are the key skills that inspiring philanthropists or social entrepreneurs should seek to develop to give themselves the best chance of succeeding in their chosen field?

Jacqueline Novogratz: My book *Manifesto for Moral Revolution* has 12 practices, and therefore 12 skills, which we think are essential. The reason I wrote it in the first place was because when I think about those social entrepreneurs that succeed not only in building companies, but in changing overall systems, it comes back to this set of skills and attributes.

The most important is what I would call the moral imagination, this idea that you have the humility to see that you're working in tough markets, often markets that are corrupt, full of bureaucracy and complacency; a status quo that you must fight against. And yet, if you cannot hold on to the vision of what can be, it will be almost impossible to develop the kind of grit and resilience that's needed to get others to come on the journey with you to build the right kind of organisation.

Connected to moral imagination is listening, not just with your ears, but with all parts of yourself. We're seeing too little of it in the world. The best entrepreneurs, particularly those that serve low-income populations, start by understanding how people see themselves, what their needs are, what their hopes are, so that they can build products and services that meet those needs, in ways that people can value and can afford.

Third, I would say, the ability to hold opposing values in tension. That is hard right now, because everywhere we look, people are standing on great certainty, whether it's business ideology versus government ideology, or if it's just tribalism, like the kind we're seeing in the United States and other countries around the world.

Yet the social entrepreneurs who have the character to realise that there's often, if not always, some small truth even on the opposing side, are the ones that are more able to build partnerships between the private sector and government. They are the ones that can go into communities and gain trust, although they may not have anything to do with them and they may even be mistrusted when they first approached them.

Finally, you must learn to tell the stories that matter. Storytelling is fundamental to fundraising, to changing mindsets, to finding followers and keeping them. We do too little skill building for entrepreneurs of all sorts, particularly social entrepreneurs, around telling stories that matter, that change narratives and build momentum.

Badr Jafar: What advice would you give to someone who's thinking about leaving their job on Wall Street today or the equivalent in their own country to go to a career in the philanthropic sector as you did?

Jacqueline Novogratz: In terms of advice to a young social entrepreneur setting out I would say number one, see the myriad problems around us as opportunities waiting for you to solve them. And then go towards the ones that meet your deeper yearning. The Jesuits say, 'Go to where your deepest yearning meets the world's great needs.' I would say if you see it, take a step forward towards it, just start, be curious and follow your thread of curiosity.

That gets you on the path. Once you have the courage to start and take a step on that path, the work will teach you the next place that you must go. And then the path begins to unfold. In some ways, although we're all about quantitative metrics and dollars and cents and building companies that serve millions, it's also the Sufi Way. It's daring to seek the unknown and having the courage to believe in yourself, and believing in a deep sense of purpose and letting that purpose guide you.

Badr Jafar: I might add to that the importance of being disciplined and rigorous about understanding not just the nature

of the problem, but the different solutions that might exist to tackle that problem.

Jacqueline Novogratz: I think you're right. Otherwise, it's just that hallucination again, it's a recklessness, that you see something and then you think you know the answer. That action comes with arrogance, rather than having the humility to immerse and understand a problem and move from there. I really appreciate that.

Badr Jafar: Acumen has a strong presence on the ground in many emerging market economies. In the work that you're doing in these parts of the world, are you witnessing a rise in the amount of philanthropic activity?

Jacqueline Novogratz: I'm definitely seeing a rise both on the philanthropic side and in terms of social entrepreneurs. I have always believed that the greatest innovation happens at the edges. I've been giving speeches in the United States about how we must look to the emerging markets, because it is here, in areas that have traditionally been more resource-scarce, where we're seeing the greatest amount of innovation to solve our biggest problems, like healthcare, like education, like access to electricity and improving agriculture. I'm deeply heartened by that.

There is such a hunger in the next generation to use the tools of business to solve these problems, and they need the right kind of capital to match it. How do we build momentum because the opportunities are so great? I do believe that these are the markets to follow for all of us who care about innovation and change, and the poor and the environment.

At the end of the day, what we're really talking about in your work and mine is to shift our definition of success from money, fame and power,

"What we're really talking about in your work and mine is to shift our definition of success from money, fame and power, to building systems that put our shared humanity and the sustainability of the Earth at the centre."

to building systems that put our shared humanity and the sustainability of the Earth at the centre. The next generation understands that this is where we must go. It's up to our generation to accompany them, support them and help them build this new world.

Professor Muhammad Yunus

Founder, Grameen Bank

Professor Muhammad Yunus established Grameen Bank in Bangladesh in 1983 to help the vulnerable exit poverty with microloans and by teaching sound financial principles. Today, replicas of Grameen Bank operate in over 100 countries. He is also the father of microcredit, an economic movement that has helped lift millions of families around the world out of poverty. Today, Grameen Bank has over 8.4 million members – 97% of whom are female – and has lent over US$12.5 billion since its inception. In 2006, the Norwegian Nobel Committee awarded the Nobel Peace Prize to Professor Yunus and Grameen Bank 'for their efforts to create economic and social development from below'.

Yunus also co-founded Yunus Social Business and serves as the chairman of the board. He has written four books about micro-lending and social business: *Banker to the Poor* (2003); *A World Without Poverty: Social Business and the Future of Capitalism* (2008); *Building Social Business* (2010); and *A World of Three Zeros* (2017). He has been awarded the Presidential Citizens Medal, the Presidential Medal of Freedom and the Congressional Gold Medal.

Badr Jafar: Professor Yunus, Grameen began with your original personal loan of US$27 to 42 women. Fast-forward to today, and Grameen Bank has well over nine million members, 97% of whom are women. Would you consider

this journey a philanthropic one? How compatible is it with more traditional business principles?

Muhammad Yunus: Grameen has always made it very clear that it is a business organisation, not philanthropy in a traditional sense, because philanthropy somehow is equated with charity, although its broader meaning is quite different. Grameen Bank is not a charity organisation; it is very much a financial organisation. It has its own shareholders, and the owners of the bank are the borrowers of the bank and a small percentage for the government also. They get dividends every year with the profit and so on. It has all the features of any commercial organisation with the difference that it belongs to the borrowers themselves, 97% of whom happen to be female. It follows all the rules of finance, except that it doesn't take any collateral. It charges interest and gets the cost recovered to its own income, and the surplus is a profit distributed to the borrowers who are the owners of the bank.

Badr Jafar: Ten years ago, you co-founded Yunus Social Business to create and empower social businesses that are solving global problems. Today, Yunus funds grow local social businesses that provide employment, education, healthcare and clean water to nine million people in East Africa, Latin America and India. Are you happy with how social impact is being embraced by businesses across the world today? Since the social business model that you champion is a zero-dividend business, are you not alienating those who might want to pursue social goals while at the same time generating financial rewards for themselves?

Muhammad Yunus: The conventional business is designed on the objective of maximisation of profit because economics created the framework, because economists imagine human beings as driven by self-interest, so self-interest, translated into business, is a maximisation of profit. If you follow that path, you ignore many social needs. We have been saying that the definition of a human being in economics is done in a very subjective, limited and damaging way. A human being is not only driven by self-interest, but also by collective interest. That part is not included in economics.

We need a different kind of business to promote the collective interest and to solve social problems. That's a business that is not interested in making personal profit, or driven by self-interested needs and the maximisation of profit. Business driven by collective interest needs no personal profit at all. That's what we call social business; it's a non-dividend company to solve human problems.

> "We need a different kind of business to promote the collective interest and to solve social problems."

When we introduced that kind of business, people said that it was not possible. Why should anybody invest in a business where they don't make money at all? They said that would be crazy but I said, 'People are crazier than that.' They give away their money, and not only small amounts of money, trillions of dollars, as charity. I'm giving them an option to invest in a social business, so that it continues to function and grow, and in the process solves human problems. Charity is a wonderful idea; it has been saving people over centuries, but it has limitations. Money goes out and does wonderful work, but never comes back. Social business money goes out, achieves the same objective, and it comes back. Then you can reuse the money to do the same thing, or do something new, again and again. Money grows in the process, and whatever profit you have is ploughed back into the business. So, you have a chance to expand your business. Compared with charity, social business gives you much better mileage for your money. I'm not denying that charity is a very important thing. In many cases, where you cannot use a social business idea to address a problem, charity is the only way.

With commercial business, you cannot address these issues, because your mind is totally focused on maximisation of profit. In a way, economists have made us into money-making robots.

We are not human beings anymore, because the word 'human' doesn't exist in economic jargon. Humanity doesn't exist. Business is about making money. So, I put humanity back in. We need a different kind of business in addition to money-making businesses. We can do social business where you don't want to make personal profit.

People are responding. We have created many social businesses in Bangladesh, and many companies are coming forward who are helping to create social businesses. You mentioned the Olympic Laurel that I was given at the 2020 Tokyo Olympics. That's because we are inviting the sports world to use its power to bring social business in to solve societal problems, and problems within the sports world, and they love that.

Badr Jafar: Moving from the role of business to the role of government, does the government in these markets need to do more to encourage this form of business and nurture more impactful giving in general, and if so, how?

Muhammad Yunus: One big role government can play is to become the cheerleader, saying that this is a good thing to do. Society has always dumped its problems at the door of the government to solve, and governments have no clue how to solve every single problem. When you create a social business, you are taking a share in solving problems. It is a tough job, but people come up with creative ideas. Social business can also create jobs, converting young people into entrepreneurs and social business funds can put the money in their hands so that they can translate their ideas into action.

Government can do a lot in recognising and encouraging the creation of social business. Government can require companies to create parallel social businesses and give them priority, because they're taking a burden from the government and solving social problems. Governments can give priority to social business banks and purchase from social business companies. The government has financial power, and the power to make these kinds of laws. They can also add social business into the educational curriculum, introducing the idea that you can solve people's problem by creating social business and that business is not only about profit. For example, in the Muslim religious requirement of *zakat*, you have to give away 2.5% of your wealth every year. We can encourage using this money to invest in social business if the religious requirement is fulfilled by that. These are the kinds of things government can do: encouragement; be a cheerleader; and use the policy tools in their hands.

Badr Jafar: In what way do you think that the next generation of strategic philanthropists, and social entrepreneurs, will change how social and environmental impact is pursued?

Muhammad Yunus: Young people will change the world; the older generation have failed, because the planet is already threatened almost to the verge of extinction. I remind everybody that our house is burning, but inside the house we are having parties, enjoying our economic growth and our technological successes, totally ignoring the fact that the house itself will not exist very soon.

Today's young people are the most powerful generation in human history. Not because they are smarter than previous generations, but because they have the power of technology, which no other generation ever had. I say to them, 'You have an Aladdin's Lamp in your hand. You can do anything you want, but if you're not aware of the power, and you're not touching the lamp, that power will be gone. So, be aware of your power and ask yourself what you want to use it for.'

These are the three zeros to create a new world: zero net carbon emission, zero wealth concentration and zero unemployment, where we are entrepreneurs, rather than job seekers. Young people should turn their attention to this; they can make it happen.

"These are the three zeros to create a new world: zero net carbon emission, zero wealth concentration and zero unemployment."

Badr Jafar: You've voiced concerns around artificial intelligence, making once-needed jobs obsolete. I'm interested in your views on how technology has changed the nature of social investing in the time that you have been engaged in this space.

Muhammad Yunus: So far, the technology that we are talking about, it doesn't have its own mind. It's people who use the technology to fulfil their objectives; technology is a supporting tool. For example, if I want to go over the ocean, then I design a ship. Technology is not achieving anything by itself; human beings are creating technology to achieve their goals. That's why having an objective is the most important thing.

Badr Jafar: Are you hopeful that we will succeed in overcoming the challenge of climate change? For the aspiring philanthropist and social investor who's passionate about this, what is the most useful thing that they can do today to help address this global issue?

Muhammad Yunus: On the first part of your question, I would say that I'm a compulsive optimist. Yes, human beings will survive. But the urgency to act is completely missing; it's business as usual. If you're desperate to stop the fire in your house, you will do crazy things. Fossil fuel use is destroying our planet and endangering our future. We have become the most endangered species on this planet right now. So, we should stop fossil fuel use right away. But governments and banks are putting a lot of money into fossil fuels, and it is difficult for them to stop. So, because young people want to survive, they will decide that we cannot rely on our leaders, we must take the responsibility ourselves and refuse to use fossil fuels, refuse to use anything that is destructive to the planet. That's the only way out and this time is coming very soon. Youth voices will be raised to make sure that the governments and the political parties are forced to take hard decisions and action.

Haifa Fahoum Al Kaylani

President and Founder, Arab International Women's Forum

Haifa Fahoum Al Kaylani is well known in international government, business and non-governmental organisation circles as a
high-impact-change agent focusing on women's leadership, youth
empowerment and working for progress, inclusion, peace and
security in the Arab region. A development economist, she
brings a wide range of skills and experience to her personal
mission of encouraging greater cultural understanding and
sustainable economic growth and reform, supporting a strong
role for women and young leaders at the heart of that process.

Al Kaylani founded the Arab International Women's Forum in
London in 2001, as a development organisation committed to
supporting women's leadership in social and economic growth in
the MENA region and internationally, and creating equality of
opportunity for all. She became a Fellow of the Harvard
Advanced Leadership Initiative 2017 and was appointed as the
only Commissioner from the Arab world to serve on the ILO
Global Commission on the Future of Work from 2017 to 2019.
She also served on the Commission on Global Security, Justice
and Governance chaired by former US Secretary of State Mad-
eleine Albright.

In December 2023, Al Kaylani was appointed an Officer of the
Most Excellent Order of the British Empire in King Charles's New
Year Honours List 2024 in recognition of services to women, to
young people and to the cultural relations between the UK and
countries of the Middle East and North Africa region.

**Badr Jafar: How and why did you establish the Arab Inter-
national Women's Forum in the first place? Has your vision
for it changed over time, especially regarding recent macro
themes, such as climate change, digitisation and technological disruption?**

Haifa Al Kaylani: I'm a development economist and setting up the Arab International Women's Forum was based on two key principles that are very dear to my heart. First and foremost, I have always believed that there is no economic, political or social development in any community without the empowerment of women. Simply, we cannot move forward without optimising and capitalising on that 50% of the population. Number two, I have always believed that the Arab world is part of the global community

> "I have always believed that there is no economic, political or social development in any community without the empowerment of women."

and it's so important for women in the region to connect. We are 22 Arab countries, and we are rich in our diversity, but it's very important for women in the region to connect and to connect with women in the international community.

Women can be bridge-builders between nations, and women in the Arab world can be bridge-builders and community-builders within their own communities. It is important for them to share knowledge and experience. When I started AIWF in 2001 in London, I felt there was a lot of stereotyping about women in the region, based mainly on ignorance. Through knowledge, understanding grows, and this is why I set up the forum. I'm very proud of the initiative and proud to lead AIWF as its president and founder.

You asked about our vision to empower women in the region in all sectors. This is why the forum is the Arab International Women's Forum. We did not say businesswomen. We wanted to engage women in every aspect as homemakers, as business leaders, as parliamentarians and as professionals. We wanted to empower women and give them their space and rights in every sector. When we started AIWF, we could see there were windows of opportunity opening for women in the region thanks to the investment in education by Arab governments. We found that we had many educated young women, but they were not able to enter the workforce, or their talents were not recognised. So, we focused on women as drivers of change. We wanted to see more women in parliament, in the business sector, in civil society, in the media, in academia and in every sector that they opt to engage in. A few years onwards, we were looking at the economic situation in the Arab region and we found that we had a huge level of unemployment, which remains. We thought it was very important to focus on the role of women as engines of economic growth in the region, women's role in the economy and the private sector. Without a vibrant private sector, the Arab region will not be able to create the jobs required for the talented youth that we have, nor will we be able to achieve the sustainable economic development, peace and prosperity and security that the people of the region deserve and are waiting for.

We focus on women and economic growth, because we could see in Europe and in the US, women were setting up very successful small and medium-sized businesses. Why couldn't Arab women do the same? That has become our focus, because without a prosperous economy, we will not have stability in our region. In 2011, with the Arab Spring, we looked at our youth and we launched an initiative for young women leaders; the voice of the future. The young women in our region from 20 to 40 years of age have graduated or are about to graduate. How can we help them open doors? How can we help them with training? If they want to set up a business, how can we help them get the funding, get the technology that they need? We were very focused on the young women leaders. We held conferences and meetings for young women across the Middle East, as well as in London, and then we also led on the role of women in STEM. We see more Arab women proudly entering and studying STEM subjects and graduating with STEM degrees. We wanted to see how they could secure their rightful place in the workplace and in the professions.

Last but not least, we are well aware of climate change and climate challenges. Don't forget, we come from a region that suffers from water scarcity, apart from the challenges of climate change. We launched initiatives on women and water, addressing the role of women in the farming communities in the Arab region, and their influence in the rural communities. We worked with the World Bank on some of these initiatives, on digitising agriculture and how women in the farming community can learn the new technologies to help them prosper. We're very proud of the timely initiatives that we have led and continue to lead with support of our partners in all sectors.

Badr Jafar: In 2017, you accepted a year-long fellowship from the Advanced Leadership Initiative at Harvard University, and one of the outcomes of this experience was a social enterprise named Haseel, which you've been piloting. Can you tell us about this enterprise, what the idea behind it is? How did you set about launching it, and what's next for the initiative?

Haifa Al Kaylani: I was proud and honoured to join the Harvard Advanced Leadership Initiative as a Fellow. This was a great opportunity for me to focus as a development economist on economic security, water security and food security, key challenges for our region. I developed a project that addresses these challenges through an innovative model for sustainable agriculture in the MENA region. I called my project Ploughing New Ground. I chose to pilot the project in Jordan. Why Jordan? Because it is the second-poorest country in the world in terms of water resources, and with the influx of refugees in Jordan they have depleted the underground water reserves.

It was important to start that project in the country that needs it most, and to see how we could pilot it. I went to Washington, DC and met the World Bank, I introduced my project and secured their support, as well as a grant to start the pilot. In 2018, I was in Jordan, immediately after graduation, and I set up Haseel, which means 'harvest' in Arabic, for sustainable agriculture. I wanted to start Haseel as a social enterprise, because this was something that I had learned a great deal more about at Harvard. Unfortunately, we do not yet have a law in Jordan, nor in many Arab countries, where you can set up a social enterprise – a business that is there to make a difference and impact social change, but at the same time can make a profit. The choice we had was to set up as a commercial business or a not-for-profit. So, I set up a not-for-profit.

I'm proud that the project and the pilot received tremendous support from all stakeholders I met in Jordan. All the ministries – Food, Agriculture, Social Development, International Cooperation – the farming community, the private sector and the chambers of commerce, everybody was excited. The project was about introducing new technology into the oldest industry in the world, which is farming. My project was to cover a farm of one hectare. We divided the land into three areas, one farmed with traditional agriculture so the farmer can carry on doing what they are used to doing, while we trained them in low-tech and high-tech hydroponics.

My project was to produce high-yield fruits and vegetables, which we can do 12 months a year using this technology, saving 70% water, and at the same time creating jobs for people who work in the farms and opening new local, regional or global markets for the produce. What was special about the project was two key things: training our farmers and the local farming community through a training centre on the farm; and attracting youth. They got excited about this project because for them it was entrepreneurial, and it had technology. Otherwise, we were finding in our region and in Jordan that the youth were not interested in agriculture. They wanted to move to the urban areas. Haseel and the model that we were launching in Jordan fired their imagination.

We also opened the farm for university students, for schools, for visits by the private sector, by women's associations and others to get people excited, and to show them that it is affordable to invest in agriculture, because our project was small, replicable, scalable and doable. Of course, there was a delay in moving forward with the project because of the pandemic. But there are now two projects being implemented in Jordan by the Ministry of Agriculture, based on the pilot that I launched, with the help and support of the World Bank. I'm very proud as founder and director of Haseel to have been asked by the World Bank to be a senior strategic advisor for both projects. It took time, but things are happening and I'm excited to see it getting replicated, not only in Jordan, but in other countries in the region.

Badr Jafar: In many of the initiatives that you continue to spearhead, you have a great ability to bring together non-profits, businesses, governments and other stakeholders, and to get them working together towards shared goals. How important are these kinds of multi-sector partnerships in what you do, and what do you think the key features are to make them successful?

Haifa Al Kaylani: From the beginning, I truly believe that you only succeed by working together. That has been one of my mottos; you cannot succeed by working alone. I couldn't have set up the Arab International Women's Forum on my own. I am grateful for the founder board members who shared my vision, and to the current board members who have joined, both men and women. You need partners, and you need board members to join you. The private sector is very important when you are setting up a not-for-profit because you need the funding, which provides you with the ability to maintain and enhance your programmes and impact.

But we also need government support. AIWF has been a convener, a catalyst and an advocate for women's rights. All our reports were presented to governments. How can we present our reports to government at our meetings, if they are not present in the meetings themselves? Every conference, every meeting had at least three or four – if not more – cabinet members, not only from the Arab region, but internationally, as well as people from the private sector, civil society, the media, universities and students themselves. You can only do it with all these stakeholders. One of the key ingredients for success is that we all share the same objective, and we are all committed to achieving the empowerment of women, job creation and the empowerment of our youth. We want to see equality of opportunity in the region for our young men and women and so we share these objectives together.

Allow me to add, we are grateful for the global institutional partners like the World Bank, the EBRD, the OECD, the ILO and the UN organisations. We work with them consistently on all our programmes. They have a huge impact on all policies in the world so it's important that they are aligned with us and provide support. I'm not talking about funding; I'm talking about their ideas and their input and their presence with us in all these functions. The same with Haseel – I could not have done what I have done without the amazing support, starting with my Harvard professors and my peers, but also Jordan itself. When I arrived, I had support and interest from the highest sources, all the way down to the farming communities I visited across the country, as well as all the government ministers, the private sector, the media and everybody. We brought them together and learned from them and adapted the pilot, because it was a learning experience to get it right. Without it, there is no way anybody can succeed.

Badr Jafar: You bring a variety of perspectives to your work as an Arab woman, as the leader of a prominent global organisation and as a trained economist. As we look at the many social and economic issues facing Arab countries, and Arab youth in particular, I'd like to ask you about the role that strategic philanthropists can play. There is a major role for governments, as you said, and I'd like to think people increasingly understand the important role that businesses play, but I'm also interested in how you think about the role of philanthropists in helping to address some of the region's most pressing social, economic and environmental challenges.

Haifa Al Kaylani: Philanthropy is in our hearts in the Arab region. It's an intrinsic part of our upbringing, our culture and our ethos. I am very proud of how the young high-net-worth individuals and individuals in general in the region are engaged not only in the usual charitable giving that they and their parents do, but also trying to effect change with their charitable giving. I call it strategic impact giving. They have ideas, they see the problems that our communities are facing, whether it's to do with the environment, or lack of opportunities, lack of jobs and lack of education, they want to come in with projects that address these social challenges, and they don't want to use a band-aid approach. They want a long-term, sustainable approach. This way, there is also transparency and accountability, so they can measure the impact of their giving. We're seeing a lot of that now. It is still in its early stages in the region, to move from the usual philanthropy into strategic impact philanthropy, but it's happening as we speak.

Badr Jafar: What advice would you give to youth in the Arab world and beyond who might be thinking about founding their own non-profit ventures? What are some of the things that they should think about if they want the longevity and impact that you have had with AIWF?

"Our youth are the future of the region, and they have outstanding ideas about the social changes that they want to see happen in their communities and in their countries."

Haifa Al Kaylani: This is a very important question. Our youth are the future of the region, and they have outstanding ideas about the social changes that they want to see happen in their communities and in their countries. They should be fully encouraged to set up their NGOs or social enterprises. I hope we will see the introduction of laws in the region so they can set up their social enterprises or NGOs.

What advice? Have a vision. Understand exactly what you want to achieve. It's important to identify clearly what you want to achieve, and to be knowledgeable about it because if you're not convinced yourself, you cannot convince others. If you go to seek funding or support for any of your projects, no matter how wonderful they are, you need to be convincing. You must have ticked everything to do with your project through studying and research; being ready before you launch is extremely important.

You need to get the right partners to come on board, whether you are working with colleagues or forming a small board, you need to work to bring in others. Do not attempt to do too much at the beginning. I am a great believer in the step-by-step approach: secure and move forward, gather momentum, bring more friends on board, more stakeholders, more supporters, let the project become more known and then move forward. Finally, I always believe if you've done something good, you must talk about it. If you have a good story, tell it, let others learn from it. Let others come to help you with it. Let others bring you helpful additional information. A good story must be told.

SEVEN
FOUNDATIONS AND LONG-TERM PHILANTHROPY

In North America and Europe, philanthropic foundations are established vehicles for philanthropy. Foundations in Europe have existed since medieval times, originally run by religious orders or by large trading houses and banks, and lately by individuals, by corporations and even by the state. In North America, private foundations such as Gates, Ford, Rockefeller and Carnegie are globally renowned names in philanthropy. The existence of a foundation sector is not characteristic of the emerging economies, although wealthy individuals and companies in many high-growth countries have created charitable endowments. Yet, structured and staffed foundations remain a relatively recent phenomenon in these countries for a number of reasons: significant wealth has been created only in the past few decades; philanthropy has been practised quietly, in private, with donations made from individual to individual; governments have not set up regulatory laws and frameworks that recognise the foundation as a corporate body or that require registration; and the wealthy have not traditionally chosen to address systemic issues over a long period of time with the help of structured foundations.

While not necessarily applicable in all settings, institutionalis-
ing philanthropic giving in the form of a foundation yields
various benefits with time horizons, risk and impact. A foundation can take a longer time perspective, especially if it is working
through an invested trust or endowment. This in turn might
enable it to take more calculated risks, including, for example, to
fund untested initiatives that may only bear results over time. It
can set out targets and measure impact based on progress towards
these targets, in a way that most individual donors do not have
the resources or inclination to do.

I reached out to leaders of foundations in North America,
Europe, Africa, the Middle East and Asia to get a sense of how
philanthropy within a foundation structure differs from individual philanthropy, and what some of the advantages of foundations may be. Some of these foundations are independent, others
are driven by families or individuals. Some are corporate. Some
have been in existence for decades; others were started more
recently and are at different stages of development. All are investing for the long term and taking on projects at scale.

I spoke to three philanthropic funders in India with ambitious
and original ideas about how they make their social investments.
India is, of course, one of the largest growth markets in the world,
and its philanthropists have been bold and creative in their
approach to collaboration with government and the creation of
social systems and structures to improve social wellbeing and
strengthen society. Nandan and Rohini Nilekani are business
leaders who provide outstanding examples of innovative philanthropy, taking risks to create new models in education with the
use of digital platforms. Azim Premji is a leader in the information technology field, and has devoted his assets and philanthropic efforts over the past two decades to improving
educational opportunities at scale for millions of Indian students.

I spoke with two highly committed women leaders in the
Middle East, who believe strongly in the importance of formalised philanthropy as a way of contributing to and changing their
societies for the better. Muna Al Gurg in the UAE and Her Royal
Highness Princess Lamia bint Majid Al Saud of Saudi Arabia are

models of next-generation philanthropic leadership and are proponents of a form of philanthropy that can take on major social issues, use all assets creatively, invest for the long term and communicate impact transparently.

I had a compelling conversation with a leading African philanthropist, Mo Ibrahim, who has created a namesake foundation to invest in governance and leadership across Africa. He took his success in business and transformed it into strategic philanthropy, addressing issues of fundamental importance across African societies such as how to defeat corruption, support good leaders and build strong and accountable public sectors.

I conversed with a man who is a sports champion, a teacher, a mentor and a philanthropist. Wladimir Klitschko of Ukraine, a former world heavyweight-boxing champion, together with his brother Vitali, created a foundation whose mission is to deliver impact through sports, science, education and medicine for children in Ukraine. Wladimir has developed a systematised approach to his philanthropy that he hopes others in similar settings can take inspiration from. Wladimir and Vitali are sports champions with hearts of gold who believe in sharing what they have learned to help others succeed.

Finally, I had a wide-ranging conversation with Mike Milken, an American philanthropist who has had a very significant impact over the past three decades with his private foundation and the Milken Institute. In his conversation with me, he described his interests in medical research and public health, and his approach to catalysing innovation, focusing on the potential of young people and leveraging the philanthropic work of his Institute by recognising excellence, fostering expertise, and convening and bringing different views to the table.

These philanthropists serve as models for others. They have chosen to work through organised philanthropic institutions that foster continuity, build data and knowledge and train staff to implement their vision and build relevant skills. They have used their foundations as vehicles for engaging in some of the most important challenges in their own communities and regions, and, in so doing, are improving prospects across the globe.

Rohini and Nandan Nilekani

Chair, Rohini Nilekani Philanthropies

Co-founder and Chairman of the Board, Infosys Limited

Rohini and Nandan Nilekani are philanthropic leaders, known in India and across Asia for their innovative contributions to their community. In 2017, they signed the Giving Pledge, which commits half their wealth to philanthropic causes over their lifetimes.

Rohini Nilekani is the chairperson of Rohini Nilekani Philanthropies and co-founder and Director of the EkStep Foundation. She is also the founder of Arghyam, set up to improve sustainable water and sanitation, which funds initiatives across India. From 2004 to 2014, she was founder-chairperson and chief funder of Pratham Books, a non-profit children's publisher that reached millions of children during her tenure. She serves on the Eminent Persons Advisory Group of the Competition Commission of India. She has also co-chaired the Akshara Foundation, which was established by the government in partnership with civil society in 2000 to work with community organisations and NGOs, to provide educational programmes to children.

A former journalist, Rohini has written for many leading publications such as *The Times of India*, *India Today* and *Mint*. Penguin Books India published her first book, a medical thriller called *Stillborn*, and her second non-fiction book, *Uncommon Ground*, based on her eponymous TV show. She has written several books for young children, published by Pratham Books.

Nandan Nilekani, an Indian entrepreneur and technologist, co-founded Infosys Technologies Limited in 1981, where he now serves as chairman of the board. He was the chairman of the Unique Identification Authority of India (UIDAI) in the rank of a cabinet minister from 2009 to 2014. In January 2023, he was appointed as the co-chair of the 'G20 Task Force on Digital

Public Infrastructure for Economic Transformation, Financial Inclusion and Development'.

Nandan is the author of *Imagining India: The Idea of a Renewed Nation* (2008); co-author with Viral Shah of *Rebooting India: Realizing a Billion Aspirations* (2015); and co-author with Tanuj Bhojwani of *The Art of Bitfulness* (2022).

In 2014, Nandan and Rohini co-founded EkStep (of which Nandan is chairman), a digital infrastructure platform for early learning. EkStep has enabled tens of millions of children to improve their literacy and numeracy skills.

Badr Jafar: Rohini and Nandan, the programmes and initiatives of your philanthropies are very diverse, spanning water, education, the environment and the arts, to name a few. How did you come to be involved in so many different fields over the past 20 years? How do you manage such a diverse portfolio of charitable activities?

Rohini Nilekani: Yes, I've been in this field for almost 30 years. What holds my entire philanthropy portfolio together is one simple but powerful idea. My entire focus is on strengthening society, or as we call it 'samaj', because I truly believe that markets and the state must be responsive to society. To make the state and market accountable to the public interest, we need very strong leadership and social institutions, and we need to coordinate ordinary people's efforts so that they become and remain part of the solution, rather than victims of the problem. Whether I'm working in environment, in water, in education or in the arts and culture, it's all about finding institutions, individuals and ideas that strengthen *samaj*, or society. That's the common thread for my philanthropy.

> "My entire focus is on strengthening society, or as we call it 'samaj', because I truly believe that markets and the state must be responsive to society."

Nandan Nilekani: My philanthropy is focused on a few issues. One is education, and EkStep is the biggest initiative for that. I also support institutions. I co-founded an institution called the Indian Institute of Human Settlements, which is trying to set up a university for sustainable urbanisation in India. I have founded and supported the eGov Foundation, which is building a tech platform for Indian cities so that they can use technology to move forward. I am also the president of NCAER, which is India's pre-eminent economic think tank. I tend to focus on education, and where tech can have a multiplier effect.

Badr Jafar: Are there common or universal principles that you seek to apply in your philanthropic efforts across all these different areas? Are there some golden rules that underpin your personal approach to philanthropy and the way in which you invest philanthropic capital and track impact over time?

Nandan Nilekani: Yes, we look for strategic outcomes. For us, getting impact at scale and speed is very important in many of the things we do. At the same time, diversity is important because one solution does not fit all. And we are also big into collabora-tive philanthropy. We work with groups like Co-Impact, where we fund along with other philanthropists.

Badr Jafar: Rohini, through initiatives such as the Akshara Foundation, you've been very successful at collaborating with different stakeholders across government, the commu-nity and other NGOs. For aspiring philanthropists from emerging markets, where formal collaborative mechanisms are undeveloped, can you tell us what you have found to be the keys to creating successful collaborations between busi-ness, government and the social sector within India?

Rohini Nilekani: From the beginning, it was patently obvious to us that you cannot solve issues in silos. As Nandan said, if you're interested in having impact at the scale of the problem, then you have to work with *samaj*, *bazar* and *sarkar* – society, market and state. Beginning with issues that are common to everybody's welfare, such as education, it's easy to draw in the state because it is their mandate to provide basic services. We have found governments are open to coming in as partners and accepting our help in getting them to the first mile, which governments find hard to reach. There are setbacks, but you find the champions

> "If you're interested in having impact at the scale of the problem, then you have to work with *samaj, bazar* and *sarkar* - society, market and state."

inside government. You very clearly articulate the common goals. And the same goes for markets. In India, companies, once they have profits, must share them back with society through our Corporate Social Responsibility laws. So, they are eager to participate.

This work that we have done for so many decades has led us to a slightly more structured way of reducing the friction to collaborate between state, markets and society. We call it society platform thinking. We focus on how we can be technology-enabled because you need technology to create scale at speed, as Nandan says. But we are not technology-led, we want to be people-led, to be problem-led. We want to create a unified but not uniform solution so that multiple people can engage, in their own context, to solve their own problems. You find that when you do that the government can come in, markets can come in, civil society can thrive and individuals can find a way to build back agency. That's what we're trying to achieve.

Nandan Nilekani: The philosophy that underpins our work is how to increase access. How do we increase access to opportunity and to services? Particularly those of us who live in countries like India, where there are still so many people who are not able to participate formally in the economy due to lack of education; we need to think about how we bring them into the fold and give them ways to improve their lives.

Badr Jafar: What long-term consequences do you think that the pandemic will have, not just in India, but around the

world on the social sector? Do you think that it might change the way that people and even governments think of the role of private philanthropy in responding to complex challenges?

Nandan Nilekani: The pandemic was a big blow in terms of pushing people back into poverty. Many of the gains over the past few years are being unwound, as people lack jobs and income. If we really want to achieve our SDG goals by 2030, we have to work even harder, even faster and even more at scale to make up for what we have lost in progress. At the same time, the very magnitude of this health crisis has made everybody more receptive and flexible to new ideas and innovations. Because of the pandemic there's been an acceleration of adoption of the work that we have done.

Rohini Nilekani: Nandan is quite right. It's been devastating. Especially in India it's heart-breaking, because so many people have just lifted themselves out of poverty in a stable way. But you asked about the role of philanthropy. I think that's going to get a big boost. We do need private philanthropy to try out new things now and underwrite a lot of risk so that the next time, and there will be a next time, whether it's climate change or another pandemic, we are much better prepared. Who else can invest in figuring out what worked where in the world, do rapid studies, do some scoping, then support institutions who will be able to come together for a rapid response next time around? Private philanthropy has the space, the time and the resources to do it. That's one thing in terms of COVID-19 and philanthropy.

You asked about the long-term impact on society. We must remember that we have to keep focusing on society and communities. Who were the first responders all over the world? It was citizens' groups; it was people who knew their neighbourhoods. Government came, health workers came, but the first responders were civil institutions. Strengthening those and building networks of trust well in advance, I think that is a big thing that has come out of this pandemic. Second, we have seen, to

Nandan's delight, the rise of the acceptance of digital technology. At EkStep we are quite taken aback. The government had already asked us to help with setting up a national infrastructure to train teachers, to create content and allow students to come online for learning resources. The kind of rapid uptake we saw has staggered our own teams as well. We have tried our best to watch out for those on the other side of the digital divide, and a lot of innovation has flourished there as well. So, the impacts of this pandemic seem to be the uptake of digital, the knowledge that citizens' groups are the first responders and the ability of philanthropy to take new risks with a new imagination so that we are better prepared next time.

Badr Jafar: Are you witnessing a growth in philanthropic activity in the emerging markets, and especially in India? What are some of the most distinctive characteristics of philanthropy in India that people should be aware of?

Rohini Nilekani: Over the past few years there's been an increasing awareness and interest in philanthropy. Wealthy people in India have concluded that we must give forward, and that there are many structured opportunities to do so. Whether it is through the India Philanthropy Initiative, or through the many business bodies in India, or just informal networks that we have been able to work with, there is an acceleration of the intent to cooperate among the Indian philanthropists. I find that very heartening. I've been lucky enough to also see a flourishing of international cooperation. We are together in the Giving Pledge circles, and many more people from the South are joining, which is very hopeful. Looking eastwards from India, the Asian philanthropists have come together in several networks, and we have been exchanging a lot of information. There are some cultural similarities here. Seeing a new way for Asia to come together, I find that very exciting. And the Western philanthropists have also been part of those discussions. Something is happening. When I add the global collaborative platforms like Co-Impact and others, I think we may be at an interesting new point. But this is not the time to sit back, this is the time to push forward and not let the momentum stop.

Badr Jafar: You've both been at the forefront of technological shifts. You've integrated technology with great impact into several of your philanthropic initiatives. I'm interested in your views on how technology has changed the nature of philanthropy in the time that you've been involved in the sector. What do you think might be the next big technological disruption to impact the social sector? What should philanthropists be doing to prepare for that?

Nandan Nilekani: I think the role of technology in philanthropy has gained importance after COVID-19 because everything is being digitised, including the way we deliver things to people. We believe that it enables scale. If you really want to solve the problems of a billion people, you need technology to reach everyone. It enables speed, because time is of the essence. It enables you to have a common platform and at the same time deal with the diverse changes that are required across the world. I think the role of technology is very important. Generally, I find more and more philanthropists are realising this and are applying it in their philanthropy. Also, I think a lot of work is happening on AI. For example, if you want to deliver better education, you can use AI to figure out what the children are learning or what they're not learning and how it can be fixed. You can use AI to deliver better healthcare to a billion people by improving the ability to diagnose. I think AI will come into philanthropy or will come into societal platform solving, which in turn will be funded by philanthropy.

Rohini Nilekani: I'm by no means a 'techie'. But thanks to working with Nandan for the past few years, I've understood how using technology appropriately, and that's a very big word, can amplify our good intent. Because there's no point in not acknowledging all the dangers that come from technology. How do you take the power of your intent and build a grammar around that intent through good technologies? I think philanthropists need to start thinking about how they will support civil society with more technology tools to be able to participate fully in the digital age. Civil society institutions, especially in India, and some around the world, have been a little technophobic, thinking that technol-

> "For philanthropy, it's very important to understand how to support civil society institutions to be technology-enabled, but not technology-led."

ogy and power get woven too intricately and against the interests of the masses. But I feel it is a very important thing for them to participate fully in the digital age and democratise technologies. Whatever problems you have about technology can be solved, but not by shunning it. Instead, we can improve the way technology serves society. So, for philanthropy, it's very important to understand how to support civil society institutions to be technology-enabled, but not technology-led. It's a super opportunity. Good technologies will amplify good intent and we must use them.

Azim Premji

Founder and Chair, Wipro

Azim Premji has been at the helm of Wipro Limited since the late 1960s, turning it into an IT, BPO (business process outsourcing) and R&D services organisation generating close to US$8.5 billion in revenue, with a presence in 58 countries. Other Wipro companies led by Premji have revenues close to US$2 billion and span sectors like consumer goods, precision engineering and healthcare systems. Wipro is recognised as a global leader in sustainability for its social and environmental initiatives spanning all countries across its operational footprint.

In 2001, Premji established the Azim Premji Foundation, a not-for-profit organisation focused on enhancing quality and equity in India's public school system. The foundation works

with over 350,000 schools across seven Indian states. It also runs
the Azim Premji University, which focuses on teaching and
research programmes in education and other areas of human
development. Azim Premji Philanthropic Initiatives support
not-for-profits working in areas of human development and
education, such as nutrition, local governance and the wellbeing
of vulnerable groups. Premji's US$15 billion donation to the
foundation's endowment makes it one of the largest foundations
in the world.

**Badr Jafar: Your foundation has been on the front line of
responding to the pandemic in India, addressing urgent
needs from healthcare and humanitarian perspectives. Do
you think the pandemic is changing the way that people
think about the role of private philanthropic organisations
and helping communities respond to this kind of
emergency?**

Azim Premji: We have been involved quite actively in helping
tackle COVID-19 across the country on many fronts; this
includes immediate humanitarian response and long-term
support for revival of livelihoods. It also includes a comprehensive healthcare response; testing is only one part of it. I don't
think the pandemic will have a lasting impact on how people
think about private philanthropy; however, it will have significant impact on two crucial fronts.

Now people appreciate much more the importance of public
systems. This includes not just the public healthcare system, but
also systems that emphasise social security, systems for data
collection and research. Even if it is not clearly articulated by
many people, there is a greater acceptance now that we must
cooperate and have solidarity; we cannot leave everyone to
themselves. And it is possible that this may have an effect on
philanthropy, which could be lasting.

**Badr Jafar: How did you go about setting up your foundation
and working out where and how you could have the most**

impact as a philanthropist? What led you to focus on education specifically? And what advice would you give aspiring philanthropists in emerging markets who are thinking about their own philanthropic journey?

Azim Premji: When I set up the foundation, there were three things that I was clear about. First, that we must contribute towards developing a just, equitable and humane society, as envisioned in the Constitution of India, and for this there is no single path. Second, we must approach this whole matter with humility. I knew social issues were far more complex than business issues, so we went about listening to people and being guided by the wisdom of many. Also, we must retain the culture of humility.

Third, we must set up a very strong organisation with people of dedication and competence, and build it as an institution. And we must trust those people to do the right thing. I knew that setting up this professional ethic of an institution would be the most crucial thing for the long-term contribution of the foundation; my advice would be the same. Set up a professional institution, empower it with people you trust and have humility to accept that you may have the money, but others know a lot more about social issues and how to tackle them.

> "Set up a professional institution, empower it with people you trust and have humility to accept that you may have the money, but others know a lot more about social issues and how to tackle them."

Badr Jafar: A new generation of philanthropists is beginning to emerge in parts of Africa, the Middle East and Asia. What impact do you think that this could have on the global economy and society over the next few decades?

Azim Premji: I think the philanthropy in this part of the world needs to scale up significantly. Here I'm referring to the newly wealthy people who seemed the most generous. Many of these countries have their own old traditions of philanthropy, and I'm not referring to that.

Badr Jafar: India is a country with very rich cultures and vibrant social structures. How would you describe the general culture of giving and philanthropy and how are attitudes to institutional philanthropy in India evolving over time?

Azim Premji: In my view, there are two kinds of long-standing cultures of philanthropy in India. First, the traditional giving back of businesses to their communities. This has been a very strong tradition, but it is not talked about adequately, because many of these people don't want to talk about their philanthropy. The size of this philanthropy may vary from very small to significant, but it is a very strong culture. One of the issues is that such people are very self-effacing, and don't talk fancy language; they get satisfaction from what they do and not by publicising it.

Second is the large-scale philanthropy deeply committed to nation building, starting in the 20th century with the Tatas, the Sarabhai and the Jamnalal Bajaj. There was significant philanthropy from big business, which contributed both to the Indian independence movement and the building of institutions in the country. This was truly remarkable. All of us can see the effects of that, even now.

In India, given the wealth that has been generated over the past two or three decades, we could be doing a lot more in philanthropy. I would not like to mention specific names, because the urge to do philanthropy must come from the inside. But I certainly think that we can be doing a lot more. I particularly think that philanthropy should contribute to developing and sustaining institutions at all levels.

Badr Jafar: What are your views on the evolving role of the private sector? What else do business leaders need to be doing not just in India, but around the world, to help address

some of our world's biggest challenges, both now and in the future?

Azim Premji: I don't think the business and private sector is doing enough, quite truly. First, businesses must become a lot more sustainable, which has to do with their environmental responsibility and climate change. They must also contribute towards social matters because they are citizens of this world. Second, on individual philanthropy, a lot more should be done.

Badr Jafar: With respect to Muslim philanthropy, anywhere between US$400 billion to a US$1 trillion is donated by Muslims around the world through *zakat* and *sadaqah* every single year, yet one in three Muslims around the world live below the poverty line. How can we better harness the power of Islamic giving in a more strategic and coordinated way with a view to maximising philanthropic impact?

Azim Premji: I'm not sure there's any simple answer to this question. I would just recommend that this money should go towards the neediest and it should go towards developing high-quality institutions that have humility. Also, it would be good if the benefit of this giving is non-sectarian.

Muna Al Gurg

Founder, Meem Foundation

Muna Al Gurg is an Emirati philanthropist and businesswoman. She is vice chairperson and Director of Retail at the Easa Saleh Al Gurg Group. Al Gurg is on the board of directors of several companies, including HSBC Bank Middle East Limited. She was chairwoman of Young Arab Leaders UAE, where she promoted education, entrepreneurship and youth development. She also advocates for a greater role for women in business. In 2015, she launched the Muna Al Gurg Scholarship at London Business

School, supporting female students studying in the school's MBA and Executive MBA programme.

She serves on the board of her family's foundation, the Easa Saleh Al Gurg Charity Foundation. She is a founding board member of Endeavor UAE, a non-profit organisation promoting high-impact entrepreneurship in emerging and growth markets, and she has served on the board of the Emirates Youth Foundation. In 2023, she founded the Meem Foundation, dedicated to addressing the unique challenges faced by women and girls in the Middle East and North Africa.

Badr Jafar: The Easa Saleh Al Gurg Charity Foundation was set up a decade ago and has been very active across numerous causes. What led to the creation of your family foundation? How did you select the areas to focus on and what, if anything, would you have done differently with the experience that you've gained over the years?

Muna Al Gurg: The Easa Saleh Al Gurg Foundation was established by my father in 2010. It is one of Dubai's first private charitable foundations. It has taken a quite traditional approach to philanthropy as it is generally practised in the Middle East, with an emphasis on access to basic services, including clean water, health, primary and secondary education and university education, and religious aspects such as mosques in the UAE, East Africa, Palestine and India. My father was born in 1927. His views on philanthropy have largely steered the foundation to date. He wanted to build a foundation that went beyond his lifetime. My personal journey with philanthropy has taken me through traditional Middle East philanthropy to the point where I am today thinking about notions such as sustainability and impact. I have been developing my ideas, taking inspiration from how philanthropy is practised globally, and what can be learned to help us improve the state of philanthropy in the Middle East.

Badr Jafar: How would you describe the state of strategic philanthropy in the Middle East region? Do you think that the role of private philanthropy is changing in the region?

Muna Al Gurg: I do see a trend in Arab philanthropy moving from being charitable and often religious in nature to having a more developmental approach. However, I feel it's still far from being strategic philanthropy for social justice. Most local philanthropy support goes to relatively safe issues like education and youth unemployment through direct income-generating projects, but not to changes in legislation towards women's empowerment, for example.

There are some areas of improvement. First, finding high-quality national and local staff. This is crucial to the giving that we do and the foundations that we build. Second, measuring impact and creating reports. This can lead to the tremendous success of foundations and the philanthropic work done in the Middle East. People can learn from research papers how to improve upon their giving and the locations that they're giving in. I think foundations need to start working on and enabling these processes for others to learn. Philanthropy has typically been a private activity, which is fine and understandable. However, there are significant gains to be had by sharing experiences and knowledge, and generally a more collaborative approach.

Badr Jafar: You and I are both concerned about corporate governance challenges in our region. The Pearl Initiative, as you know, was launched a decade ago as a non-profit to address this challenge. The Pearl Initiative has a programme dedicated to governance in philanthropic organisations to help empower and streamline the impact of the sector. Can you describe your vision of a better-governed philanthropic sector in the Middle East and where are we today on this journey?

Muna Al Gurg: It would be great to see a more institutionalised giving approach emerge in the Middle East. Many of the discussions we had with the Pearl Initiative fostered debate around best practices and how approaches to philanthropy have evolved elsewhere in the world, and why. I really feel that institutionalisation can give good governance a permanent front-row seat in determining how philanthropy happens.

It's probably worth describing what philanthropic good governance entails. I would emphasise some important aspects. It is essential to have a clear charter to start off with that describes the culture and philosophy of a foundation, and then establishing a transparent and robust process for conducting due diligence on grantees, for example. Implementing a toolbox of KPIs [key performance indicators] that allow for measurement and structuring important feedback – that is often overlooked. And lastly, the valuable role of independent oversight through a suitably appointed board of directors; try to work with people who aren't afraid of giving independent advice and pulling you up when you're going wrong. There are many corporate governance lessons that can be applied equally to philanthropy. Let's start treating our philanthropy as we would our investments.

> "There are many corporate governance lessons that can be applied equally to philanthropy. Let's start treating our philanthropy as we would our investments."

Badr Jafar: You work a lot with talented young women and men in the early stages of their careers who seek guidance and mentorship as they chart their future. What advice would you give to youth who are considering a career in the social sector today?

Muna Al Gurg: Securing a job in an NGO is usually very competitive. You would not think it, but it is just like joining a corporate. I think this is justifiable, as NGOs are, in many instances, less well funded. Hiring mistakes can be very costly to the organisation, as you can imagine. I think it's critical that candidates believe in the organisation's mission statement, perhaps even more so than when joining a corporate. It's important to be really vested in it. Look for jobs you might be interested in and note what skills or experience they're looking for. NGOs tend to look at these transferable skills in a way that other corporate organisations perhaps don't.

Working for an NGO often requires multitasking and is therefore a good way to broaden out your skill set rather than getting siloed into one area of business, which might happen in a corporate. On a CV, experience with an NGO can demonstrate depth, adaptive abilities and on-the-job learning, something most employers like to see. Working with passion for a cause can show commitment, while an NGO's work can often lead overseas. Broadening experience further with different languages and cultures is very enriching.

Ultimately, it will be your personal qualities, your skills, your knowledge and your experience that will determine whether you can get your foot on that first step of the ladder. Invest in yourself and develop skills that are valuable to the role you want. Another really important point is networking. Working for an NGO can lead to interaction with senior figures from the world of business, working in partnerships on projects as part of their CSR initiatives. These contacts can prove valuable for becoming more senior within the NGO, or should you decide to re-enter the corporate world. I've seen this first-hand, and it has proven to be extremely beneficial to a young person's career.

Finally, consider languages and embrace new cultures. Naturally, it will depend on the locations in which you wish to work, but NGOs appreciate multi-linguists, because of the international nature of their work, so this is a good excuse to brush up any existing language skills you have.

Badr Jafar: Do you think that culturally in the Arab region we are prepared to embrace careers in the social sector as

viable and respected career choices for youth? Sometimes there are impediments within families and within societies as to what's considered a respectable job or not. And this is something that has changed and evolved over time.

Muna al Gurg: The more governments and private philanthropists talk about the valuable work that comes out of foundations and non-profits, the more families are inclined to say to their youth, it's an honour for you to be part of such a cause. It's important that we start speaking about this valuable work. We need to share the impact of the work that we're doing, and that encourages more young people and more families to want to be part of it.

Badr Jafar: In what ways do you think that the next generation of strategic philanthropists will change how the practice of philanthropy develops in the future, and how might technological shifts accelerate these changes?

Muna Al Gurg: This is a topic that really interests me, as I have a daughter who has already started expressing a keen interest in philanthropy. At her age, I recall having a somewhat one-dimensional perspective of philanthropy, which was more in line with traditional charity. This next generation are already showing that they're more aware of their physical and social environment, and their relationship with it and their desire to impact it. As a truly digital generation, their capacity to share ideas and data with others in their field is unprecedented. This holistic thinking is something that I believe will continue to shape philanthropy well beyond the 2020s. The progress that has been made in recent years in creating strategic philanthropy gives plenty for the next

"The progress that has been made in recent years in creating strategic philanthropy gives plenty for the next generation to expand upon with an exciting array of technological tools to aid them."

generation to expand upon with an exciting array of technological tools to aid them.

Technology and software have taken the limelight in the pandemic. Digital technology has catalysed video connectivity anywhere in the world. It gives us almost in-person contact with colleagues and thought leaders, as well as grantees. So, it dramatically reduces the need for travel. And it's associated with lower environmental impact, which is great. Other progress in the field of collaboration databases has allowed strategic philanthropy to adopt many tools at a low cost. These are the tools that were used by corporates, for example, in the past. These are also the tools that the next generation are very comfortable with and will use going forward. Strategic philanthropy is still in its early days, but progress is rapidly being made and there is a lot of innovation taking place related to operating models, knowledge sharing, data analysis and impact measurement that I believe will only accelerate from here.

To be honest, in a world that is increasingly digitised, there's going to be more data than we know what to do with, which in the world of philanthropy is a high-quality problem to have.

Badr Jafar: I'm just as excited as you are about the way in which technology can help to boost impact and create that multiplier effect on impact. Do you see any potential pitfalls or downsides of increasing use of technology in helping to channel and direct philanthropic capital across borders?

Muna Al Gurg: I think we need to have balance. The experience of being on the ground and hearing from your grantees is crucial. We will use technology because it has a greater impact from the perspective of numbers, and you can reach many more people more quickly. But it is even more important to have on-the-ground experience and to be present as a philanthropist to hear from the grantees.

Her Royal Highness Princess Lamia bint Majed Saud Al Saud

Secretary General, Alwaleed Philanthropies

Princess Lamia was appointed Secretary General of Alwaleed Philanthropies in April 2016, having previously served as Executive Manager of Media & Public Relations. Alwaleed Philanthropies was founded in the 1980s by HRH Prince Alwaleed bin Talal. It consists of three philanthropic organisations: Alwaleed Philanthropies Global, focusing on philanthropic and humanitarian projects around the world; Alwaleed Philanthropies Lebanon, which is focused on the social and community needs of Lebanon; and Alwaleed Philanthropies Saudi Arabia, which focuses on the needs of the Kingdom of Saudi Arabia.

Under her leadership, the foundation has enabled new opportunities for women in Saudi Arabia, including supporting the training of women ride-share drivers and enabling employment for women law graduates.

In 2003, Princess Lamia started the publishing company Sada Al Arab. In 2010, she published her first novel, *Children & Blood*, on the complex issue of honour killings.

Badr Jafar: Your Royal Highness, how would you describe the philanthropic mission and philosophy of Alwaleed Philanthropies? How has it evolved over the past four decades to cater to changing needs and priorities of society here in the Middle East and beyond?

Her Royal Highness Princess Lamia: There are many kind-hearted people around the world who are donating their time, money and effort to do good and to make the world a better place. Some of these people have a strategic vision of how to deliver their funds, to help and support. We're very blessed to have one of them as our chairman. Prince Alwaleed started this foundation the day he started Kingdom Holding Company. The same day he got the first project he decided that a portion of this project, beside the *zakat*, will go to people in need. I learned a lot personally from him. You get a view on how to give back to the community, do good, promote tolerance, understanding and acceptance of others.

I asked His Royal Highness, 'Why didn't you specialise in something?' And he said, 'Why should I specialise in something? Let us help as much as we need.' As Secretary General and honoured to be so, I'm very happy with my team, with one billion beneficiaries, with US$4.4 billion in 190 countries around the world. It's only ten Saudi women who are doing all that. This success, and the recognition that I'm getting personally, is because of this team, and I'm very grateful to be one of them.

Badr Jafar: I understand that Alwaleed Philanthropies has invested over US$30 million to help communities in the Middle East and North Africa respond to COVID-19. Can you describe how you designed and implemented your response to the pandemic? Do you think that this experience might affect how people think about the role of strategic philanthropy in responding to these kinds of crises in the future?

Princess Lamia: Well, as you said, we always strategise our moves. We didn't announce our commitment in the beginning. We waited for a couple of months just to see where the need was. This is the beauty of our type of work. We don't work with our own hands. We strategise, we see the gap, and we try our best to narrow it or work with others to help people in need. That's what happened with COVID-19. We had six initiatives in the Middle East and Africa. In the beginning of the pandemic, everybody was worried about the Gulf area, the United States, Europe and Asia. No one was worrying about the Middle East or the refugees in Africa,

"This is the beauty of our type of work. We don't work with our own hands. We strategise, we see the gap, and we try our best to narrow it or work with others to help people in need."

and how they were going to face it. We were successful in collaborating with some of our old partners such as Gavi the Vaccine Alliance, Bill Gates, Splash, ICESCO and UNICEF. We redirected some of the funds towards the COVID-19 pandemic response. We put another almost US$21 million as a new project to improve testing and for a public health initiative.

We also looked at the post-pandemic and what people in Africa could do who could not get access to vaccinations for years. We needed to help get the community ready with masks, sanitation and protective equipment. For them, that's a huge thing. So, we built small factories in countries in Africa for the mothers and the youth to produce sanitation and masks for the community, which also increased their income.

Of course, we are working with the World Health Organization and the Centers for Disease Control. We worked in accelerators to improve the testing. We worked on many scientific projects, but we also tried to meet the needs of people. And we work with UN Habitat to build shelters. For refugees, isolation during the pandemic is not an option, unfortunately.

Badr Jafar: How do you think that the nature and practice of philanthropy in the Middle East and North Africa have changed during the time that you've been involved in the sector? Do you think that the youth of today will change the way that philanthropy is practised?

Princess Lamia: As Muslims in this part of the world, we have this as a core in our beliefs and religion – giving back to the community and helping others. Even if you smile at a person, this is doing good at the end of the day, that is what we believe.

I have been working in this area since 2012 and I see a huge transformation in this area. I'm not very good with technology. Maybe my daughters are much more knowledgeable than me. But honestly, technology makes philanthropy much easier. Helping people, reaching out and creating awareness, it's easy. It's not what we used to do before. And it gives you a wider perspective on how you can help. We're not using the old methods. Now you just can go online. There are communities on Facebook that you can enter, and you can understand from refugees, displaced people and special needs people what they want in certain areas of the world.

So, what's changing? I know that poverty is increasing. But God has given us the tools to serve better. I'm always positive. I like to see the solution more than the problem. You try to have a unique solution that can be sustainable, which is very important. Before we did not think about sustainable philanthropy. You donate to a *masjid*, you donate for elders, for sick people, for orphans, but we never thought of a sustainable project that can benefit people moving forward, and how you can have a positive impact on people's lives. What I see now, even with companies and their corporate social responsibility efforts, they are saying, 'I don't want to just be a sponsor in an event. I want to do something that will help the community and we will gain from it by creating loyalty for our brand,' which is very smart marketing. I care that they start being involved in communities and even though they're going to create loyalty for their brand, at the end of the day, they're benefiting the community.

Badr Jafar: The Kingdom of Saudi Arabia is the largest economy in the Arab region. It launched the Saudi Vision 2030, which is a strategic framework to diversify its economy, and develop public service sectors such as health, education and tourism. I've heard you speak about the role of organisations such as Alwaleed Philanthropies in helping to support these national strategies. What do you think makes for successful collaboration between business, government and the social sector?

Princess Lamia: To be successful, we need a shared goal. This is where we come in as Alwaleed Philanthropies. Because we are dealing a lot with international partners, we have this kind of approach and knowhow to leverage several partners on the same project and give everyone what they want.

I'll give you an example. His Royal Highness is a big investor in Careem [a ride-sharing app] and Uber. We took an initiative in support of women after His Majesty declared that women could drive. Forty-eight hours after the announcement we collaborated with Careem, we donated cars for women to drive, we gave them the licence, and now there are almost 70 of them on the streets as drivers, Careem Captains. We wanted to do something more that would help the community. So, we were collaborating with an entity called Harakia for physically disabled people. We went to them and said, 'We want disabled people to be Careem Captains.' They said, 'What are you talking about?' And we said, 'There is a car that they can drive with their hands, they don't need their legs.' We donated cars. Now we have almost 100 of them as Careem Captains. You don't understand how their life changed. The Ministry of Labour of Saudi Arabia is also involved in that. Their aim is to provide physically disabled individuals with creative opportunities. It's our role as a philanthropic organisation to go the extra mile, and to give people in need economic support and technical support. For us, it's helping people. You have to understand the players, and what they want, and you have to be smart, and satisfy everyone.

> "It's our role as a philanthropic organisation to go the extra mile, and to give people in need economic support and technical support."

Badr Jafar: Throughout your career, you've been a very strong advocate for advancing the role of women across a wide range of fields. What advice would you give to the next generation of women leaders who might be considering a career in the philanthropic sector?

Princess Lamia: I advise them not to fall into the trap of being a victim. Women in this part of the world have been raised to be a victim and to play this role well. I was one of them. But I realised that I have everything that can make me a successful person. What I want from the next generation is to understand that we're not in a fight with men. Men are our partners, our fathers, our brothers, who will always support us. We want to work together towards a better future. Do not depend on anyone. You are capable to achieve what you want. So do not underestimate yourself. That's my message.

Mo Ibrahim

Founder and Chairman, Mo Ibrahim Foundation

Sudanese-born, Dr Mo Ibrahim is the founder and chair of the Mo Ibrahim Foundation, which he established in 2006 to support good governance and exceptional leadership on the African continent. The foundation created the Ibrahim Prize for Achievement in African Leadership in 2007. Since 2007, the foundation publishes annually the Ibrahim Index of African Governance, which assesses public governance performance in each of the 54 African countries. The foundation also holds every year in a different African country the Ibrahim Governance Weekend, which gathers African and global stakeholders to debate around key challenges for Africa.

In 1989, Dr Ibrahim founded Mobile Systems International (MSI), a world-leading cellular consulting and software provider. In 1998, he created Celtel International, one of Africa's leading mobile telephone companies, which pioneered mobile services in Africa. He is also founding chairman of Satya Capital Limited, a private equity fund focused on Africa.

Dr Ibrahim is also the co-founder and co-chair of the Africa Europe Foundation, which was launched in 2020 with the think tank Friends of Europe to catalyse partnerships between Africa and Europe.

Badr Jafar: Several of the fastest-growing economies in the world are on the African continent. Are you witnessing a rise in the number of individuals and families from these countries who are becoming involved in philanthropy?

Mo Ibrahim: No, unfortunately. In Africa, and I would say in the Arab world as well, philanthropy is not widespread. Philanthropy, in principle, is selfless, or giving for people you'll never know, and you'll never meet. We have had conversations about this with many friends, and it appears to me that philanthropy or a form of philanthropy in the region is focused on relatives, families and the immediate community. Culturally speaking, in Africa, we have extended families. A family in Africa is going to be more than 300 or 400 people. Whoever gets a bit well off, will start by looking after these people. People are very cooperative and, in African culture, if you live in a village and you need to rebuild your house or your hut, everybody will come to help. This is not unusual because of the lack of social safety nets. None of our African countries have adequate social programmes or safety nets.

People look after each other within their own community, their own village and their own extended family. It's a form of cooperation, or help, but is not exactly philanthropy as we define philanthropy. Similarly in the Arab world, the only time people will step out outside the extended family is to give to something like building a mosque. I always say, we have a lot of mosques so maybe we should look after needier people. I think God will reward you more for doing that. But it is a question of culture.

Badr Jafar: Would you say that the practice of institutional philanthropy is at a very early stage, and that the general attitude towards governance of the sector requires more work? Is there a trend in that direction?

Mo Ibrahim: There's not much of a trend in our regions because, as I said, philanthropy is not really a recognised institution. If there is flooding in our country, the president will make an appeal, he will ask well-off people to help, to give the government some money to look after people. This is a form of social cooperation, but we don't have the concept of philanthropy or even the concept of non-profits. Several sites have started to emerge, but mainly focusing on politics, corruption and human rights. This is the scene in our country.

I remember having a discussion with Bill Gates, who travelled to the Gulf and Saudi Arabia to recruit for the Giving Pledge. He said to me, 'There are a lot of billionaires in the region, and we cannot find people who are willing to join us. What is wrong?' I tried to explain to him, 'It's not necessarily wrong. But people have a completely different approach to generosity.' I must say, I was a bit ashamed. I think our wealthy people are not really looking beyond their noses.

Badr Jafar: Your foundation publishes an annual index of African governance, concerned with state governance and governance of national institutions. It obviously varies by country. How would you describe the current state of governance on the African continent? What are you most encouraged by? And conversely, what are you most concerned about?

Mo Ibrahim: We have collected data for the past two decades. There was a marked improvement in governance, especially in the first ten years of our work, then we started to see stagnation, which is unfortunate. Three-quarters of our people today live in better-governed societies than 20 years ago, so that's a step forward. But it has been slow and at times stagnant, and that is worrying. It is hard work; we must keep pushing. Thank God, we're not going backwards. But we're stagnating, and that's not good enough.

> "Three-quarters of our people today live in better-governed societies than 20 years ago."

Badr Jafar: Do you think that the pandemic will have a lasting impact on how people around the world think about the role of private philanthropy in responding to global challenges?

Mo Ibrahim: It's a very strange situation and strange times. Apparently, the economic impact of the virus is far greater than the health impact. In Africa, we have lost about 35,000 lives from almost 1.3 billion people. However, we lose just under 400,000 people every year to malaria. Looking at the two numbers, losing 400,000 people annually to malaria is far worse, and nobody talks about this. Some philanthropists, especially the Gates Foundation, are doing a lot of good work in the malaria area, as well as the global funds and others. But it's obviously not enough because we are still losing a lot of people.

The health impact of COVID-19 is far less in my view than the economic impact. Wealthy countries responded by writing big cheques and they have no problem creating debt, or just printing money. But in the emerging world, and Africa specifically, we don't have that fiscal space. So, the impact on Africa is severe. And the progress of the past 15 years is now threatened. When we had the banking crisis in 2009, there was some leadership, and we all recall how the G20 played a very decisive role. This time, there is no international leadership and philanthropy on its own cannot play a major role. The capacity that is required is far greater than the resources available to philanthropy. So, I'm worried about the economic impact; and we'll have to live with this for some time. We have been humbled as a human race. We thought that we were masters of this universe. And then this little thing played havoc with us.

It also shows a lack of preparedness. Our health systems are inadequate and completely underfunded in emerging countries and in rich countries. The main worry in the UK, France and other European countries was the possible collapse of the health system because we did not prepare ourselves for such a pandemic. In the end, this virus is relatively benign; the mortality rate is below 1%. Imagine if it was something more serious. What would have happened? I hope this emphasises our limits, as one of the species that live on this planet. We need to be more respectful of the environment around us. Otherwise, we're in danger.

Badr Jafar: I wanted to ask you about technology. You have a lot of experience in telecoms and networks. How is the

so-called information and digital age changing the nature of giving today, in your view?

Mo Ibrahim: Technology is already changing our lives. Suddenly, we're much more productive than ever before. This pandemic has shown us that we can teach, study or go to school online. We can buy our stuff online; we can communicate with others. In the past, one of us would have to travel 4,000 miles to sit down and have a talk. Of course, it lacks the human touch, of shaking hands, hugging or whatever, but the content is there.

So, technology has opened a lot of opportunities. We are more aware of what's going on around us in the world. Today, if something happens in Vietnam, in China, in India or the United States, we're all informed. Technology is bringing us closer together. It makes it much easier for us to organise ourselves and to act. It's very easy to bring a group of people together to cooperate, and it cuts the cost of acting together to almost zero. So, that opens a lot of avenues to act together, to organise together and to learn from each other. Yes, technology is affecting all aspects of our life, including philanthropy.

Badr Jafar: Your leadership fellowship and scholarship programmes are committed to identifying and mentoring promising leaders in a range of fields. What's different about emerging leaders of today, compared with when you first embarked on your own career?

Mo Ibrahim: I think younger generations now are better equipped to deal with issues of society. Let me give you an example. When I was a young man in Sudan, many years ago, we had only one TV channel, which was run by the government. The first item in the news was always what the president had for lunch or who he met. So, information was controlled by a government ministry, which chose what to tell us and what information we received. Our channels of information were very limited. One newspaper was owned by the army and one by the government; there were only one, maybe two, that were independent, and they had to be careful what they published. Our chance to get information was to buy *Newsweek* and *Time* magazines, which were very popular at the time, although sometimes they didn't arrive. We tried to listen to the BBC World Service, but our access to information was really limited and, in many cases, effectively censored by design, or just as a by-product of this narrow channel of flow of information. Today, information is everywhere. We have information fatigue because we cannot process all this information available to us. I have umpteen things to see on my computer from various news channels, to YouTube to WhatsApp, some personal, some organised. You have a deluge of information. Our problem now is not information but processing of information.

The scope of issues in an earlier time was very limited. For most of us, the main issue was independence and how to get rid of colonial rule. So, matters were simple; there was a colonial power, and we were fighting for independence. Today it's a much more complex world, where we are fighting on multiple fronts. Development, human rights, climate change – there are so many issues which require an array of policies.

Badr Jafar: For the aspiring philanthropist, any tips you can impart in relation to the what, where and, importantly, the how of giving?

Mo Ibrahim: As you mentioned, the word is 'strategic'. What are you trying to do with your philanthropy? What's your objective? Who do you want to help and how do you want to help? When we started our foundation, because we made some money in Africa from business, we said, 'Let's give back to Africa.' But, how to give back? There are many options. We have a lot of refugees in camps, so we can give baby milk or blankets, and other supplies. We can open some schools to help educate younger generations.

But the question we faced was, and that's specific to Africa, why do we have so many poor people, what is wrong with Africa?

You look at Africa, it's a rich continent. The number of people living in Africa is very small. You can take India and China and North America and Europe together, and Africans have more space. So, why are we poor? Mandela used to say: 'Africa is rich, but Africans are poor.'

The answer we came up with was that it's the way we run our countries. It's governance and leadership. That is a problem with our countries. That's why we are backward. Many African countries were far better than South Korea, than China, than Malaysia at the time of independence. If you go back to the late 1940s and early 1950s, GDP per capita in Africa was higher than many of those countries. So why have these countries moved to a much higher level of development and we're still backward?

Clearly it is about governance. So, we decided to focus on that area. You may say this is not philanthropy but I think it's a higher form of philanthropy because to help the poor, we need to change what is happening in the country; that is the best way to move the education system and improve the health system, through to real governance and self-reliance on our resources. Fighting corruption, supporting good leadership and improving governance; that is the best way to help the poor in our countries.

> "Fighting corruption, supporting good leadership and improving governance; that is the best way to help the poor in our countries."

Our work doesn't look like giving, because we don't give grants, except scholarships, but we believe we're helping the poor in a significant way by building systems so that young philanthropists really think about what they're trying to achieve, and what is the best way to achieve that. We want them to ask questions such as: Is it a direct or indirect attack on the problem? Is it leveraging, is it collaboration? How can you achieve what you want to do in the most effective way? You want a big bang for every dollar you put in. It is like business. Investing in human beings is a wonderful investment.

Wladimir Klitschko*

Founder of Klitschko Foundation, Company Founder, Author, Lecturer, Boxing Champion

In 2003, Dr Wladimir Klitschko and his brother Vitali founded the Klitschko Foundation, a charity whose mission is to create opportunities for the development of young people who change local communities through their own projects. So far, the foundation has helped more than two million children.

Wladimir Klitschko is a former professional boxer who competed from 1996 to 2017, winning the Super Heavyweight gold medal for Ukraine at the 1996 Olympics as well as becoming the longest-reigning world heavyweight champion. His mission is to pass on the knowledge he has gained from many years in professional sport to other areas of life and show people how to achieve willpower using his method FACE the Challenge. To this end, he founded Klitschko Ventures in 2016.

In 2003, Wladimir and Vitali founded the boxing promotion company K2 Promotions. Wladimir also founded the Klitschko Management Group, a sports marketing agency. Together with the University of St Gallen in Switzerland, in 2016, he set up the CAS Change and Innovation Management programme and the Competence Center for Intrapreneurship. He is the author of *Challenge Management: What Managers Can Learn from the Top Athlete* (2018); *FACE the Challenge – Discover the Willpower in You* (2020); and *Stolen Lives – The Abducted Children of Ukraine* (2023, in German). He has been awarded the UNESCO Heroes for Kids Award.

---

* This interview was conducted at the end of 2021 before the Russian invasion of Ukraine. Dr Wladimir Klitschko's focus since then has been on supporting his country and the city of Kyiv. The work of the Klitschko Foundation has also expanded to include humanitarian aid. It still focuses on the welfare of children and young people, but its projects differ from those described in the interview. Some updates have therefore been added to the following conversation.

Badr Jafar: Wladimir, more than two million children are receiving assistance from the foundation that you founded with your brother in 2003. Tell us about this journey, and the mission to deliver impact through sports, science, education and medicine for children in Ukraine.

Wladimir Klitschko: It's 20 years now since we created the Klitschko Foundation with my brother Vitali, and we were supported by many people. This support is crucially important. I truly believe that self-made men or women don't exist. If someone says, 'I'm a self-made man,' that is totally wrong. It's wrong because there were two parents who made that self-made person, and that's just the beginning. When you want to achieve goals, you need to have allies, you need to have partners and you need to have friends. Sometimes your competitors can become your partners; it's called coopetition in business, instead of competition in sports. Since we are receiving so much support, we decided it was time to give back.

The foundation is a non-profit organisation to support present and future generations, but we wanted to do it systematically, sustainably. We were thinking of questions: What can we do, and how can we identify what we stand for? There are a lot of things that you can stand for. We came from sport. Sport is crucially important for young men and women, because through competition you learn a lot about yourself and about your competitors as well. I believe that sport gives you a sense of respect for opponents and for yourself. Sport teaches you about having a powerful body. But on the brain side, you need education.

Education was important for us, because knowledge gives us a chance to avoid the mistakes that we made before and learn from the mistakes of others. Even though you learn from others' mistakes, you are still going to make your own mistakes, which you can learn from. That's why we decided to take care of education and sports, the duality of body and mind. It's so important for any person if they want to achieve any goal in life.

Badr Jafar: What is the most useful role that private philan-thropists can play in making children's dreams come true whether that's in Ukraine or in other regions of the world? What does strategic philanthropy look like in this critical space?

Wladimir Klitschko: I believe that the world has become more global. Through the pandemic and the war in Ukraine we under-stood that we're united, and whatever region, country or contin-ent we live in, we are connected with each other. We need to understand what is going on in the world, because eventually a local problem could become a global problem.

I believe that entrepreneurs and philanthropists need to come together. When you act together, you get different perspectives. It's very important to communicate with the rest of the world and collaborate with each other, and I think it's crucially important that we focus the effort. We need to come together, identify where the threat is coming from, localise it and eliminate any chances to spread it. Whether it's a health threat, or poverty or lack of educa-tion; many different things affect our society. I truly believe that philanthropy is something that should be focused. We need to focus and systematise our efforts. It's crucially important that we communicate with each other, collecting examples of how similar challenges were solved and share them so as to learn from other philanthropists' methods and systems. This will help us to identify quickly, localise quickly and solve issues quickly.

The Klitschko Foundation is in Kyiv, the capital of Ukraine, but we also have a great network. We have, for instance, children from Kazakhstan travelling to Ukraine, and having summer camps with Ukrainian children and children from North America. Basically, you have different geographic, cultural and religious backgrounds. We had the summer camp with the Klitschko Foundation, where children were given tasks. They were supposed to make short films and produce those films in teams and the best film was broadcast on national television. It was a truly collaborative project; they learned how to work with each other, who was responsible in front of the camera and behind the camera, who was responsible for editing, for lights, for microphones and for writing the script. Eventually, with a common effort, they made a short film that they were allowed to keep and which will stay with them forever.

Badr Jafar: Your foundation has been successful in rallying the business community to create a space for social, emotional and physical development for children. Are you happy with the state of business engagement with your cause and with organisations like the Klitschko Foundation, and what specific things can business and philanthropy do to enhance and get the most out of that relationship?

Wladimir Klitschko: I want to say thank you for the previous support. Business is a crucially important part. But as a businessperson, you also need to think how to do more to support your community. Receiving is nice, but giving is even nicer. It gives you motivation and a better sense for the future.

Since I became a parent, I better understand the circle of life. I thought I understood my parents, or well enough, but when you see that you are in the chain of generations and you are receiving support from parents you care about passing it to future generations. So, when you're a businessperson, obviously it's important to take care of your own business and make it as good as possible, but it's also important not to forget the community, family, your city, your country and the world, because we're facing global challenges.

How can I make a better future for the next generation? As soon as you understand this question, you will act differently. I'm happy to receive business support, but I want to motivate business to do it even better. That's why I believe we need to structure and focus our efforts. With this, we are going to get better communication with each other. We will identify the issues in this world and in our communities and address them.

Badr Jafar: What does success look like to you in terms of the work that you're doing at the Klitschko Foundation? How do

you measure progress over time? Can you imagine a day when the foundation's support will no longer be necessary?

Wladimir Klitschko: Success is tricky. In sports, it's like a medal with two sides. It gives you satisfaction, but it numbs your motivation. The more success you have, the more motivation gets dull. I have been a champion for 12 years and I was always trying to figure out how to repeat the success.

At some point, everything has an end. We've seen great empires coming to an end in history. But how can we make our philanthropy work more sustainable? We need to handle philanthropy as a business. I believe in this system of endowment, and eventual compounding of the endowment, so the more financially secure you are, the better future you could have. I love Alfred Nobel's idea of creating the Nobel Prize. Alfred is not with us, but the prize is still there, and people are being supported as the organisation continues. At some point Vitali and I will not be present in this world, but the organisation must function and that's why we are trying to build more endowment into our foundation. Beyond our time, and with the methodology that I've created – FACE the Challenge – it can be passed to the future directors of the foundation. The principles will remain the same and that gives me a good feeling of a brighter future.

Badr Jafar: You have a diverse exposure to philanthropy in both Eastern and Western Europe. How would you describe the current state of the non-profit landscape in countries like Ukraine versus, say, Germany? Do you think that there is more scope for collaboration?

Wladimir Klitschko: Totally different worlds and totally different approach. I believe that Ukrainians and Ukraine can improve a lot in philanthropy, compared with Germans. I think there is a lot to learn for us Ukrainians to do things better.

We're trying to build bridges. With the Klitschko Foundation as an example, we work with the DFB Stiftung, the Foundation of the German Football Association, one of the largest organisations in the world of football, and football is huge. We're collaborating on exchanges where Ukrainian children are going to Germany and the other way around on different projects and exchanges. We've been collaborating, and those bridges are extremely important. We're not far away geographically from each other but we're far away in our approaches. Our current generation and future generations will learn from each other through such exchanges; they create lifelong memories, especially as they are in person. Zoom calls and digital communication are important, but it's still necessary to feel it. Theory and practice, they're similar, but different. I think we'll continue to get more experience and knowledge and share this knowledge in Ukraine. The expertise that we have collected we will also share with local organisations. I think Germans can learn from Ukrainians too, there's always a different angle on something.

Badr Jafar: You've told me about your challenge management philosophy and methodology that you've been developing, and now teaching. Could you summarise what that is, but also how it can be applied across different aspects of what you do, including within the philanthropic sector?

Wladimir Klitschko: I believe that a system is very important. I learned it as an athlete; you need to be disciplined, you need to remain consistent and you need to improve with consistency. It doesn't mean that you need to do the same thing over and over. But, like a golfer, who practises a swing billions of times during his lifespan, every swing is better; it's a never-ending process. I think that we will improve if we work systematically and sustainably. FACE the Challenge is based on four core skills: focus, agility, coordination and endurance. It's based on my experience as an athlete that has been implemented on a personal level as well as on corporate level. Large corporations are using it in their ecosystem, and you can use it even in finance, with FACE Capital (our multi-family office service). Methodology is also important in philanthropy; to identify the goal, just as we identified what the Klitschko Foundation stands for – sport and education. I believe that a system will help us to improve our approach as entrepreneurs and philanthropists.

FACE is based on my athletic background and my consideration of how to pass on my knowledge to future generations in a systematic way. Unfortunately, a negative event triggered it. My Hall of Fame coach Emanuel Steward passed away during my training camp. I had finished my first workout when I got the call, just as I was going up to a cabin in the Austrian Alps; suddenly the world crashed. In addition to the devastating personal loss, it made me ponder. Emanuel had so much expertise; he was a genius in boxing, and when he died, all his knowledge was gone. He passed knowledge on to us athletes, but when we are gone, what will happen to all the expertise? It will also go.

So, I was thinking about how important it is to pass on expertise, so that the same mistakes will not be repeated. We need to learn from history so we can improve and accelerate change. In 2016, I got into the methodology of Challenge Management at the University of St Gallen and I've been sharing it ever since. That's the philosophy of my life and philosophy of the method FACE the Challenge. The CAS-certified study course is called Change and Innovation Management. Additionally, the Harvard Business School [HBS] has made and published a case study, which is based on my athletic background, as well as FACE the Challenge method. It's important to pass it to the future generations in different shapes and forms. Two study books and a workbook came out within six years and are translated in different languages. The University of St Gallen shared the methodology in the German language for the HBS. Now it's in English, and I believe that we will eventually digitalise the experience. So, you can learn the methodology and how to tackle challenges and conquer them; to be the winner in the end.

"It's crucial to empower the younger generation by equipping them with the skills to navigate today's challenges."

Badr Jafar: Where do you think the greatest opportunities will be for philanthropists and non-profit organisations and foundations to generate the biggest impact in the years ahead?

Wladimir Klitschko: I believe that it's crucial to empower the younger generation by equipping them with the skills to navigate today's challenges. In our foundation projects, we focus on teaching participants how to address community issues, such as waste sorting problems and the lack of opportunities in their villages and cities. The Klitschko Foundation has always been a dependable resource for the young people of Ukraine. I advocate for an emphasis on practical education, providing young people with the necessary tools to overcome obstacles both in their personal lives and within their communities. Regarding the greatest opportunities for philanthropic organisations, I believe that leveraging technology and innovation for social projects is crucial. The younger generation will live in a completely different world, and non-profit organisations can be pioneers in teaching them how to use digital technologies and tools.

> "I advocate for an emphasis on practical education, providing young people with the necessary tools to overcome obstacles both in their personal lives and within their communities."

Mike Milken

Chairman, Milken Institute

In 1991, Mike Milken founded the Milken Institute, whose mission is to help people build meaningful lives with access to good healthcare, education and employment, and the resources to create opportunities for themselves and their communities. The Milken Institute hosts more than 200 annual events and conferences in North America, Europe, Asia and the Middle East.

As a financier, Milken revolutionised modern capital markets by pricing and rewarding risk more efficiently. He has been at the forefront of successful initiatives in medical research, education, public health and access to capital for more than four decades. *Fortune* called him 'The Man Who Changed Medicine' and

Forbes listed him among 'Visionaries Reimagining Our Children's Future'. In 1982, he formalised his philanthropy by co-founding the Milken Family Foundation, which focuses on educational reform.

Milken's latest book is *Faster Cures: Accelerating the Future of Health* (2023).

Badr Jafar: The work of the Milken Institute keeps human, financial and social capital at the centre of its operations. From your decades of experience with the institute, how can we better engage philanthropic capital as a partner alongside business and government in addressing our world's greatest challenges? What can we do to enhance effective collaboration between philanthropy, business and government?

Mike Milken: I think people underestimate the true assets of the world. You're used to reading a balance sheet or financial statement, even if it's for a philanthropic foundation, and it focuses on financial or real capital assets such as real estate. These make up a very small part of the true assets of the world.

In 1965, I wrote down a formula where, essentially, access to financial capital, which could be philanthropic or non-philanthropic, served to multiply the world's greatest and most important asset, which is human potential, often referred to as human capital. The second-largest asset in the world is social capital, which includes universal education, access to healthcare and even creditor rights that come into play. And third, the real assets you find on the balance sheet. With the founding of the Milken Institute, a decade or so after the founding of the Milken Family Foundation, we focused on human and social capital.

The value of human capital is measured in many ways. But it is in hundreds or thousands of trillions of dollars. When you think about what is going to propel our society and the emerging markets of South Asia, sub-Saharan Africa and parts of the Middle East, you're focused on the potential of human beings. Building this capital takes different forms. One important form is health; lengthening life and improving the quality of life. And next, it takes education. Like a glass of water, you don't really see it as you go through different levels of education. But you're filling up the glass of water, and it becomes more valuable.

And then there is the value of social capital. Everyone should have a feeling of upward mobility. I think I was eight years old when my father told me that his grandchildren would not have an opportunity unless all children felt they had a chance and an opportunity. The role of government becomes very important in creating the social capital element.

The sustainability of the environment in many ways has taken more importance today. It was 1968 when we received the pictures of this little blue planet from a satellite. We don't have any alternative; there's no other place where we can live. The closest star is about four light years away. It might have a planet like Earth that could sustain life, but it is not going to be reached in our lifetime. I think this gives you this appreciation of the importance of a sustainable environment.

In some ways, it's very easy to create collaboration. In the medical field, we told researchers we would not fund them unless they collaborated. But each of these elements to which you refer, philanthropy, government and business, has its importance. Philanthropy can take enormous risks and try new things to get things going. And then, government agencies can develop the ideas into action. Lastly, if it's sustainable, business or industry can get involved.

Many years ago, we let medical researchers know we would fund them for five years. After that we would no longer fund them. This gave them the understanding that they had to be able to stand on their own feet, or search for other sources.

Badr Jafar: Mike, you've previously said, 'Philanthropy is far more than just writing cheques. It takes an entrepreneurial approach that seeks out best practices and empowers people that change the world.' How do you think that the next

> "Philanthropy is far more than just writing cheques. It takes an entrepreneurial approach that seeks out best practices and empowers people that change the world."

generation of socially conscious consumers and investors is changing the way that the world relates to business practice and philanthropic practice?

Mike Milken: We often talk only about money when we talk about philanthropy. But giving your time, even in a financial sense, is far greater, if you calculate the hours that people give. If you can give one person opportunity by being a mentor, you have a chance to change the world. People need to understand the importance of giving time – a high school student helping an elementary student or a college student helping a high school student as a mentor.

What we've tried to do is figure out how to get leverage. In the United States, the world's largest economy, US$600 billion to US$700 billion a year is spent on K-12 education. There is no foundation, even the largest – the Gates Foundation with support from Warren Buffett – that can make a financial difference that is substantial in the educational system. In education, our leverage point was to raise the self-respect of the teaching profession through a National Educator Award programme. If we changed how education and the teacher are viewed in society by bringing more respect and self-confidence to the profession, that would provide a lot of leverage.

The other element is technology. We launched a programme raising money for cancer research, where the average donation was US$2. If you mailed it in, if you wrote a cheque, the cost of processing would far exceed the value. But by using digital means, small donations can be made at lower cost. For young people who are much more likely to be technology-oriented, the idea that a billion people giving you US$1 is a billion dollars has far greater effect than one person giving you a billion dollars. Large numbers of small amounts can change the world.

I think people don't realise how much one person can influence another person's life. When you talk to people who have a successful path, often they identify one teacher in their life who gave them a love of reading, or mathematics, or gave them the confidence that they could succeed. When I look at places like sub-Saharan Africa, I see millions of young people who are optimistic, if given the opportunity to succeed. Technology can help. If you look at many of the new technology companies, such as Salesforce or Google, many of them set aside 1% of their revenue or a percentage of their profits to go towards philanthropy. If you look at a company like PayPal, my guess is they will have raised US$6 million to US$8 million for philanthropy in donations that are probably less than one dollar. So, they will have raised more money for philanthropy than Gates and Buffett will give away in donations.

Badr Jafar: You established the Center for Strategic Philanthropy at the Milken Institute several years ago to advise philanthropists and foundations seeking to develop and implement transformative giving strategies. In the world's fastest-growing markets, including the emerging economies of Africa, the Middle East and developing Asia, a lot of new wealth is being generated and will be passed on to the next generation in the coming decade or so. What impact do you think these geographic and generational shifts will have on our global economy and social sector more specifically?

Mike Milken: One of the things in philanthropy that we were concerned about, as I look back over 50 years, is to do no harm. Many well-meaning programmes often have the opposite effect. One example was school busing for racial equality in the United States. It had certain positive objectives, and many leading philanthropists endorsed it. But it broke down the neighbourhood school. Lower-middle-income or middle-income parents, when they were told that their seven-year-old child was going to be bused for more than an hour to school every day each way, moved because they couldn't afford private school alternatives.

One of the key questions that we see with philanthropy is: Is it positive or negative? Have you thought of the potential consequences of that philanthropy? Next, is your philanthropy productive? Are you doing something that someone has already tried? Particularly in education, and in medical research, a great deal of all philanthropy is either unproductive or wasted. In medical research, if a person had a serious life-threatening disease and was treated by a doctor, that grateful patient would fund the doctor. Now, the doctor was a clinician, not a researcher, and might not necessarily be qualified for it. So, there was a very low return.

We discovered in our own philanthropy that the highest return comes from supporting young people. We were focused on talented people with long careers. If I pick medical research as an example, we used to give a lot of funds to people at the peak of their career after they had accomplished much. Very little was ever accomplished after that. Someone who has gone to medical school, earned a PhD fellowship, taken part in internships and residencies, they're often in higher education for 15 years. When we talk about a young investigator, they might be 33 or 35 years old. What we discovered is every young scientist whom we funded was later funded by government or business. When you look at Nobel Prizes that are awarded, many times you'll see a person who is 60 or 70 years old winning that Nobel Prize for ideas that they had when they were in their 20s or 30s. To me, one of the great challenges is to get money out earlier in this process, and to identify individuals who can change the world.

"The highest return comes from supporting young people."

It is no different in business; to identify an individual who has the talent to build a business, an industry, a real pioneer. There are many people who have chosen a philanthropic path in their life who could have run a company, but by empowering them, they could change the world. Part of the effort in strategic philanthropy is to try to make sure your philanthropy is productive, that you're not reinvesting in something, or an area that would have been funded anyway. You're looking for areas that have not been funded. And that is one of the key roles, particularly in emerging markets, in sub-Saharan Africa, South Asia and the Middle East.

The question as we look at philanthropy is: What is the most effective form of this philanthropy and is it sustainable? Our centre has looked at very interesting ideas and projects, but they're not all sustainable. The cost per person is too great. That is the exciting thing about what you're seeing in India, or in other parts of the world where you have to figure out how to operate at a cost that is realistic for those societies. One of the most important things a centre for strategic philanthropy can do is to advise people on enormous wealth creation, particularly in Asia, in the Middle East and other parts of the world, which is far greater than people realise.

Badr Jafar: You have a long history of practising strategic philanthropy focused on medical research and public health. What is the optimal role for private philanthropy in the field of medical research? What advice would you give to philanthropists on how best to engage in the space when they may not always understand the intricacies of the science behind it?

Mike Milken: More than 50% of all economic growth in the world over the past two centuries can be traced to advances in public health and medical research. The greatest thing that humankind has created has been a doubling of life expectancy over the past 120 years. Life expectancy on our planet was only 31 years in 1900, increasing by only 11 years over millions of years. We've now gone from 31 to the mid-70s over a very short period with a 100% increase in life expectancy in South Asia – this is not only an increase in life expectancy, but also quality of life.

When you look at some of the countries in sub-Saharan Africa, their median population age is 15 to 16 years old. They're about to see, with medical advances, a doubling of life expectancy in one generation. We constantly focus on how important it is for a child to go to school, who's had food, who's healthy and is not dealing with very serious medical issues. This changes the world for them.

When you look at the response on COVID-19, 3% of R&D or medical research is funded by philanthropy. But it is risk capital. Many years ago, we tried to change the paradigm for medical research, realising that philanthropy is the venture capital, the start-up capital for new ideas; if these ideas work, then they're supported in a larger way by business and government. In emergencies, philanthropic capital can move more quickly than governments or even businesses. To me, it is impossible to have a strong society if you don't have a healthy society. For example, years ago we saw AIDS ravaging sub-Saharan Africa. Only 20 to 25 years ago, a woman had a 95% to 98% probability of passing AIDS on to her children in childbirth. Now, with technology and advances in AIDS research, she has a 95% to 98% chance of avoiding it. Just imagine a whole generation of children who are not born with AIDS. These changes are benefiting the fast-growing parts of the world.

The vaccines that prevent people from getting diseases were around long before philanthropy focused on the COVID-19 vaccine. The efforts on a polio vaccine were driven by philanthropy, for example. We underestimate the importance of public health. For a government, the highest rate of return on government money is public health. Being able to drink water that doesn't give you a disease, that's healthy. You don't have to be an expert in molecular biology. When the Chan Zuckerberg Initiative was launched, neither of them was an expert in molecular biology. But they hired individuals to lead that effort for them. So once again, in many ways, philanthropy is dependent on picking people to represent you in areas that require great technical knowledge, to find those who can change the world.

Badr Jafar: What have you found to be some of the most effective ways to ensure discussions convened by the Milken

Institute are inclusive by nature, and to ensure that these conversations lead to action?

Mike Milken: This is an extremely important question. Many years ago, I became a strong believer that demographics was destiny. Someday most people in the United States will be of Asian or Latin American ancestry. In a state like California today, more than 50% is of Latin American ancestry and more than 70% of the children in the Los Angeles school system are of Latin American ancestry. The growth of the Islamic population and how it views philanthropy is also exceedingly important to the world. As the wealth of individuals from Indonesia and other countries in the world increases, how are they going to deploy their philanthropy?

What we've done might not make any difference if we don't create opportunities in sub-Saharan Africa. The UN is projecting an increase in the world's population from 7 billion to 11 billion people in this century, and almost all of that increase will be in sub-Saharan Africa. When I look at Nigeria today, a country whose population is around 60% that of the United States, they have twice as many children born in Nigeria as born in the United States. At the current birth rate, they have the highest birth rate of any country that has 200 million people or more today. That is why the United Nations and others have projected that, in fact, Nigeria 100 years from now might be the most populous country. What are the opportunities for the people in Nigeria?

What we have tried to do from a diversity standpoint in all our philanthropic programmes is to ask: How do you see the world through new eyes? If I look at our Milken scholars, they were born in more than 40 countries, their parents were born in more than 70 countries. As they convene, they have very different views of the world. One of the qualities of a great philanthropist is the ability to see the world through someone else's eyes; to understand from other people's viewpoints. The United States had the benefit, for more than 100 years, of enormous immigration. To me, this diversity is strength. To make an analogy, the strongest metals today are alloys, which are a mixture of different ingredients. The strength of a society is its diversity. What we find is if the philanthropists themselves have diversity, and they search for diversity in their efforts, then you get these viewpoints that are quite different.

We can see the world today through so many different viewpoints. There is an app today where you can read newspapers from 54 countries. You don't have to read how the world is reported from your local newspaper; you can see how the world is reported from any place in the world. But it starts with diversity in the philanthropic organisation itself. If you look at the centres of the Milken Institute, and they've grown from seven to ten and most people that lead those centres are women; they view the world differently. We have an enormously diverse group of people. The executive director of our Milken Institute Faster-Cures Center, Esther Krofah, was born in Nigeria. How she views healthcare, medical research, public health might be quite different from someone who grew up in New York City. It's very hard to get diversity if your organisation is not diverse.

EIGHT
CATALYSING SOCIAL INNOVATION

Social innovation has been defined as 'a novel solution to a social problem that is more effective, efficient, sustainable and just than existing solutions and for which the value created accrues primarily to society as a whole rather than private individuals'.[1]

Innovation comes from the minds of creative people in any discipline. Social innovation is the result of individual imagination applied to the common good. And as with all forms of innovation, it requires cultivation and support to thrive. This support can be provided in the form of financial capital. It can also be provided as knowledge, influence and expertise. Strategic philanthropy has the ability to support social innovators on a sustained basis. A philanthropist's investment can be the spark that catalyses the innovator to demonstrate the evidence required for other investors to move in at scale. And in some cases, the philanthropist and the innovator are one and the same.

I spoke to five exceptional social innovators, who might not describe themselves in this way but who have all launched innovative platforms to benefit others. One of these innovators has used creative philanthropy to engage and motivate other donors. Two are committed to improving society and economies by empowering women. And two have chosen arts and culture as a means of enriching their communities. In all cases, their initiative has improved the lives of individuals and the wellbeing of society.

Her Excellency Sheikha Bodour Al Qasimi from the Emirate of Sharjah in the UAE wears multiple hats. She is a professional publisher, and recently led the International Publishers Association as its president. As chancellor of the American University of Sharjah, she champions academic excellence and inclusion. She has created networks and organisations to support women in publishing, to foster entrepreneurial start-ups and to advance literacy among refugee children.

Rasha Alturki is another innovative female leader who has dedicated herself to women's empowerment in her home country of Saudi Arabia. Through her leadership of Alnahda Society, one of the oldest non-profits in Saudi Arabia, she has worked to help women become effective partners in the development of Saudi society, using research, advocacy and development programmes to help women out of poverty and to support women's rights.

Sanjit 'Bunker' Roy is the founder of Barefoot College, which he started in 1972, initially to provide rural Indian communities with basic services and solutions to support them on their journey to self-sufficiency. Over the past half century, the model that underpins the Barefoot College has proven to be highly transferable. Today, there are programmes and initiatives in more than 90 countries, and many of them focus on empowering women and girls in rural villages who have had no access to education or skills training but who are helped by Barefoot College to become catalysts for change in their communities.

Finally, I spoke with two extraordinary cultural philanthropists and innovators, both of whom work in the Middle East region and have influence and impact that extend beyond national borders.

Her Excellency Huda Alkhamis Kanoo is an Emirati philanthropist who is the founder of the Abu Dhabi Music and Arts Foundation, which she established in 1996. She launched the Abu Dhabi Festival in 2004 and has served as its artistic director ever since. The objectives of the foundation are to embed creativity and innovation among the people of the UAE, to enable access to arts and culture, and to build cultural bridges between the UAE and the rest of the world. Through her work, Huda Kanoo has built partnerships with many of the leading global cultural organisations and has helped put the UAE on the global cultural map.

Sultan Al Qassemi from the UAE has dedicated himself to building an appreciation of Arab art and culture throughout the diverse Arab region. He created the Barjeel Art Foundation in 2010 as a pan-Arab project to contribute to the intellectual development of modern and contemporary Arab art by building a publicly accessible collection. The foundation has more than 1,100 pieces in its collection and, since 2013, has mounted over 25 exhibitions across the world.

Her Excellency Sheikha Bodour bint Sultan Al Qasimi

Founder and Chief Executive Officer, Kalimat Publishing Group

In 2007, Her Excellency Sheikha Bodour Al Qasimi founded the Kalimat Publishing Group, based in the United Arab Emirates. It is now a global, multi-imprint publishing and educational technology company publishing over 400 titles, with licensing and distribution in 15 countries. Kalimat is recognised as an industry pioneer for books highlighting traditional Arabic culture alongside the modern challenges faced by children, as well as Arabic translations of titles that deal with themes that occasionally push socio-cultural boundaries.

Al Qasimi is also involved in several regional and international initiatives to promote youth and children's empowerment, economic development, creative industry development and cross-cultural exchange. The Kalimat Foundation, the non-profit arm of Kalimat Group, is involved in promoting literacy, reading culture and book accessibility, particularly among children who are victims of war and displacement and who are visually disabled.

Badr Jafar: Your Excellency, could you explain the thinking behind the Ubuntu Foundation, and how this new project came about? I'm particularly interested in the five elements and ancestral framework that guide the work of the foundation, and how they are applied in practice.

Sheikha Bodour: The Ubuntu Foundation is something that I hope will create positive change across the Middle East and Africa. The seeds of the Ubuntu Foundation were planted when the Ubuntu Love Challenge campaign developed strong momentum after the beginning of the pandemic lockdown in early 2020. The idea of the Ubuntu Love Challenge is simple, yet powerful. It's built on African ancestral wisdom. The word *'ubuntu'* reflects that. It means 'I am because we are.' This spirit of togetherness and interconnectedness was needed as the world was hit with the most difficult crisis in living history.

The Ubuntu Love Challenge took off quickly, with celebrities, businesspeople and philanthropists joining the challenge and offering something back to the community. The success and the impact of the Ubuntu Love Challenge encouraged us to continue and to multiply that effect globally. We also wanted to sustain our efforts beyond the pandemic.

As a human family, we learned a few lessons during this pandemic. We know the world needs more we-thinking and less I-thinking. We know the world needs more collaboration and less competition. It needs more interconnection and less exclusion. In that context, we decided that the best way to sustain this project in the future was to set up the Ubuntu Foundation. The Ubuntu Foundation aims to elevate human consciousness, while supporting the regeneration of our planet. It also adopts a holistic approach, a different one from other philanthropic organisations. We want to support and promote innovative social business initiatives that will help regenerate the five elements necessary for human upliftment, which are air, fire, water, earth and love.   —

Love is about culture, education, healthcare and ancient wisdom which tap into our heart centre. Under earth, we will look for sustainable projects in agriculture and mining. Under air, we will look into projects that are connected to wind power, energy and cleantech. Under water, we will look into structured resources of water. And under fire, we will look into alternative sources of clean energy.

We want to be proactive in creating a new vision for our planet; a new Earth, if you will. And we will support sustainable projects around these five elements that are connected deeply to the Ubuntu philosophy. To achieve that we will empower and promote local heroes, making a difference in their communities, and will offer them a global platform for greater support and sharing best practices for the benefit of everyone.

Badr Jafar: Are you seeing evidence that the nature of philanthropy is changing in Africa and the Middle East? And what do you think might be driving that change?

Sheikha Bodour: Yes, absolutely. Changes are indeed happening in philanthropy in the Middle East and Africa. This was the case even before the pandemic, but I think the COVID-19 crisis has elevated the voice of philanthropists from our region. For at least a decade now, we've seen movement; charitable giving has morphed into strategic philanthropy and hybrid models, where commercial capital is mixed with social investment and structures such as impact investing, which is an important development, in my opinion.

In emerging markets, this process has taken longer and has been less institutionalised than in countries where capital markets are more mature. But even in this region, and in Africa, we've seen a move towards more innovative ways of financing philanthropy, moving from grants, for example, to interest-based loans, coupled with a new drive towards more entrepreneurial models, such as social enterprises. These new models are driven by the growing understanding of the opportunity of philanthropic capital and the greater sense of social purpose, presented by these youth-dominated regions. As you know, both in Africa and in the Arab region, we have very young populations. These populations are digitally savvy, they're entrepreneurially minded and they're socially driven. And they've clearly brought new ideas to the sector. I think we should welcome and encourage that.

The days of simply establishing a foundation and giving out hundreds of random grants are over. Today, young people want to see fast, technologically-smart systems, changing the ways of creating social value. The gravity and urgency of the pandemic have further entrenched this trend and meant that effective and efficient delivery of social solutions is more critical. Ideas that the youth have been championing are coming into their own.

Badr Jafar: There are 80 million or more forcibly displaced people in our world and many of them live in the Middle East. Through the Kalimat Foundation, you've sought to meet some of the most basic needs of refugee children through literacy. What are some of the challenges facing refugee children that you're working on? What can philanthropists and businesses be doing to help address some of these needs in a practical way?

Sheikha Bodour: Refugee communities are perhaps the most vulnerable and often most hidden communities. This is one of the reasons we decided in the Kalimat Foundation to focus on sharing books and encouraging a culture of reading in refugee communities. We wanted to give children tools to express their voices, assert their existence and give them a fighting chance to create a better future. I think what they need most are quality education and accessible healthcare services. These two elements will give them the opportunity to obtain and retain employment and build a secure life for themselves and their families. Although COVID-19 stopped all travel and prevented us from accessing the analogue world, it forced us to use the tools and platforms of cyberspace. I think this shift needs to move vertically across all philanthropic efforts, to the communities that we're trying to serve. In that context, connectivity issues are still a major problem in many of the refugee communities. The rapid adoption of digital technology can radically transform the way we engage and the way we serve these communities. The need to digitise education has been paramount across the globe. And we've seen multiple foundations working with local governments to fast track the digitisation of education.

> "The rapid adoption of digital technology can radically transform the way we engage and the way we serve these communities."

I believe that this can provide an opportunity for innovation around how we deliver quality education to children and refugee communities that might not be able to access, or even have, a local school. We need to make sure that connectivity is not an issue. The potential to use software to improve access to education for these communities, in my opinion, is huge.

Equally, telemedicine is trending across the globe now, and we can offset the shortage of medical facilities prevalent in refugee communities. We must leverage the power of technology to better support these communities. Digital education, connectivity and telemedicine are just some of the aspects that need to be explored further by governments, businesses and philanthropists to maximise the opportunities of the digital revolution to serve these vulnerable communities better.

Badr Jafar: You created PublisHer a few years ago, to increase the number of women in leadership roles within the publishing industry. What advice would you give to young women around the world who might be considering a career in the publishing sector, or in the social sector?

Sheikha Bodour: PublisHer is close to my heart. I'll give you a quick introduction to why I set up PublisHer. I frequently found myself the only woman in publishing circles around the world. Wherever I went, whether it was Italy, Frankfurt or London, I would look around and men would dominate the room. I thought that we need to support women in leadership positions in publishing.

I've been working in publishing for quite some time. The best advice I could give is to say to aspiring young women, first, value yourself and your achievements, however insignificant they may be to you. Also, spend time and effort learning about yourself. To be successful, you have to start from understanding the kind of person you are and go from there; build on the good parts and learn how to deal with weaknesses. I believe that confidence is extremely important. In a world where gender balance is far from achieved, I think confidence is key to moving up the ladder and making a difference.

So, I tell women, be confident, be bold, don't undersell yourself. And remember to help other women. But also, be authentic. People will see through you if you're not 100% genuine and committed to what you do. And finally, I would add, take care of yourself. You can't always achieve everything that you want when you want. So, take time to stand back, relax, take care of yourself and be flexible, to make any necessary adjustments to your career path.

Badr Jafar: You are known for being passionate about supporting entrepreneurship and cultivating the local start-up scene. Have you found an intersection between entrepreneurship and what is driving social change in our region? How do you think that technology and youth participation is changing the nature of philanthropy and social entrepreneurship across the Middle East and North Africa?

Sheikha Bodour: I really love this question. I believe that technology is now a catalyst for enterprise. We've seen this globally, and especially in our region. So many of the social enterprises that we come across are built on technology platforms and have digital built into their DNA. Obviously, this has two huge pluses. First, it means that the opportunity to scale is inordinate and goes way beyond their analogue predecessors. And second, by underwriting these businesses with technology, we can ride the wave of the data revolution, bringing with it much better evidence-based products, improved ways of capturing our

impact, better sharing of social needs and perhaps, most importantly, the opportunity to share data quickly and cheaply across
borders. This will help to avoid the mistakes of the past. We've
seen this during COVID-19, where the crisis forced organisations to capture, analyse and share data perhaps more quickly
and more efficiently than they had historically.

Trying to figure out which community needed what at the
start of the crisis, in the absence of travel, conferences and face-
to-face meetings, was hugely dependent on digital platforms,
digital sharing and the wholesale adoption of technology tools
such as Zoom. This, in turn, feeds naturally into the space of
digital natives, who are quickly and naturally able to adopt a fully
virtual approach to living and working where earlier generations
might not have.

In our region, we know that enterprise has been driven mainly
by youth. Most enterprises in the Middle East, unlike other parts
of the world, are established and scaled by young people. And we
also know that these entities intrinsically have a sense of social
purpose, even if they're commercial ventures. This is quite a
departure from the past, where CSR might have been bolted on
to a business. Now we see it built in, and that's why we see an
emergence of more and more dedicated social enterprises in the
region.

This is hugely encouraging, but we need to support the development of an ecosystem for them. In other markets, we see a flow
of capital where traditional charitable giving connects with
philanthropy, which in turn connects with the community of
enterprises such as VC [venture capital] and angel investors. This
ecosystem is less well developed in our region, with less connectivity along the continuum, which undermines our ability to see
where capital is most needed and can be most effective.

If entrepreneurs, philanthropists and social entrepreneurs
can work closely together to share data, pool capital and ensure
sectoral alignment, there is an opportunity for technology to
better target social investment. And that's something governments can also help with by ensuring that the regulatory
framework supports the emergence of this ecosystem, and that

this alternative to public-sector spending is encouraged and facilitated.

Badr Jafar: You're someone who has worn multiple hats in business, government, philanthropy and in the international publishing sector. What advice would you give to aspiring philanthropists and social change makers? How do you choose where and how to invest your time, energy and resources to generate the most impact that you can?

Sheikha Bodour: I would say that social investors and change makers can look at three key elements. The first would be need; where is the most need in society or the area you want to work in, and where are others fearing to tread?

"Philanthropy is risk capital; we can and should take risks and go where others are unable to."

Philanthropy is risk capital; we can and should take risks and go where others are unable to. Do your research and understand not only which elements of society need most help, but also where there are gaps. If governments are already working extensively on a specific socio-economic challenge, that might not be the best place to start. Research can be hugely helpful here by identifying the gaps and ensuring philanthropy is well targeted to the right sector, community, location and issue.

The second element is aligning with the national plan. It's important to know what the national government development plan is for the country, to create a multiplier effect while avoiding duplication. If governments have powerful plans for developing education, for example, ask where philanthropy can provide innovation and new ideas, rather than simply adding to what's already planned.

Finally, I would assess my own technical capabilities, expertise and passion. Where can I add value best? What's my passion? Where are my strengths? What kinds of expertise can I bring to the table that would make a difference in people's lives? Philanthropy shouldn't be a question of value added based only on financial contribution, but also on non-financial contribution. If I can maximise my impact, while also delivering a professional activity that I'm likely to stick with over the long term, then that's a successful story.

Rasha Alturki

CEO, Alnahda Society

Between 2013 and 2021, Rasha Alturki held the position of CEO of Alnahda Society, a non-profit organisation established in 1963 in the Kingdom of Saudi Arabia, dedicated to women's social and economic empowerment. Prior to this, she was the society's chief projects officer for three years, overseeing the running, development and evaluation of projects in the fields of financial and social development, professional and vocational training and employment. In 2019, Alnahda gained consultative status at the UN Economic and Social Council and was appointed by Royal Decree to lead the Women 20 (W20) Summit and its related activities as part of the Kingdom's G20 presidency. Alturki was appointed in 2016 by Royal Decree to the board of trustees at the Human Rights Commission, where she served on a part-time basis. Her career interests lie in positively contributing to Saudi Arabia's development, with a particular focus on women's empowerment.

Badr Jafar: Alnahda Society is an organisation with a fascinating history and an increasingly important role to play in the evolution of Saudi society. Could you explain what Alnahda Society is and how it goes about fulfilling its mission?

Rasha Alturki: Alnahda was established in the early 1960s. It's the oldest organisation in Riyadh and one of the two oldest organisations in Saudi Arabia. Interestingly, the earliest charitable organisations in Saudi Arabia were predominantly

established and run by women. It has been a field in which
women have been able to flourish, and to develop themselves.
We have always focused on making sure that women have a role
and have impact on the development of their country and are
true partners. How we have done so has changed over time,
according to women's unmet needs, according to local legislation
and according to capabilities, both financial and human.

The dedication has always been to the cause, and less to the
programming. The programming is only a tool, the project is
only a tool, the end goal is what we all work towards. I always say
we must remain nimble and dynamic, and not get stuck in our
ways, but rather try to see better ways of achieving results.
Currently, our focus is purely on women's socio-economic
empowerment. We have our historic programmes or fields that
we have worked in since the beginning, and which are usually
associated with non-profit or charitable organisations. That is
our development programming; we also work in research and in
advocacy.

With our development programming, we focus on developing female-headed households on a grassroots level in a holistic fashion. It's our belief that if you solve the systemic
development problems for the less fortunate, who don't have
the financial means, then you are finding solutions for women
on all levels. Some women might be able to address certain
problems because they're able to pay for a lawyer or a teacher.
But for those who don't have that, then how well can they
access public services? And how are they able to develop themselves and their families? That's what we do with regards to
development programming. We focus mostly on social and
financial support and development, skill building and employment readiness, which is mostly college and career counselling
for the younger generation. Our aim is to break the cycle of
poverty, to make sure that it's not inherited from one generation to another.

With regards to research, we look at monitoring and evaluat-
ing our programmes and improving them based on that. But we
also see research as a tool. We create original research as a tool for

increasing the body of knowledge, which is very sparse in the field, especially in Saudi Arabia, but then also to work as a tool for our advocacy. We have worked in advocacy for a very long time but now we're really focusing on it in a systematic way with goals and research, so that it's evidence based and not just feelings based. Working those three fields together, we hope we will push the cause forward and this will lead to more systemic development in the future.

Badr Jafar: How would you describe the current state of the non-profit landscape in the Kingdom of Saudi Arabia, or even the Gulf region more broadly?

Rasha Alturki: I think it's changing. I'll speak mostly of Saudi Arabia because that's my experience, but I wouldn't be surprised if the rest of the Gulf is experiencing similar changes. The landscape is maturing in many ways. The number of non-profits has been increasing and with that comes competition, growth and so forth. It's come from above and below. With Vision 2030, there is an increased appreciation of the non-profit sector. There has been a push for it to be more productive and to increasingly assist in the country's development.

Since 2015, there are new forms and new ways in which the non-profit sector can develop. One of these new forms is the endowed company. It has opened a new way for people wanting to work within the non-profit sector. Even more so for philanthropists, it's a new way for them to set up organisations that will fulfil and achieve their philanthropic goals, creating an endowment and then creating the company to fulfil those objectives. This development gives more options and has encouraged a lot of people to enter the field.

I know some people who worked in a company and considered it a non-profit but didn't have a model or didn't have a legal structure to establish it as a non-profit. They were telling everybody that they were non-profit, but they didn't have the actual licensing. So now with this, there are organisations or companies that have created endowments and then set up as endowed companies, which in other areas are called non-profit organisations. This has been a real boost to the sector.

There has also been a shift in funds from generation to generation. I'm finding that the new generation who have inherited large sums of money are preferring to go the endowment route, to professionalise and systematise their giving, and to make sure that they are working towards very clear goals that are important to them and what they value. I'm also finding that, in addition to the Islamic responsibility of paying *zakat*, there is more of an understanding of social impact, the need for people to participate and give back within their society, whether that be in time or money. I also think the criteria for good corporate ESG practice is affecting the way large companies do business, especially those who want to go public. This boosts the sector and brings in new people who might not have been as active in the past. These changes within society and within institutional structures are working towards strengthening and maturing the sector.

Badr Jafar: What advice would you give to individuals who might be interested in engaging in philanthropy or non-profits work in the region either on their own or in collaboration with organisations like yours?

Rasha Alturki: My advice for people is to get to know the people in the non-profit sector who share your values. Determine your values and what you want to achieve and find those people who can help you. They have to share your values in life as well as your business values, because in the end a non-profit organisation is a business as well. When non-profit work turns into an organisation, it becomes a business, and you must treat it that way. Not to treat philanthropic organisations as businesses is to underestimate their importance.

> "Not to treat philanthropic organisations as businesses is to underestimate their importance."

It's also important, with regards to Saudi Arabia in particular, to look at the ratings of organisations. The government gives governance ratings [*Makeen*] to different non-profits. And I think checking those out is a good first step for people who want to work with non-profit organisations.

Badr Jafar: What is the most useful role that private philanthropists can play in support of women's social and economic participation, whether in the Kingdom of Saudi Arabia specifically, or elsewhere in the region? It's obviously not something that can be addressed with money alone. How can strategic philanthropists maximise their chances of making a meaningful impact in this space?

Rasha Alturki: There are two ways. The first way doesn't require any money, and that's influence. No matter what your circle of influence is, whether small or large, whether on the level of states or on the level of your family, everybody has influence. I think if you work within your circles of influence to push the message or the cause, that's very important. Making sure that even within your own organisation women are represented on every level will go a long way to achieving that goal. Just being aware of your own surroundings and working to rectify any injustice is important.

Now to the other way. Money is extremely important. It's what helps empower organisations. Without proper funding, organisations cannot get proper staff, cannot get proper leadership. This has become more and more acute for us in Saudi Arabia. Before, there weren't that many options for women and so Alnahda was always one of the first places that women started their career. We had the best of the best. However, women are now highly prized employees everywhere. We have to pay dearly to get good female leadership. And so, money does help.

I would highly recommend to investors to invest in the non-profit organisation itself, in those things that most people don't want to invest in. For example, people like to give us their *zakat* because we're professional, we're organised, but then they don't want to pay for the computer systems, they don't want to pay for our CRM [customer relationship management] systems, they don't want to pay for the social workers who have to find out if people should get the benefits from their *zakat*. Like any company, it's important to invest in the people who are running the organisations and the systems. That's the only way you're going to get the proper monitoring, reporting and assessment that are required by a savvy investor.

Badr Jafar: Alnahda was founded – and continues to be led and run – by women, including yourself as its CEO. To what extent do you think that the philanthropic sector has its own house in order in terms of gender equity, and providing qualified women with meaningful opportunities to pursue their own careers and to fulfil their own potential? What advice would you give to young women considering a career in the social sector?

Rasha Alturki: There is definitely a role for women in the social sector. Traditionally, until five years ago, we were very separate. Any women in gender-mixed organisations were in a bubble, and they never reached leadership positions. Now, with the transfer of inheritance and funds, as well as the opening of Saudi Arabia to mixed-gender working environments, there's a very strong role for women, as board members and investors as well as professionals working in the field. We need to understand that the non-profit sector is a sector that you can enter and leave, that you can bring skill sets from other work experiences into the sector to benefit it and then you can move out. This concept of moving from one sector to another, taking your skill sets to enrich whatever environment you choose to work in, is something that we still need to develop in Saudi Arabia, and maybe in the Gulf.

Badr Jafar: Where do you think the greatest opportunities will be for philanthropists and non-profit organisations and impact entrepreneurs to make the most meaningful impact in the years ahead?

Rasha Alturki: We should be investing in education for a creative mindset on every single level, among those running organisations and among those bene-fiting from organisations. We should be pushing ourselves out of our comfort zone, thinking in a different way, coming up with creative solu- **"We should be pushing ourselves out of our comfort zone."** tions. It's not a natural instinct among many. People need to be pushed, to be taught and to be placed in an environment in which they can be creative. We've seen this with our beneficiaries. Sometimes when you give them the knowledge of the basic tools and inspire them by stories and experiences of others or best practices from other places, they come up with the best solutions for themselves. Empowering that kind of thinking, breaking the mould, that's where more investment needs to happen.

Sanjit 'Bunker' Roy

Founder, Barefoot College

Sanjit 'Bunker' Roy founded Barefoot College in 1972, following the workstyle and lifestyle of Mahatma Gandhi. What makes the college unique is the focus on providing basic needs to improve the quality of life of the rural poor living on less than US$1 a day through inexpensive, community-based 'barefoot solutions', stressing the application of traditional knowledge, practical skills and village wisdom.

Born in India, Roy is a social activist, entrepreneur and educator, and has become a leading and inspiring figure for sustainable development. In 2008, the *Guardian* identified him as one of the 100 most influential people in the world. In 2017, he received an honorary degree from Princeton University.

Badr Jafar: You established the Barefoot College more than four decades ago. Have the fundamental principles behind the mission remained the same? What do you know now that

could have made a difference in how you designed or imple-mented the Barefoot College's work?

Bunker Roy: We haven't changed the philosophy and the princi-ples of the Barefoot College for 50 years because it is so simple, so down to earth. Everyone in the community understands that. It's a question of focusing on basic minimum needs like water, education, health and employment required everywhere in the 600,000 villages of India. There isn't one region in India that can say that they're self-sufficient with these basic needs. We have kept to that mission from the very beginning.

Traditional knowledge, village skills and practical wisdom are available everywhere in India. What the Barefoot College has done is to bring them into the mainstream. We say this cannot be ignored. It is indigenous knowledge of the highest order because it has stood the test of time. Why not replicate this approach everywhere in India as well as abroad? We have not changed our mission or philosophy because what Mahatma Gandhi said is still very dear to us, which is that you must reach the last man and woman, you cannot look only at some communities in India. What about the lower castes? What about the untouchables? Who are the people who have been marginalised? They're the ones the Barefoot College is focusing on.

We started in about 13 states of India with small grassroots projects. Our philosophy is never to start a project in a city or in a district. It must be based in a village, because you must be closer to the people, to the poor, to understand the way they think and what they want. That is what the Barefoot College has managed to do. We are in 23 states of India today and all our projects started from villages. The Barefoot College mission will continue because it's so easy to understand. You don't need a high-powered study to say what you need in a village. Common sense is required. That's all.

Badr Jafar: In your experience, what are the challenges that come with scaling up a philanthropic initiative of this nature across different markets? What would you advise other

philanthropists and social sector entrepreneurs to think about before they begin to scale up their own initiatives?

Bunker Roy: You have to start from the grassroots, from the remotest villages, whether they're the remote islands in the Pacific or the remote villages in Africa. The Barefoot solution concentrates on one village at a time, and one year at a time, because no one looks at five years; it must be something which is doable, something which is within one year that you can achieve and get dramatic results. And it's simple. How do you get drinking water? How do you get basic services to the community? You don't need something very elaborate or hierarchical. You need something which is face-to-face with the communities. You also must have faith in the community. We are so reluctant and sceptical because someone is illiterate and has never been to school and college, but the Barefoot College has always treated them as equals. The moment you communicate that, then the job is easy, because they know that we will do it together.

We took this Gandhian model abroad. In the communities where we went, we showed that we have confidence in their capacity and competence to do it without anyone from outside. This was a very powerful message, and one that they understood. First, they said, 'We are illiterate. We need someone from outside.' We said, 'No, that's not what you need. How much faith have you got in yourself to be able to do this? So what if you don't know how to read and write, you can become a solar engineer, you can become a communicator, you can become an architect, anything is possible provided you have the confidence that you don't need anyone from outside to tell you how to do it.'

The Barefoot College has managed to communicate that message. We've gone to 36 countries in Africa, and not one has said they can't do it. In six months, women who cannot read and write have learned 21st-century technology and they've solar powered their villages. There are now over 50,000 houses in Africa powered by these newly skilled women whom the Indian prime minister called 'Solar Mamas'. These Solar Mamas said, 'We learned by doing, we don't need theory. If you tell me there are 68 parts in a solar charge controller, I can put together the 68 parts without learning theory. And I can make it work.'

When I went to Peru, I asked if they would prefer a Solar Mama, who can put this solar lantern together in half an hour, or someone from Stanford who's looking after the whole electric programme. They all said the Solar Mama, because the guy from Stanford only knows the theory, not the practice. That has given them dignity, confidence and self-respect, and this is a part of the Barefoot approach. We have given dignity and self-respect to people who've been marginalised and who've never been given responsibility or recognition.

Badr Jafar: Are you seeing evidence that the nature and prevalence of philanthropy is changing in these emerging regions of the world? What do you think is driving this sort of change?

Bunker Roy: I think the driving change is the pressure being applied by the communities on the ground. They see injustice, exploitation and inequality and they don't have time to wait. They are asking philanthropists to show that they can deliver on the ground, so philanthropists know they must start working directly with grassroots communities, not through intermediaries.

How do you work with grassroots communities? Both the philanthropist and the community must change mindsets. There must be a meeting point where they can say, 'Yes, we will work together.' There's such a gap between the philanthropists and the people on the ground and I think the gap is getting larger, because we are not actually getting to the villages and the communities that need this most. This is the biggest problem. Why aren't some philanthropists saying, 'All right, we've done some due diligence with X organisation which has got a widespread and scaled-up model which is provable, which is effective, why don't we work through them directly? Why don't we choose an X organisation, which is working in 60 villages all over India? Why don't we invest in that organisation?'

I think the philanthropist must say, 'We must change the way we are working today.' It's too slow. It's too cumbersome. There are too many levels, there are too many layers, there are too many people in between. Why can't you have a direct approach with the communities? And your due diligence process can be very exhaustive, but once you're convinced that this organisation is something that you can work with, just go directly to them. That can be done so easily, when there is trust, but that trust must be developed directly.

Badr Jafar: You've spoken about the importance of finding homegrown solutions to local problems and listening closely to people on the ground. The Barefoot College has worked on the ground in many different communities around the world. What are some of the key things that you have learned from the people that you've met in these communities and how have these lessons helped shape your own mindset?

Bunker Roy: We have found that the only sustainable solution is to decentralise and demystify. Decentralise your skills, right down to the village level, where it matters the most. Demystify technology so that it can be used for improving the quality of life. That is one message we have learned very clearly from our work in villages all over the world. The second is that women are the agents of change. Everywhere, in the villages where we went, people have migrated into the cities. Who are left? Only the old women. So why not invest in old women? Why not give them the skills? When we talked about solar energy with illiterate women, everyone was aghast. But they have courage and tenacity, so I said, 'Let's give them a chance, don't prejudge them and say it's not possible because they're supposed to be in the kitchen and looking after grandchildren. Take them out of their habitat and let's see how they perform.' Since 2008, there are now over 3,000

> "The only sustainable solution is to decentralise and demystify. Women are the agents of change."

Solar Mamas and not one has proved a failure. The third lesson is that there is a difference between literacy and education. Literacy is where you learn how to read and write, education is what you get from your family, from your environment and from your community. I think that is very important. When we went back to the women in these villages, they all said that now they've got status. They've got respect.

So, on a large scale and to keep the work sustainable, we continue to ask, How do we keep it simple? How do we demystify technology? How do we get the communities involved, so that the management control and ownership is in the hands of the communities, not someone in Delhi or someone in Zurich? It is a simple message but so difficult to make the World Bank understand or the UNDP understand that investing in these women can change communities from the grassroots up.

Badr Jafar: One of the consequences of the pandemic has been to remind people that they belong to a community, and that their safety and wellbeing is often dependent on the resilience and collaborative nature of their community. This is not a new lesson for many of the people that you have worked with, whose survival really depends on community. What are some of the lasting impacts of the pandemic, specifically on the social sector?

Bunker Roy: The lasting impact of COVID-19 in India has been the massive reverse migration that has taken place from the cities to the villages. That has been enormous. Now most of them want to stay in the village rather than go into the slums of Mumbai or Calcutta. We have also seen traditional knowledge and skills that were dying being revived. Now, artisans like carpenters and leather workers, women who went to work in the slums in Mumbai in some factory, they have come back to the village. And they want to revive their craft, revive all the work that they used to do, that their fathers used to do. They want to make sure that this is happening in the village itself.

I think the labour force that the industry had in India is going to be in very short supply, because now they want to stay in the village. They want to get into government relief programmes. There's something called the Rural Employment Guarantee Programme in India, which is giving jobs to 800 million people in the villages – they get guaranteed work for 100 days in a year, and if they don't get 100 days of work, then the government has to compensate. This is a remarkable programme. I think most of them are thinking, 'Why go back to the cities, why not stay in the villages?' This is one thing that COVID-19 has done, and I think that has been an added point for the communities and for the villages. If they get work, if they're treated decently, they get clean water, a health system and school for the kids. Why should they go back? With millions of people back in their villages, the whole demography has changed. In a way, COVID-19 has been good for some of these villages. I see many people saying, 'Thank God, I'm not going back to Bombay. Let me do some work in the villages.'

Badr Jafar: You talked about technology, but also communication. In 2011, you gave a powerful TED Talk that's now been viewed by well over half a million people. Fifty years ago, it wouldn't have been possible for one individual to communicate so easily with so many different people in so many places. How has the ability to reach many people with your message changed the nature of the work that you do, and how can philanthropists and change-makers harness the power of these technologies without becoming distracted by them?

Bunker Roy: Small correction – the TED Talk has been viewed 4.4 million times in 45 languages and got more hits in 2015 than Bill Gates and President Clinton and Al Gore combined, so I've not done badly at all!

You know, the 3,000 women in 96 countries have generated 1.4 gigawatts of power, which is the power generated by one nuclear power station. How do you decentralise? How do you spread it? Mahatma Gandhi said the answer to India is not mass production, but production by the masses. Decentralised development is going to be the answer for India. I think the philanthropists must start a dialogue with practitioners on the ground.

I went for five years to the World Economic Forum meetings at Davos from 2002 to 2008 and they asked me, 'What are you doing here? You're not supposed to be here, you're not a billionaire.' I said, 'No, I'm not. I was invited by Klaus Schwab, because Klaus felt that the philanthropy industry should meet the grassroots practitioner and change their minds about us. We're not all waving flags on the road, we want to work with you guys and how do we manage to do that?' By the time I left in 2008, there were many people who were working with us, who wanted to do something with us. But not one industrialist from India came to me. Not one of them said, 'Let's do something together.' What is wrong with us? Why are we so suspicious about people? We have to break barriers somehow, to bring us together and do something which is worthwhile and doable on the ground. Research and studies are all very well, but we know what the basic problems are. Let's get on with it.

You asked me about what the First and Second World can learn from the Barefoot College. Can we apply the model to the First and Second World? I concluded that the First and Second Worlds are too hung up on degrees and paper qualifications, and there's too much hierarchy. The Third World has much to teach the First and Second Worlds: compassion, generosity, simplicity and austerity. Leonardo da Vinci said, 'Simplicity is the ultimate sophistication.' I believe it.

"Simplicity is the ultimate sophistication."

Her Excellency Huda Alkhamis-Kanoo

Founder, Abu Dhabi Music and Arts Foundation, Founder & Artistic Director, Abu Dhabi Festival

Her Excellency Huda Alkhamis-Kanoo is a philanthropist and patron of the arts who has dedicated her life to inspiring artists to create, and communities to unite and prosper. She worked tirelessly to establish the Abu Dhabi Music and Arts Foundation (ADMAF) in 1996. The foundation has been nurturing creativity across the United Arab Emirates through arts education, community arts and special projects. It enables creative expression through a wide range of programmes and projects.

Alkhamis-Kanoo is the founder and artistic director of the Abu Dhabi Festival, which she established in 2004. It is an annual multidisciplinary festival, the largest cultural celebration in the region. It strives to deepen cross-cultural dialogue while inspiring a deeper interest in the cultures of the Arab world. She is also a founding member of the American Ballet Theatre Global Council.

She has received numerous awards, including the Abu Dhabi Award and Abu Dhabi Medal, the United Nations Women Together Award, the Aspen Institute Emerging Voice Award for Cultural Stewardship, the Puccini Festival Foundation Award and the Middle East Institute Visionary Award.

Badr Jafar: Your Excellency, you have dedicated your focus to three universal themes that touch human lives, namely inspiring arts, innovation and unity. You established the Abu Dhabi Music and Arts Foundation in 1996. I'd like to start by asking about your journey with ADMAF and whether your vision for it has changed over the past two and a half decades.

Huda Alkhamis-Kanoo: I was driven by instinct and passion. I had no idea of being a philanthropist. I had no clue what philanthropic work takes to do or to achieve. When I started, I didn't know that I needed a strategic and financial plan. I didn't know about governance or audit, and I used my own finances. I did what I thought was right and I didn't know if I was going to be successful. Today, we are a registered foundation with proper governance and strategic plans in place. After 25 years, I'm more determined than ever, and my vision is clearer than ever. What keeps me going? I would say, what carries my vision and transforms our ideas into reality is craftsmanship.

For me, being able to craft an ecosystem that embraces mutual understanding and nurtures creativity will always be my mission, my driving force. I have been privileged to be involved with visionary artists, who allow me every year to achieve this process of craftsmanship, of achieving the goals. I try to do that with wisdom, patience and humility. I strive to extend and amplify the vision of the United Arab Emirates, a cultural nation, diverse yet united. This is how we are, rooted yet open to the world, strong yet peaceful, traditional yet innovative.

With this DNA that we have, I continue to open the gateway to knowledge. Education will always be at the heart of my mission, and I will forever be dedicated to it. We at ADMAF remain committed to providing a wide variety of education programmes. I do that through scholarships and fellowships for university and PhD students abroad, as well as grants and mentorship for young artists, writers, musicians and filmmakers to produce new work. We continue to open doors for emerging artists, and reward excellence with awards and programmes that make a difference. So, we continue to nurture free creative thinking.

Today, I'm proud to say that thousands of students and artists from the Arab world have moved forward with our help to create, innovate and make a difference. What we give is the opportunity. In the end, the mission and vision are there, more consolidated, and I will join with every person who believes in investing in the young to create the future. We unite with the world to make a difference and to build up civilisation.

Badr Jafar: Could you share your vision on how to create lasting impact through music and the arts, and the role that strategic philanthropy plays to propagate and maximise such impact?

Huda Alkhamis-Kanoo: It's a very deep question, and it means the world to keep on reinforcing the role of music. We all know that it takes a village to raise a child, but we don't know that it takes a nation to make music and bring it to life. Developing music does not start with the individual; it starts with the society. The challenge in our part of the world is for arts in general, and music in particular, to evolve into a serious pursuit for the future of a child. Part of the challenge that ADMAF is still facing today is to help families and individuals to understand that music is a respectable career.

For music to hold an important place in people's life, ADMAF had to change perceptions on the ground, and many initiatives were needed. This brings us back to education. In every direction I go, it's education. It's enlightenment; it's knowledge. So, this brings us back to giving music a place at schools, and a possibility for higher education in music as well. Also, supporting composers to publish their work and musicians to perform these new compositions, especially from the Arab world.

Let me share with you two recent examples of our investment in musicians and composers to produce new work and how we maximise the impact of our support. Abu Dhabi Festival produced Emirati composer Mohammed Fairouz's Fifth Symphony, a call for peace celebrating the vision of Sheikh Zayed, the UAE's founding father. This was performed by the London Symphony Orchestra from its home in London. The LSO is one of the great orchestras of the world. For them to perform the work of Mohammed Fairouz, an Emirati composer and Arab composer, is an endorsement and a great achievement.

It took me 25 years of hard work to be able to reach this point. I have work today that can be performed, that can be heard and seen by everyone in the world. Emirati composers are perhaps more underprivileged than others because we don't have the education system. They had to find higher education on their own. This was not an easy path and they had to fight their battles on their own for a very long time.

Another Emirati composer that I would like to mention is Ihab Darwish, who wrote *Hekayat* last year. It was commissioned and produced by Abu Dhabi Festival, broadcast online and reached millions. This is the power of the digital era, if we use it properly. We can popularise our classical music; we can make it accessible to everyone. It doesn't cancel or take over real-life experience, nothing takes over real-life experience. The power and the energy of connecting with everyone at the same moment in real-life experience are incredible. Also, we don't invest once and leave; our support is ongoing. This year, Ihab is producing his second symphony, the Abrahamic Symphony, celebrating the founding of the Abrahamic house in Abu Dhabi. What's special about this composition is we were able to bring world-renowned Grammy and Academy Award-winning composers and producers together with Ihab to compose the Symphony of Three. It has three movements – Peace, Love and Tolerance. I must mention their names: John Debney, who wrote the score of *The Passion of Christ*; David Shire, who wrote part of the score of *Saturday Night Fever*; and Robert Townson, who produced the recording and scores of *Game of Thrones*. They all came to work with Ihab Darwish. Our power here as philanthropists is that we were able to connect them.

So, we have two world premières with Ihab and Mohammed Fairouz. What we were able to achieve was to nurture our own Arab talent but also present it on the world stage and online for everyone to know and to listen. We partnered with the greatest institutions and halls of the world to present new art, to present a new production and new compositions. The latest was at the Lincoln Center Opera House with *The Flying Dutchman* – it was a new production that we did with the Lincoln Center, the Canadian Opera House and the Dutch Opera House. It took us more than five years.

We're the only one from the Arab world who are working in the international arena in new productions, commissions, co-commissions and with content that will stay for humanity forever. It doesn't matter if it premières from New York or from Abu Dhabi, what matters is what we leave behind – the content. So, this is what we do in the world of music. What's needed is to continue joining hands; we need infrastructure, we need facilities, more halls. There is always a place for innovation, but we must have the will to unite and work for the betterment of humanity through the arts and music. Without that, we have nothing.

> "There is always a place for innovation, but we must have the will to unite and work for the betterment of humanity through the arts and music."

Badr Jafar: You've been recognised on the global stage as an advocate for women's rights and empowerment through education, career development and equality of opportunity. What role can philanthropy play as an enabler for gender equality, and how can we catalyse more philanthropic capital towards this important cause?

Huda Alkhamis-Kanoo: ADMAF advocates for the needs of both women and men in the arts and provides equal opportunity for them to create their work and present it. We will always strive to empower artists to be part of the decision-making process and reform policies relating to the arts. This is the mission. Listen to their needs, understand their needs and then support them.

We do support women in many ways. An example is the exhibition *Beyond Narrative*, which tells the story of the contemporary art movement in the UAE for the past 50 years. Almost half of the artists represented are women. We have supported women artists by funding their education as we did with the first Emirati visual artist PhD, Karima Al Shomali, who studied for her doctorate in London with ADMAF support.

We have funds for higher education for women, from master's to PhD and internships. We have supported many women so that their work is in museums abroad. In the world of music, we have a young soprano – Nass El Ghiwane – whom we have supported in building her career and internships abroad.

It's a continuous investment and there is no end. With the ones who are ready, we give them the opportunity, and with the ones who are not ready, we invest in their education, in their potential, and champion their work. This is what women need today, in my opinion.

Badr Jafar: For those philanthropists who are passionate about generating positive social impact in the UAE, what advice can you share with them as they define their philanthropic purpose and priorities? What are some of the things that you have learned over time when pursuing a lifelong mission dedicated towards a higher purpose?

Huda Alkhamis-Kanoo: The lesson I've learned from the past 25 years is to stay faithful to my vision and mission. I learned to work with humility in the pursuit of my mission. Challenges will always come, but we cannot let them defeat us. If we fall, we must rise again and ask for help. I've learned to ask for help.

Also, find ways to persevere. We will walk on a path of thorns, and we will bleed and this will not change. But we will learn how to heal and keep on moving. Not everyone will value our work, but the true value of our work remains in what we can give and share, and where we can make a difference. I believe that if we are to lead, as philanthropists, we must be an unshakable bridge for people to cross over from problems to solutions.

> "If we are to lead, as philanthropists, we must be an unshakable bridge for people to cross over from problems to solutions."

We are the bridge. People trust us, follow us, confident that we will help them reach their goal and solve their problems. Our work, my fellow philanthropists, is hard work and this is never going to change. It's not going to be an easy drive. But this work brings joy, it brings joy to the hearts of people, and this is an act of love and, therefore, the ultimate blessing. This is who we are as philanthropists.

Sultan Sooud Al Qassemi

Founder, Barjeel Art Foundation

Sultan Sooud Al Qassemi is the founder of the Barjeel Art Foundation, an independent initiative established in 2010 to contribute to the intellectual development of the art scene in the Arab region by building a prominent and publicly accessible art collection in the United Arab Emirates. Since 2013, the foundation has mounted over 40 exhibitions across the world, including in Egypt, the UK, Jordan, the US, Kuwait, Singapore and Iran. In 2018, 100 works from the collection were hosted on a long-term basis at the Sharjah Art Museum.

Al Qassemi is an Emirati columnist and researcher on social, political and cultural affairs in the Arab Gulf States whose articles have appeared in many notable publications including the *Financial Times, Independent, Guardian, Huffington Post, New York Times, Foreign Policy, Open Democracy, The National* and *The Globe and Mail*.

Al Qassemi is a frequent visiting instructor and senior lecturer at major universities in the United States, Europe and the Middle East. With Todd Reisz, he is co-author of *Building Sharjah* (2021).

Badr Jafar: Could you explain how the Barjeel Art Foundation goes about fulfilling its mission and how you track its overall impact? Do you think that the foundation is on the track that you envisaged for it back in 2010?

Sultan Al Qassemi: Barjeel was founded with the idea of promoting art from the Arab world. The Arab world is a multicultural, multi-ethnic and multi-religious region of our planet. It includes 22 countries, dozens of nations and many ethnic groups that are represented in the Arab world culturally, but never represented politically. There was a pan-Arab project in the 1950s and

1960s to bring the region together, but it neglected our minorities, neglected the diversity within the region. This is something I tried to make sure that we didn't repeat in terms of a cultural project. So, the foundation's ethos, its drive, is to promote art from these 22 Arab states, but to include all the different minorities in the organisation. We try to show artists who are, of course, ethnically Arab and Muslim, but just because that is most of the region, it doesn't mean that this is the sole representation of the region.

We have diverse religious communities. As well as Islam, we have a sizeable Christian minority. We have Jewish minorities. We have ethnic groups like Turkmen, Farsi, Persians, Amazigh and so many other groups. We make sure that they are represented in all our exhibitions. Hopefully it has succeeded in the two or three dozen exhibitions that we have done to promote art from our part of the world. It's a small organisation, we're only a team of five or six, but we've mounted exhibitions in about 15 countries. I am proud of where we are.

To answer the second part of your question, has it fulfilled the original mission and is it where I want it to be? Yes, very much. We have a touring exhibition in the US, we are negotiating with one or two museums around the world. At the same time, while initially I had thought that I wanted to promote Arab art internationally, it turns out that what we need to do is promote Arab art locally and regionally. This is where the understanding must come from. If we want young people from the Arab world to be proud of their art and culture, they need to see it. So, it's great to show it in Singapore, and in the US, but we also must think about showing it regionally and locally. This is where I think we've slightly adjusted the mission of the foundation.

Badr Jafar: Looking back to the so-called Islamic Golden Age during the eighth and the ninth centuries, innovation happened at the intersection between the arts and humanities and the sciences. Today, it often feels as if the arts are ornamental rather than fundamental. Do you see a

correlation between socio-economic development and the arts? How does one work on making that correlation better appreciated in mainstream policymaking and business decisions?

Sultan Al Qassemi: There is certainly a very strong correlation. We need to emphasise that at the height of the Islamic Renaissance era, a key theme was diversity and inclusion. Many scientists were Jewish, for example, but they felt part of society, they were promoted equally as much as the Christians and the Muslims. The idea of diversity, inclusion and respect for the other is integral for the success of any society. The other thing is that art plays an important role, because art gives people a sense of ownership in society. When you think of countries as diverse as Iraq, Iran, Egypt and Morocco, you will notice that at the peak of their scientific innovation was a unifying cultural and socio-political identity.

"Art gives people a sense of ownership in society."

The way this was achieved was to go back in time, reaching for heritage that brought everyone together.

The way that you saw it manifested in Egypt, for example, is that there was a theme of neo-Pharaonism, as they call it. In the 1920s, Egyptian artists and sculptors who were Jewish, or Muslim, or Christian, Baha'i, or any other religion, looked towards Egyptian heritage, because that was a way of unifying everybody. Rather than an emphasis on contemporary politics and modern politics, they looked at heritage. The Iraqis did the same with Sumerian and Babylonian history. The Moroccans did the same, and the Algerians did the same with their Amazigh history. This also applied to Iranian, Assyrian and the other cultures of Persia. It's important

"If you want people to innovate, you need to give them a sense of belonging."

to find a unified sense of identity that everybody can aspire to. Of course, if you want people to innovate, you need to give them a sense of belonging. This is something that I think that we lack in many parts of the Arab world. I feel that the UAE is trying to give this sense of belonging, or at least a sense of semi-permanence, if not of ultimate permanence to people from the region. This could be an interesting model to look at, and I wonder if any other countries are doing the same.

Badr Jafar: How would you describe the current state of the non-profit landscape in the Arab region? What issues do you think strategic philanthropists in the Arab region and around the world should be turning their attention to?

Sultan Al Qassemi: I think that the state of philanthropy in the region is complex because people are very generous and willing to give to specific causes. They give for religious causes, for example, they want to give to build a mosque, they want to give to build an institution that is affiliated to a religious cause. This is integral to the identity of many people in the region, but it's not the only thing that we need. We need to give to religious institutions, but maybe rather than build the new mosque, we should renovate an existing mosque. We need to preserve our historical mosques and that is where there is a lack of giving.

Another avenue where there is a lack of giving is in the education sector. People think that there is more reward from the hereafter and from God when you build a religious institute or a mosque, rather than build a hospital, or an educational institute, or an orphanage, or a technology hub or infrastructure. The reality is, yes, there is a reward, because people can get to work, they can earn money if you create jobs. There is also some kind of religious reward if you give people the avenues to earn money. This is something that we need to capitalise on.

People are very generous. Whenever there's a drive to raise money, for example, an earthquake takes place somewhere in the world, a lot of people are willing to give and help. Our societies in the Arab world and in the Muslim world are generous, but sometimes they're overly generous to a certain cause, and less generous to other causes. We don't have the idea of philanthropy as the West understands it. Many people in the Arab world are too shy to say that they have given to an organisation or institution. It's a new phenomenon that some people are willing to talk about philanthropy, although I feel like it's still frowned upon, that people ask why this family is putting their name on this organisation, or this building, or this chair or this institute. We need to tell people that this is to encourage others. It's not only because this family wants the credit, and there is nothing wrong with having credit, but it's also because you're encouraging others to do it.

Also, our tax system needs to be modified to give people tax breaks for giving. If you think, for instance, of the charitable donations in the US, why is the US overtaking Europe when it comes to institutions and organisations that have endowments? Why does Yale have a US$30 billion endowment, whereas a typical university in the UK has a few US$100 million? It's because US institutions are able to take advantage of the tax system in the US. Now we have a VAT tax and other forms of tax in the UAE. Oman, Qatar, Saudi Arabia and other countries are introducing tax. We need to introduce this idea of tax breaks if you give to certain institutes or sectors. The final thing I will say about philanthropy is that it is not structured properly. You don't know how to get a licence or how to get registered. Many non-profits don't have a board of advisors or a board of directors. Many non-profits don't hold themselves accountable to the outside world, which is important because they are public-good organisations. So there needs to be accountability and regulation. In the UAE, there are nine ways of getting a non-profit licence, and each one of them is very complicated. It could be an Emiri decree, it could be through the Chamber of Commerce, it could also be through a foreign embassy, which is how several schools are registered in the UAE, like the British, American, French and German schools. You need to have a workable structured policy when it comes to non-profits, because you need to encourage non-profits. The government cannot be subsidising and building everything. Philanthropists, merchants, businessmen and corporations want to engage but it needs to be very straightforward.

Badr Jafar: Would you say that there is a cultural shift, linked to the generational shift in the Middle East and North Africa in terms of how they relate to philanthropy and social impact? You come from a prominent multi-generational family business. Is this the sort of discussion you have in your own family, about how to engage in philanthropy and change habits related to giving?

Sultan Al Qassemi: This is such an interesting point. First, I believe that the previous generation was very generous. The founding generation of the modern family businesses in the Middle East and North Africa in the mid-20th century were very generous. These are huge merchant families across the Gulf, Middle East, North Africa. The giant sovereign wealth funds and other funds that were established were generous. Kuwait established a fund in the 1960s or 1970s which has been very generous with the rest of the world, helping dig wells in Africa and build dams and offer people opportunities. Another very generous country was the UAE. But there was no structure. The UAE, in its almost 50-year history, had never tallied how much foreign aid it had given since its founding in 1971. Only recently, it calculated that it had given AED 200 billion, which is about US$45 billion, as foreign aid. I spoke to somebody in the Ministry of Foreign Affairs of the UAE, and he said we will never know the true amount of foreign aid that was given because the founding father of the UAE was giving money without recording or talking about it.

Culturally, you almost are shy to tell people that you've helped somebody. But it's important to know how much is given because we realise in the Gulf States, in the region, that foreign aid and philanthropy can be a tool of soft power. When Qatar was trying to win the World Cup, it used its tool of soft power and cultural diplomacy and investments. Similarly, when the UAE was lobbying to host IRENA in Abu Dhabi and to host Expo in Dubai, the UAE's lobbyists would go meet with the representatives of nations who had received foreign aid from the UAE and say, we have built a dam and we have supported you, we have offered education opportunities, we'd like you to vote for us to host this organisation. So, it's not a quid pro quo, but I think it's a way of understanding international relations. We all depend on each other. Even the smallest countries such as Micronesia have a vote at the UN equal to that of Russia. Every country, no matter how big or small, can be an important way or avenue for you to reach your goal. The UAE is a medium-sized power, so, as they say, you need every single member of the international community.

Badr Jafar: The opportunity to understand this soft power that you talk about is one that hasn't yet been captured, not just in our region, but globally. As a committed advocate of cultural diplomacy, utilising art as an extension of social commentary on the Middle East's development, do you believe that philanthropy can play a role in advancing cultural diplomacy?

Sultan Al Qassemi: Certainly. I can give you a true-life example of a museum in the Middle East with one of the largest collections of modern art. This museum was suffering financial shortages, they were unable to pay for their staff and were on the brink of shutting down. It's one of my favourite museums, playing an important role in educating its society. They have a lot of workshops for children, for adults, they go beyond painting and art into education of the public. The staff reached out to me and said, we have not been paid for months, and there's talk about shutting us down. I contributed a small amount of money just to keep them going, but then I reached out to the UAE Ministry of Foreign Affairs and the UAE Cultural Ministry, and they offered them a sizeable donation. That is keeping the museum going for the next year or so while it finds its bearings. This is in a country that is allied to the UAE in the region, but even if it wasn't allied, the impact that this donation has had on the museum and the wider society goes beyond the immediate political advantages and benefits that we might get.

This is a medium- to long-term plan to keep a cultural organisation afloat. It's an example of where we cannot really calculate the amount of help that we are giving each other. I only use the example of the UAE because I'm familiar with them, but I am sure that there are many other people around the region – and some governments – who are trying to offer help and assistance to others in need.

Badr Jafar: For the young philanthropists who are interested in focusing their efforts in the field of art, what advice would you give them?

Sultan Al Qassemi: In the previous example, I was able to donate a small amount of money because that's what I could afford, but then my role was to find other sources because I am in touch with merchants, with corporations, businessmen and governments. So, I was able to channel more money to this organisation. I think young philanthropists should not underestimate the reach that they have through their networks. Maybe they can also help these institutions restructure through advice. It's not always financial. As a young philanthropist you can spend time with these cultural institutions because your time is also worth money. In many cases, advising these institutions can help them progress and diversify or can help them apply for international funding, if they restructure themselves, for example, or apply for registration somewhere globally. There are many things that young philanthropists can do beyond just financial assistance.

NINE

PHILANTHROPY AND THE DIGITAL GENERATION

One of the revolutionary changes of our times has been the spread and impact of digital technologies. These technologies have influenced every human domain. Philanthropy is no exception. Digital technologies have enormously expanded our ability to analyse data, to share information, to deliver services, to educate and to measure impact. In the past two decades we have witnessed much change in philanthropic practices as donors and charities take advantage of these new capabilities. Websites, social media, surveys, online giving platforms, direct giving and any number of other tools are expanding the philanthropic field for individuals, foundations, companies and non-profits. These tools are making it easier for donors and recipients to find each other, to collaborate and to assess impact. This, in turn, contributes to the growth of more strategic philanthropy focused on the complex systemic issues of poverty, climate disruption and inequality, which cannot be adequately resolved by philanthropists working in silos.

The forced reduction of in-person contacts during the COVID-19 pandemic only accelerated the use of digital tools and platforms in philanthropy. Some of these were already in development before the global health crisis but proved their value in the midst of lockdowns. For example, online education platforms had to be developed very quickly, and many did not have the support required to grow at speed and at scale to meet the needs. An instance of this was described to me by Kathleen Chew of the YTL Foundation in Malaysia. In her interview, she outlined her company's philanthropic support for rapid development of digital educational content and technological teaching tools. Another example was provided by His Excellency Abdul Aziz Al Ghurair, who cited his foundation's longstanding efforts to promote online education and accreditation at the university level in the Arab region. Many philanthropists in emerging markets are already focused on education as one of the crucial factors in developing the human capital of a young population. Online and digital education provides an enormous opportunity to extend access to previously remote and marginalised communities. The pandemic gave great impetus to the expansion of this approach to education.

In this chapter, I speak with four leaders who have applied their thinking, creativity and capital to take full advantage of digital platforms for social purpose.

Masami Sato is an outstanding organisational leader who has taken up the opportunity offered by applying digital technologies to giving. Originally from Japan and now based in Singapore, Sato started a social enterprise, B1G1: Business for Good, which connects businesses to charities through an online platform and through engagement tools that allow businesses to choose causes, track social impact and offer direct engagement to their customers and employees. This is a win for businesses and for charities alike. In her conversation with me, Sato describes her impressive 14-year journey to develop B1G1, which is now considered a global success.

Humanitarian emergencies caused by floods and fires due to climate change, as well as other natural disasters, are expected to occur more frequently in the decades ahead. The impetus to give and the need for more philanthropy to support such efforts have stimulated the growth of digital platforms for online giving across emerging markets. One such platform, simply named Give, emerged in Kuwait in 2019 after earthquakes in Turkey and Syria. It now helps donors find effective charities across the Middle East and in some parts of Asia and Africa. Its developer, Shayma al Sabah, is a committed young Kuwaiti who started Give as a non-profit, driven by her personal conviction of the necessity and urgency to create better and more transparent ways for charities and donors to connect. My conversation with her fills me with hope about the entrepreneurial and altruistic spirit of Shayma and her generation.

Political and business leaders across the world are increasingly focused on the potential and impact of new digital technologies for economic and social progress. His Royal Highness Sultan Nazrin Shah, the Deputy King of Malaysia, spoke with me about the ways in which digital platforms can enhance contributions in his country, particularly from Islamic philanthropy and the practice of *sadaqah* or voluntary alms giving. He also spoke about the uses of fintech for investment and development purposes, mentioning Ethis, a pioneering firm deploying technology for Islamic finance.

Finally, I had a fascinating conversation with Professor Mads Krogsgaard Thomsen, the CEO of the Novo Nordisk Foundation, a corporate foundation associated with the global pharmaceutical company Novo Nordisk, based in Denmark. The Novo Nordisk Foundation is one of the largest foundations in the world, and Professor Thomsen came to it after decades as chief scientific officer of Novo Nordisk. He has a scientist's appreciation for the revolutionary potential that technology has to improve lives, and how philanthropy that supports scientific advancement can truly contribute to solving some of the major challenges faced by humanity. The Novo Nordisk Foundation is investing in research centres tackling issues of sustainable agriculture, carbon capture and understanding the human genome. The foundation is implementing technologies that will accelerate the translation of knowledge into implementable solutions that will benefit human societies across the world.

Masami Sato

Founder, B1G1

In 2007, Masami Sato founded the Global Impact initiative and social enterprise B1G1 (originally known as Buy1GIVE1 – b1g1. com), which enables businesses to integrate effective impact creation at the core of their business operation. Her 'B1G1 Movement' has taken a completely new look at the power of giving and has inspired thousands of businesses, creating more than US$340 million in giving impacts to date.

Sato has been a serial entrepreneur since 2001, starting and running several commercial enterprises all aiming to transform the way businesses are operated today and engage their stake-holders in the collective mission to create a better future. Her first business was a fast-food takeaway venue in New Zealand, which she transformed into a wholesale frozen meal producer in Australia with the goal to make a positive social impact by helping to feed and educate disadvantaged children.

A two-time TEDx Speaker, CEO and author, Sato's career has followed her diverse talents and skills. She has been a teacher, translator, natural food chef and a farmer, and an award-winning entrepreneur. She has authored four books, including: *Joy: The Gift of Acceptance, Trust and Love*; *Giving Business: Creating the Maximum Impact in the Meaning-Driven World*; and *Better Business, Better Life, Better World*.

Badr Jafar: You are the founder and CEO of B1G1, the social enterprise, which is a global movement with more than 500 high-impact projects. Can you share with us a bit more about this journey, and the impact that you generated by bringing together over 2,300 businesses to work with B1G1?

Masami Sato: It's been 14 years since we began in 2007. We imagined a world full of giving. Imagine if every time you had a cup of coffee or tea, a child received access to life-saving water, or imagine if every time you purchased a book, so that you can learn and grow, somebody else received access to education. Imagine if every time you went to see a doctor, a child received access to healthcare. This is what inspired me to start B1G1.

I was already an entrepreneur. I started my first business 20 years ago. It was a food business because I was passionate about food, and I wanted to make sure that every person in the world would have access to healthy food and share that with their loved ones. That was my motive behind being an entrepreneur. I ran that business for five years, developing it and growing it, and it became a frozen packaged meal company, distributing frozen meals to health food stores and some of the supermarkets in Australia across multiple states.

We were doing well compared with when we began. But I realised that I wasn't doing anything beyond just running the business. I always felt that I wasn't ready, we were not successful enough, or we had to put money back into the business to grow more. At a certain moment I paused and thought, if I kept telling this story to myself, then in 10 or 20 years I will still be doing the same thing. That was when I imagined, instead of trying to do something big in the future, what if we did something small, something that we could do already, every day. We incorporated this idea of B1G1 into my own company. Several months later, I realised that maybe the world had many businesses who care, and I decided to sell my company and focus on B1G1.

B1G1 was founded in Singapore because we wanted it to be a global initiative from day one and we thought that Singapore was strategically a good place to be. Since then, we've worked with more than a thousand businesses and those businesses have already created US$250 million in giving impact. I think there is a power in the small things that we do every day.

Badr Jafar: B1G1 has been successful in rallying the business community from several sectors to support its cause, including providing access to clean water, meals, medicine, and mentoring for women and children. Are you happy with the

state of business engagement with philanthropic causes in the parts of the world that you operate in? What specific things can both sectors do to enhance this relationship?

Masami Sato: Compared with when we started in 2007, there is a stronger desire and awareness in the business community to contribute towards greater social impact and incorporate effective giving or CSR. But traditional forms of philanthropy or charitable giving are a bit ad hoc, such as doing a big charity gala dinner to raise money for a cause or donating to help in a natural disaster or doing annual fundraising. Much ad hoc giving takes place in today's world. The opportunity we are missing is how businesses can integrate social activities and effective giving into day-to-day business activities. Not only could we be creating impact regularly, it's also good for the non-profit side to have a stable income.

When we are doing something regularly, it becomes part of our identity. So, that act of giving and making an impact could uplift the spirit of businesses, and that can impact the team members, clients, customers and community. When we look at the non-profit side, I believe that traditional older non-profits are doing good work, but they tend to think about fundraising campaigns asking for immediate donations, and when something happens, and they can't continue their usual fundraising, it can be very disruptive. During the pandemic, many charity organisations lost a massive part of their regular income, because they couldn't do campaigns and events.

I think we should shift the focus on the giving side to think about the opportunity, and do the work continuously, over the long term. We can all learn and come together, almost like social ventures. Businesses can have a stronger sense of purpose, and non-profits can have a greater value proposition.

Badr Jafar: More and more entities around the world, both in the for-profit and the non-profit world, are seeing their purpose through a lens of social impact. Do you think that might be a problem going forward, that there might be

competition between entities or maybe that the way that the non-profit sector sees itself might be challenged?

Masami Sato: I don't think so at all. The more we can come together, the better we can shift our focus. The current approach is not creating value. On one side, corporations and businesses are trying to maximise profit at all costs, with leaders making decisions that create longer-term challenges and consequences. But they don't worry, because, as long as they are providing quarterly performance, they get paid well, and then they jump to another company and get paid more. On the other side, the non-profit sector is kept busy fixing the problems created because of this two-sided approach.

When we shift and come towards the middle, then the benefit is that every organisation can thrive. For the non-profit to be more sustainable, it's better to have the value proposition, and for businesses, it makes them more sustainable long-term, when they have a deeper sense of purpose, as well as taking care of people in the organisation better. So, these organisations will still thrive, it's just that we are filling in a different part of the ecosystem. Businesses are here to solve problems as well for the customers and communities. So, they are already creating good in the world. Non-profits are filling the gap to solve certain problems. There is not always a direct revenue model. These organisations will still exist in a symbiotic way to achieve results. Because we are working in alignment, I think we use less effort and fewer resources to achieve the same or even better results.

Badr Jafar: You've set a goal for B1G1 to reach a million businesses by the end of 2030. To what extent do you apply traditional entrepreneurial or business principles to the practice of philanthropy, whether that's through B1G1 or other things that you've been involved in? Has your approach to this changed over time?

Masami Sato: We tend to use a business forecast approach, even though our ultimate work is creating social impact. We've been focused on value creation because we believe that no matter what we are doing, our work itself should have a sustainable funding model that doesn't depend on donations. When businesses are choosing to support the causes that we bring on board as partners, we want to make sure 100% of their giving will go to the project. For us to make that work, we must have our own value proposition that is useful, meaningful and rewarding for the businesses we work with.

That's why we offer a platform to show the impact accounts for each business. They can embed a widget on their website, or they can generate a certificate of gratitude that they want to send, or we package giving in a way that businesses can very easily do a carbon offset. We continuously think in terms of creating value, making it easy, effective or rewarding for businesses to continue to give and to see the impact that they are creating. I came from an entrepreneurial background, and I grew up in a family business in Japan. My grandparents had a family business in Tokyo, and I was always helping them run their business. To me, thinking like a business is a very natural thing. When I was backpacking in my youth, I also saw there were lots of problems that nobody was interested in giving money for, so now, we are here to bridge this gap. I hope that one day we will be in a world where we don't even need charities anymore.

Badr Jafar: Do you believe that the pandemic will have a lasting impact on how people think about the imperative for this multi-stakeholder collaboration?

Masami Sato: Yes, because during the pandemic, we all recognised how connected we are. This issue impacted us no matter where we were. So, we also realised that we cannot move forward only thinking about ourselves, and not taking care of challenges together. We also understood the urgency of climate change and the importance of asking, if we all have the power to create an impact and influence each other, then how do we want to use that and what kind of world do we want to create? What kind of world do we want to leave for our children and grandchildren and generations to come?

I believe that we have the technology, we have the ability, resources, creativity and the uniqueness of the gifts that we individually have to solve this big global challenge. If we are aligned, we can actually make a real difference, but then the question is, can we align?

> "If we all have the power to create an impact and influence each other, then how do we want to use that and what kind of world do we want to create?"

Badr Jafar: What are some of the key issues and topics that you believe the next generation of philanthropists and social entrepreneurs should be focusing their efforts on globally?

Masami Sato: I think that because we are in this world of connection, effective learning is one of the keys. We can collate and access all the information that we have, and lots of information is free today. So, how quickly can we all learn to apply that knowledge to action? How can we create more collaboration, and bring the power that we have together to achieve the goal much faster? These two things matter, and I'm looking forward to seeing the next generation of leaders bringing their unique gifts into this mix because people like us may not be able to solve it by ourselves. We need young people to come into the space.

Shayma Al-Sabah

CEO and Founder of Give

Shayma Abdullah Al-Mubarak Al-Sabah leads Give, a Kuwait-based non-profit company that aims to improve the process of donating and encourage charitable giving. She launched the company in 2018 when she could not find the tools and information to support response efforts to a large earthquake that struck Iraq and Iran. Al-Sabah enrolled in accelerator programmes to gain the knowledge and support that she needed to pursue her specific goal of making online giving as easy and trusted as online shopping. In 2019, Give launched its online platform, which connects donors to charities in Kuwait as well as their international partners. Give is now successfully channelling support and donations to urgent causes in Kuwait, elsewhere in the Middle East and North Africa, as well as wider Asia and Europe.

Prior to founding Give, Al-Sabah, who is a graduate of the University of Oxford, worked in publishing, real estate, the Arab Fund for Economic and Social Development, and the World Bank.

Badr Jafar: I'd like to begin with the story of Give. What is Give's ultimate vision? How does it work, and what inspired you to establish this platform and put so much of your time and energy behind it?

Shayma Al-Sabah: Give is a non-profit company that aims to improve the process of donating and to encourage charitable giving. We created an online platform, which connects donors with registered Kuwaiti charities, to provide more choice, convenience and transparency. Users can donate on our app or our website. It's completely free for charities to join. A hundred per cent of the donation amount goes to charities, and we provide all the charities with access to their own portal where they can add projects and reports and monitor donations with complete transparency.

We currently have 20 charities on board and over 190 active projects, both in Kuwait and internationally. So, how does it work? We believe that by utilising technology in a very straightforward manner, we can do our part to bridge the gap between donors and charities. It used to be the case that if someone wanted to donate, they weren't aware of what was available in terms of campaigns. We'd find out about new campaigns on social media, like a sponsored ad, or through word of mouth, which is quite a haphazard way of donating. If someone had a specific cause in mind, if they saw something on the news, or they wanted to give to a specific country, they'd have to go to

Google or browse various websites until they found what they wanted. This is time-consuming, inconvenient, and the longer that this process takes, the less likely the person is to donate – they'll just forget about it.

A platform such as ours helps solve some of these problems, and it also serves to provide some added benefits. We've gathered all the campaigns by various charities in one place. The donor has easier access to information. It's also easier to filter because we have a double filter by category or by country. Our main page on the website and the app is dynamic, so whenever there is an emergency or a new campaign is launched, we highlight that. It also changes according to time of the year. For example, during Ramadan, we would focus on *iftar*, and so on.

The other wonderful thing about a platform is you can compare projects from different charities, and in that way, you can learn or find out about campaigns or charities you didn't even know about. I think older generations were much more loyal to specific charities. We're finding that with younger generations, the charity must be credible, but it's the cause that speaks to them. It's how transparent the charity is in communicating. A platform allows people to explore and find new campaigns. Content is very important. We try to engage with charities and ask them to provide more information either at the time of completion with reporting, or when they're gathering donations. We say, tell us about the beneficiaries, the scope of the project and so on. That's how we help donors.

In terms of charities, in the beginning we faced resistance because charities are very well established here and they gather a lot of donations, but we can help them attract younger segments of the population. We found the charities were not really using technology in an optimal way. Very few – less than a handful – had functional apps and some of them didn't even have payment platforms. The websites were not very easy to navigate, and some were completely in Arabic. At Give, we can help with that.

The other thing is that we want to help charities communicate their needs and their goals, but also the results and the impact. We're constantly reminding them of that. The story behind Give was born out of personal frustration and curiosity. Back in 2017, I was sitting at home watching TV, and the whole room started to shake. In Kuwait, we were fine. There wasn't much damage, but I wanted to help and donate to people who were badly affected in the epicentre, and it wasn't that easy for me to find the right information. That struck me as very strange, especially in a tech-savvy country like Kuwait, in our modern age where we can use our smartphones to buy anything from food to flowers and clothing. It's easy to consume, to buy, to get, why isn't it easy to give? This is the question that stuck with me; hence, the name of the platform.

I enrolled in an entrepreneurial boot camp, I set up a non-profit tech company and started to build a team who work remotely, all over the world. Then I started approaching charities. It took about a year from creating the company to having our MVP [minimal viable product], which was a very small launch with just a handful of charities in 2019. The original idea wasn't just a donation platform; it was supposed to be a resource for all your giving needs. You could give money, you could give your time, you could find out about volunteering opportunities, give clothes or furniture or give a second chance by becoming an organ donor, because I've also struggled with finding a way to become an organ donor. But I had to focus, so we decided to focus on monetary donations and charitable giving.

Badr Jafar: How do you see the future role of innovation in philanthropy, especially across regions like the Middle East, which has, for the most part, been operating in a very traditional way?

Shayma Al-Sabah: I find this topic of innovation and tech in philanthropy fascinating. To take a step back, I think innovation can be regarded in a variety of forms. You could have innovative thinking and creativity, and you could have innovation that relates to the tools that you use in the technology. So, just to briefly comment on creativity. Part of our vision at Give is to change people's perceptions when it comes to donating and incorporate it into our everyday lives. In this part of the world, donating is inextricably linked with a religious component. We're more likely to give during Eid, or especially Ramadan, which is the top season. At Give, we believe that giving should come from a place of gratitude, and not obligation, and that means that we'd like to make donating fun, if possible.

We can do this by introducing new features such as fundraising or gift donations. There's still lack of awareness with these features here. For example, in Europe or the US, any time anyone participates in a sporting event or marathon, they will often do it for a cause, and then get their circle involved in sponsoring them for that good cause. London Marathon runners to date have generated, I think, up to £750 million for charities. It's a wonderful experience and it's very inclusive. That's an example of creatively changing the way we think about donating.

The other thing is tools. Technology offers us the ability to be flexible and to respond rapidly to changes, as can seen following the invasion of Ukraine. Two teams from Harvard created a website in three days to match Ukrainian refugees with potential hosts in neighbouring countries. There was an outpouring of help online from people volunteering to translate the website 'Ukraine Take

> "Technology offers us the ability to be flexible and to respond rapidly to changes."

Shelter', and now there are hosts in North America and elsewhere. There was a need, they did it. The other technology that I think is fascinating and has tremendous potential in the sector is blockchain. Blockchain is a technology that allows digital information to be distributed but not copied. It mitigates against fraud, it happens in real time, there's transparency because you see every transaction along the donation cycle in this case, and it also offers a chance to reduce costs and be more efficient, because you remove the need for third-party financial services.

A great concrete example of this is the World Food Programme Building Blocks system. Building Blocks help one million people in Jordan and in Bangladesh to access multiple forms of assistance from different aid organisations. How do they do that? It used to be the case that a refugee on the system would be told when to collect their assistance, at different locations while juggling the correct documentation, the authentication forms, different forms for each charity and so on. Now with Building Blocks, they can present their QR code, or with the UNHCR I think they even do it biometrically, so they can scan your iris, and the refugee or the displaced person can visit various outlets or even retailers and buy what they need when they need it, and then that is automatically connected to their online account. There's a record of each transaction, and it doesn't have to be a specific person, as it used to be before, just one person per family. Now anyone in that family is linked to that one account. It's wonderful for the recipient of the aid, but also for the agencies. It's helped optimisation and coordination, so that you're not duplicating efforts, you see where there's a need. Where Building Blocks was operational, the World Food Programme reported that their costs for bank fees and financial fees fell by 98% because they didn't need those intermediaries any more for most of the transactions. So, it was quicker and cheaper.

I'll just mention a couple of other NGOs that I think are doing fantastic work. Each NGO can leverage their own know-how in a different way to solve a specific problem. Charity Water is a classic example of this. They saw that millions were being wasted on poorly maintained wells. Traditionally, charities used to go out physically to monitor and check the wells. It was quite difficult and infrequent because the wells are in rural areas. If a well stopped working, it just meant that people went back to drinking dirty water until the next maintenance occurred. Charity Water developed their own sensors, which they placed in the wells to monitor the flow in real time. Whenever a problem occurred, the technician could go and fix it. Then, they were able to upload information on Google Maps on their websites. Donors could see where they're operational, and they could see the communities that were being served.

Another great one close to my heart is Techfugees. It's a non-profit that organises hackathons, competitions to find tech solutions for problems facing refugees. They offered training for refugees to become AI trainers to make visual data AI-ready.

There is also a great example of a smartphone game, which is open source and free. It doesn't require an internet connection, and it helps teach refugee children how to read. These are just some wonderful ways in which technology can really help in our sector.

Badr Jafar: In what ways do you believe that the youth of today will change how philanthropy is practised tomorrow? As a philantropreneur yourself, what advice do you have to youth who wish to pursue a career in the social sector?

Shayma Al-Sabah: We can look at it in two ways when approaching the question of youth and how they can change philanthropy. One thing that we can't ignore in our area is high-net-worth donors or family firms, and the other is individual donors. In our areas, family firms are a huge source of philanthropic capital. I read a statistic that the top 100 family firms in the Gulf Cooperation Council region account for US$7 billion of annual spending on philanthropy. It used to be the case that CSR initiatives and spending might have been done in a relatively ad hoc way or in some cases it might have been for a marketing purpose and so on. Now there's more emphasis on strategic giving, and part of the reason for that could be that a new generation places a greater emphasis on impact-driven philanthropy and transparency. Also, I think many companies now are required or encouraged to share their social environmental impact, with ESG targets and so on.

In terms of individual donors and young donors, it's significant to note that millennials will represent 75% of the global workforce by 2025. According to studies in the US, they are very generous. This generation gives more than Gen Xers and baby boomers. In terms of the percentage of that segment who donate it is as high as 84 to 85%. It's quite significant considering that they have lower disposable incomes than other generations. They might still have debts to pay off. They might not have bought their house or other large purchases, but they are still very generous. When it comes to younger than millennials, these generations grew up with smartphones. The digitisation of the financial and social spheres makes it easier to learn about causes and makes it easier to donate. But we must be conscious of how we NGOs and charities communicate with them. They're already inundated with information. The messaging must be simple, personal, shareable, and it must have an impact. If they're going to spend their money, they have to know that there's an impact, and there is also the sense of community among younger people when it comes to causes that they support.

Another brilliant example of young people being involved with charity and philanthropy is Abo Flah, a Kuwaiti-based YouTuber who raised US$11 million for charity by living in a glass box for 12 days and live streaming the event. He got a Guinness World Record for the greatest number of viewers for a charity event, and the longest continuously broadcast live stream. So, the youth can be engaged and be a force for good.

Badr Jafar: You have demonstrated use of entrepreneurial skills and passions towards philanthropic causes. What advice would you have to youth who want to pursue a similar path?

Shayma Al-Sabah: I don't know if I'm the right person to offer advice, but I can share some lessons I've learned along my short journey so far. You only have one life to live. My fear of failure and my perfectionism used to hold me back from a lot of things. I had no background in start-ups, in technology, and I had very little work experience because I was in and out of work frequently as I was having my children, and so on. This project made me overcome my hesitancy because I changed my mindset.

I started looking at it in a different way. I was engaged and challenged and found it exciting, and my curiosity was sparked about how to build something from scratch, and that's what I focused on instead of being fearful of failing. I had to accept that everyone starts from step one, and it's okay to learn new things, no matter what stage of life you're in. You learn from experience, but also you can educate yourself. I think the reason for that change in mindset had to do with being in the start-up community, which is very supportive. There isn't as big a stigma attached to failure as there is in traditional businesses. Especially in a small country, where everyone knows everyone else, failure to the individual can feel like a stain on their reputation. But failure is not the opposite of success; it's part of success, because through that, you gain experience. I remember people with me in the start-up community joking about how their first start-ups failed, and they were joking about it, whereas I would have thought people don't talk about this. So, that really switched the way I started viewing things.

The second reason for me was that ego was removed from the equation. It's not about me; it's about something bigger than me. Many years ago, I would never have stood in front of a room full of people and pitched an idea, but I have had to do so for the charities multiple times. I probably would not have accepted this interview because I'm fearful of being on camera. So, that's something I've learned. In terms of young people pursuing social entrepreneurship, I think there's perhaps a false dichotomy that either you try to make as much money as possible, or you try to save the world, but you don't make any money.

There is a middle ground. There's social entrepreneurship. Social entrepreneurship tries to address some of the most difficult and pressing problems of our time, and you can earn a decent living from it because the goods or the services that you create are in demand. This is especially true nowadays with the rapid changes in biotech, infotech, AI and robotics, meaning stable jobs might become obsolete. We still need critical thinking and problem-solving creativity; there's always a need for that. It's especially pertinent in our part of the world where 60% of the population is under 25, and the rates of youth unemployment are consistently higher than the global average – approximately 23% compared with 14% in the rest of the world. The elephant in the room – the

"We need purpose in our lives. Whether we can find that in our personal life, or in our professional sphere, we all need the thing that will feed our soul, and working in the social sector is one possible way to find it."

pandemic – has changed the way we look at things. I think it's made us take stock of our lives, and has emphasised our interconnectedness. We need purpose in our lives. Whether we can find that in our personal life, or in our professional sphere, we all need the thing that will feed our soul, and working in the social sector is one possible way to find it. Personally, I have found a great deal of fulfilment in what I do.

His Royal Highness Sultan Nazrin Shah
Deputy King of Malaysia

His Royal Highness Sultan Nazrin Shah is the Deputy King of Malaysia and the hereditary ruler of the State of Perak. He is the descendant of a dynasty dating back to 1528.

In recognition of his knowledge and contribution to humanitarian issues, the United Nations Secretary-General invited Sultan Nazrin Shah to serve as co-chair of the High-Level Panel on Humanitarian Financing in 2015. The panel's recommendations for closing the funding gap for meeting the needs of complex humanitarian crises helped frame discussions at the first-ever World Humanitarian Summit, held in Istanbul in 2016. Prior to that UN role, His Royal Highness also served as Malaysia's Special Envoy for Interfaith and Inter-civilisational Dialogue at the United Nations Alliance of Civilisations (UNAOC) in 2012.

Sultan Nazrin Shah is chancellor of the University of Malaya – Malaysia's oldest university. He is an honorary fellow of Worcester College, Oxford, and of Magdalene College and St Edmund's College, Cambridge, as well as vice chairman of the board of trustees at the Oxford Centre for Islamic Studies.

As an economist, Sultan Nazrin Shah oversees and provides direction for the Economic History of Malaya project (www.ehm.my), and is the author of *Charting the Economy: Early 20th Century Malaya and Contemporary Malaysian Contrasts* (2017) and *Striving for Inclusive Development: From Pangkor to a Modern Malaysian State* (2019).

Badr Jafar: You are a renowned advocate of good governance, and you often call on institutions in Malaysia and elsewhere across Asia to leverage innovative methods to
maximise the social impact of the rapidly growing wealth
across the region. How urgent do you think it is to improve
governance when it comes to managing the flow of philanthropic capital, and what can be done to accelerate this
cultural shift?

Sultan Nazrin Shah: I've always believed that good governance
is paramount in these matters, and this is something I've spoken
about many times. To put it in very simple terms, civilisation falls
when governance fails, and since corruption is, in a very real
sense, the antithesis of effective governance, there is a duty upon
all of us who uphold civilised values to fight against corruption in
all its forms. We must use all the innovative tools at our disposal
to eradicate the scourge. I believe that transparency, accountability and justice must guide our day-to-day interactions in the
world of work, across all sectors of society.

We are living in an era of massive
wealth generation, and this presents
an exciting opportunity for the region
of Southeast Asia, but also raises
daunting challenges. Governments
and decision-makers in the region
have an increasingly urgent responsi-

> "We need to harness available technologies, work collaboratively and form productive partnerships."

bility to make the best possible use of these growing opportunities, and to direct these philanthropic capital flows so that they
benefit the largest numbers of citizens. To do that, we need to
harness available technologies, work collaboratively and form
productive partnerships with the right stakeholders from Asia
and around the world.

Badr Jafar: Between US$400 billion and US$1 trillion is
donated by Muslims around the world through *zakat*, which
is compulsory almsgiving, and *sadaqah*, discretionary
almsgiving, every single year. Yet one in three Muslims

around the world lives below the poverty line. How can we better harness and empower Islamic giving in a more strategic and coordinated way with a view to maximising philanthropic impact?

Sultan Nazrin Shah: For the benefit of our non-Muslim friends, I think it's very important to clarify that *zakat* refers to the obligatory tax for Muslims to achieve social justice through the distribution of wealth, whereas *sadaqah* is charity, or voluntary almsgiving. Those distinctions need to be kept in mind when we talk about Muslim charity. Global giving using technology can harness the power of *sadaqah*, and there are already numerous examples of this happening around the world. For instance, in Southeast Asia, we have a fintech platform called Ethis, which has grown tremendously in recent years. This platform has seen the development of a wide range of projects, from low-cost housing to agriculture and even tourism. Badr, you yourself have been involved in the establishment of HasanaH, which is based in the Middle East but has a global reach. Platforms like Ethis and HasanaH, along with others created by the UNHCR and other international organisations – both Islamic and non-Islamic – now feature *zakat* calculators that allow Muslims to channel the obligatory *zakat* using this technology, and I think that's very exciting.

In Malaysia, online and digital transfer of *zakat* is very much embedded in our *zakat* institutions. One example is the Maybank Islamic Mosque Adoption Programme, which aims to ensure transparency of giving through the use of technology, in particular QR codes. I launched this initiative in Malaysia and witnessed first-hand the disbursal of several contributions through the programme. Malaysia is fortunate in that *zakat* institutions are well established and have embraced technology to connect those performing *zakat* with the people and projects that require support. In order to keep improving, what we now need to do is use similar methods to reach recipients more widely, and to use technology to monitor progress and capacity development among *zakat* recipients.

It is worth mentioning the difference between the local and the global when we talk about giving. While there is some guidance already available on global *zakat* standards and distribution, at the present time Islamic jurisprudence is very localised, and this has practical implications for Islamic philanthropic giving. One way to overcome poverty eradication gaps is to focus on local needs, while at the same time harnessing global philanthropy from donors who live in more affluent societies. I think your platform, HasanaH, is doing a great job in that respect.

Badr Jafar: How do you think that the rapid growth of the world's emerging economies and the generational transition that's happening with trillions of dollars changing hands can be harnessed to create opportunities for youth?

Sultan Nazrin Shah: The future belongs to the young, and I think the youth must be given more voice. They must be given the skills and the knowledge to guide them in later years, when they are the world's policymakers, entrepreneurs and so forth. The older generation, people in our generation, will also need to come to terms with the destructive impact of our decisions, the harm that many of our actions have already caused the planet, and the disasters and health crises that will follow as a result. You mentioned the emerging economies, and I think Asia, particularly Southeast Asia, can take the initiative to harness innovation and new knowledge to show leadership, especially in sustainable development. What is needed is leadership to drive a new way of doing things, alongside a groundswell of citizen advocacy – particularly among the youth – to demand that change.

> "The future belongs to the young, and I think the youth must be given more voice."

Professor Mads Krogsgaard Thomsen

CEO, Novo Nordisk Foundation

With over 30 years of experience in research and development of innovative medicines for chronic diseases at Novo Nordisk, Professor Thomsen has a deep understanding of the life sciences and biotechnology sector and its potential to improve human and planetary health. He was appointed as CEO of the Novo Nordisk Foundation in 2021.

The Novo Nordisk Foundation is an independent Danish enterprise foundation. Characterised as a non-profit organisation, it supports philanthropic purposes, focusing on scientific, humanitarian and social causes. With a net worth of nearly US$100 billion, its funds derive from ownership of and investment in companies and other financial assets.

Professor Thomsen is the former Chief Scientific Officer at the Danish pharmaceutical company Novo Nordisk. During his tenure, more than 20 innovative medicines were developed and approved. His efforts contributed to Novo Nordisk's leading role as a global healthcare company, with exports to over 180 countries.

Badr Jafar: As the CEO of the Novo Nordisk Foundation, an independent foundation that's proud of its corporate links with Novo Nordisk the company, how important is the nexus between business and philanthropic capital, in your view?

Mads Thomsen: I think it's very important. You've talked about the development of insulin analogues that have made pharmacotherapy within diabetes more convenient and safer and more efficacious. I believe that there is a good balance and benefit from owning, or at least partly owning, a company that can invest in new technology, while making the last generation of technology available at very affordable prices throughout the world and yet retain surplus cash to invest in innovation. We are now investing in giving back to society some of the profits from the operating companies in meaningful ways both within human healthcare, global health and sustainability. It's been a jump from just making medicines to a broader societal impact, which I find extremely rewarding.

Badr Jafar: The Novo Nordisk Foundation has been very active in the fight against the COVID-19 pandemic. You donated millions of dollars for COVID-19-related measures, test centres and funded research trials for anti-inflammatory drugs. Do you think the pandemic is changing people's perception of the role of private philanthropic capital in helping communities respond to this sort of emergency?

Mads Thomsen: Yes, I think at least in little Denmark, public–private partnerships, including those with philanthropy, have been on the radar in a positive way among the political establishment. The Novo Nordisk Foundation funded many test centres throughout Denmark for COVID-19 testing, and the operating company developed the PCR technology that was then used nationwide. This is an example of philanthropy, the public system and the operating companies coming together in a way that has created a better image of what we are able to do on the business side.

Badr Jafar: Emerging markets are among the fastest-growing economies in the world. As a European organisation deeply engaged in many of these markets, have you observed the nature and attitudes of philanthropy changing in these regions of the world, and, if so, what do you believe are the main drivers of this change?

Mads Thomsen: It's a good point you're making that in these emerging market economies due to their relatively strong growth, it becomes more feasible to do meaningful philanthropy, because infrastructure is built, education and healthcare are enhanced, and it becomes possible to do things where, for instance, diseases can get diagnosed and treated. It also becomes easier to help in more established economies, with the possibility to make sure that funding and support goes to the correct places.

During my 30-year tenure at Novo, I've witnessed that our ability as a company, and now in the foundation, to operate more broadly in these emerging markets has expanded vastly, particularly over the past decade or so. It's important to reach out early on and make pharmacotherapy affordable and accessible when the economies are immature. Over time, the societies mature due to financial growth and strength, and they can also become an integral part of the more modern healthcare systems that we know from the Western world. I've seen that happening and we've tried to contribute also via the World Diabetes Foundation.

Badr Jafar: Your work at the foundation is closely tied to data- and evidence-informed grant giving. How can we ensure that this new generation of philanthropists across these growth markets – and globally – have access to the tools and knowledge that they will need to maximise their impact?

Mads Thomsen: That is a very important question. To me, everything must be evidence-based. For example, in bio-agriculture, we need a database to give us the ability to have healthier crops in a biologically reasonable way and not to have to cut down the Amazon rainforest or use all water for irrigation. I could mention many other examples.

"Everything must be evidence-based."

Even though we can do wonderful philanthropy in Denmark, and can show that it works here, it's important to have the evidence base so that when research points to new ways, whatever they may be, they must prove themselves in local environments. This is why we are extremely evidence-based, and we would like to share data. When we talk to the Bill & Melinda Gates Foundation, the Wellcome Trust and so on, we are preoccupied by the idea of sharing data so that we can generate more collective knowledge and avoid duplication of effort.

Badr Jafar: How are technology and innovation changing philanthropy to meet unfulfilled healthcare needs in the regions that you're active in?

Mads Thomsen: For us, it has changed quite a lot. In general, technologies have emerged over the past decade that are contributing insights on the human genome, on the genome of plants, carbon capture and so on. Technology is making it possible to move to an industrial scale. We're starting to be able to use, for instance, high-performance computing, maybe even quantum computing, in modelling of the future, weather forecasts of the global climate and the ability to understand microbial populations in our guts, and so on.

Today we don't have the computational power to make all these technologies reach their maximum potential. But technologies are emerging in the climate area, in human health and in computing, which will help us get there by around 2030. So, we are investing heavily in some of these technologies by creating research centres that are dedicated to bio-agriculture, to quantum computing, to carbon emission, carbon capture and things like that.

Badr Jafar: Novo Nordisk has long been open to partnerships. Do you believe that the pandemic will have a lasting impact on how people think about the imperative for multi-stakeholder collaboration and true partnerships?

Mads Thomsen: I sincerely hope so, because what has been painfully evident during the pandemic is that just like we have built a network within a non-communicable disease called type 2 diabetes, we need to build infrastructure so that remedies and therapies can get to the population in emerging markets. We've seen that just getting the vaccines out there to do the job of vaccinating local populations has been a huge dilemma, and very often the data infrastructure and the logistics have simply not been in place.

There is a lot of ongoing effort between the WHO and the UN system and some of the big foundations and trusts to prepare for the next round. Luckily, we now have the technologies, the mRNA technology and a couple of others, which have revolutionised our ability to counteract pandemics like COVID-19 in a way that was unforeseen. Now, we just need global outreach and to get the systems up and running in a way that we're better prepared for next time.

> "One of the roles that private philanthropy can play, and the Novo Nordisk Foundation is playing in a big way through several research centres at universities today, is to bridge from basic research through translation into the remedies of the future."

Badr Jafar: Is there an optimal role for private philanthropy in the field of medical research and for philanthropists who are interested in focusing their efforts here, and what advice would you give them?

Mads Thomsen: I think there's a huge role. In all honesty, if you take the private companies in the pharmaceutical industry, they are often focused on the more established paradigms, and the universities are not really focused on translating basic research into applied science. One of the roles that private philanthropy can play, and the Novo Nordisk Foundation is playing in a big way through several research centres at universities today, is to bridge from basic research through translation into the remedies of the future. We can help both with the funding, but also with the translation into something that is more than a publication in *Nature* or somewhere else, but goes all the way. We can help the whole life science ecosystem come together from the very early stages of basic research to the latest stages of applied research translation, and even into the marketplace by facilitating and catalysing this whole value chain.

TEN
BUILDING INFRASTRUCTURE FOR IMPACT

Building a stronger ecosystem of local and regional platforms and networks is fundamental to the development of collaborative philanthropy. One of the important aspects of such platforms is that they provide an opportunity for philanthropists to tell their stories and to listen to others. This would also help overcome the reticence that many feel about discussing their philanthropy. The inspiration and lessons learned from the experiences of others will also help generate trust between donors and help spur collaboration. Pooling capital among private and public funders during the pandemic was highly effective in addressing major social, environmental and economic emergencies. More such collaborative funding models can be facilitated by networks. The Asia Venture Philanthropy Network (AVPN) in Singapore has demonstrated how this can be done through its pooled Philanthropic Funds. Similarly, the Asia Philanthropy Circle (APC) has helped to form funder collectives on climate and mental wellness.

Philanthropic network leaders across emerging markets are at the forefront of strengthening collaboration and impact. In my conversation with Naina Subberwal Batra, the

CEO of AVPN, she described how to build an effective ecosystem for philanthropic venture capital. She is passionate about the way in which AVPN enables its members to benchmark, set standards and apply best practices. Through AVPN, she says they gain new perspectives and can see a roadmap to the future in their own work. This is a point also made very strongly by Laurence Lien, the co-founder of APC. Laurence is a serial founder of philanthropic networks, responsible not only for APC but also for establishing the Community Foundation of Singapore and, most recently, the Asia Community Foundation. He is passionate about creating these peer networks to share stories and examples, inspire more individual philanthropy, and, most importantly, foster collaboration and leverage collective action on the most complex issues we face.

To understand more directly how philanthropic networks can accelerate strategic philanthropy, I also spoke to two female leaders, Belinda Tanoto, a trustee of the Tanoto Foundation, one of the largest philanthropies in Indonesia, and Tsitsi Masiyiwa, chair of the Higherlife Foundation and a leading Zimbabwean philanthropist. Both women have been inspired by the opportunities offered through the networks that have promoted collaborative philanthropic projects across their respective regions. From Tanoto, I heard examples of the impact of collaborative philanthropy in Indonesia. In building her philanthropic impact as a next-generation philanthropist in her family, she has benefited greatly from the peer exchanges, collaboration opportunities, and sharing of knowledge and stories that comes with membership in networks such as AVPN and APC. From Masiyiwa, I heard about the role played by the African Philanthropy Forum, which she has chaired, in connecting philanthropists and fostering more strategic philanthropy across Africa. She spoke with great optimism about the increasing collaboration that she is seeing among philanthropists around the African continent, and the surging interest of the younger generation in using philanthropy and social investment to tackle the issues confronting African societies.

Naina Subberwal Batra

CEO, AVPN

Naina Subberwal Batra is the CEO of AVPN, based in Singapore. AVPN is the largest regional social investment network that aims to increase the flow of financial, human and intellectual capital for impact. Batra's leadership since 2013 has nurtured the AVPN community, expanding the membership base more than fourfold and elevating the organisation into a regional force for good. Under her direction, AVPN has grown from focusing only on venture philanthropy to supporting the entire ecosystem of social investors, from catalytic philanthropists to impact investors and corporate CSR professionals.

Batra is a board member of the Menzies Foundation and the Global Resilient Cities Network, and a trustee at the Bridge Institute. She was a fellow at the Bellagio Center Residency Program in 2022 and was featured on the list of Asia's Most Influential by *Tatler Asia* in 2021. She was recognised by CSRWorks as one of Asia's Top Sustainability Superwomen in 2019.

Badr Jafar: You've expanded AVPN over a short period of time from a purely venture philanthropy network to an authority and a reference for philanthropists, impact investors and CSR professionals. Can you tell us about the network, its philosophy and the efforts that it is most focused on today?

Naina Subberwal Batra: As you probably know, Asia has only a third of the social investors that exist in the US or Europe, and six times the population. If Asian leaders are to solve Asian problems in Asia, Asian capital must spend every dollar well. I believe that we must invest in the mechanisms that multiply impact like intermediaries, networks and other ecosystem builders, and scale. At AVPN, we see ourselves as an ecosystem-builder for impact capital in Asia. Over the past ten years, we have nurtured the ecosystem and created opportunities for our members to act through connecting them to unusual allies. By that I mean foundations being connected to businesspeople, to policymakers, to social entrepreneurs to learn practical insights from one another. So, learn from practitioners. And lead by taking decisive action to move capital towards impact. Many of our members are aligned in this desire to build the ecosystem and that's why we've seen success moving capital towards impact at scale. One of our biggest strengths is that we have enormous convening power in Asia, reflected in the fact that we run more than 50 events a year. Our AVPN global conference in 2020 attracted almost 7,500 attendees, making it the biggest Asian social investment conference in the world.

We influence a huge amount of capital, and I'll give you an example. During the last 20 months of the pandemic, our members moved more than US$10 billion towards COVID-19 relief efforts globally. Some of that has been with our direct support, most recently to impact organisations on the ground in India and in Southeast Asia. The most important thing for me is that our members tell us that their work with AVPN enables them to benchmark, to set standards and to apply best practices. They also tell us that their horizons expand with new perspectives, and they can see a roadmap to the future in their own work, through stories that they exchange with their peers, with other people. That's the thing of which I am most proud.

Badr Jafar: Asia represents thousands of years of traditional philanthropy and a massive growth in wealth that is bringing the continent to the forefront where trillions of dollars are in line to be passed on from one generation to an even more socially conscious next generation. How would you describe the culture of giving and philanthropy across the markets that you're engaged in? How are attitudes to institutional and collaborative giving evolving over time?

Naina Subberwal Batra: Philanthropy in Asia has been around for centuries, and we've always given, whether to the church, or to the temple, or to the mosque, or to our communities. What hasn't been there is institutional philanthropy. That is something that is new for us. There are a few philanthropic institutions like the Tata Trust, for example, in India, which has been doing institutional giving for more than a hundred years, but they are a rarity.

For most, philanthropy has been a private individual-giving exercise, because their conscience motivates them to do it, or they feel a need to give back to their communities. Most high-net-worth Asians don't like to talk about their giving. Because we don't talk about our giving as they do in the West, we are unable to inspire or be role models for a new generation of givers, and that is where institutional philanthropy networks and intermediaries need to come in. Unless we have a more formal structure for giving, it tends to be ad hoc, linked more to emotional than to logical, practical decision-making.

This is true for a lot of new givers. Our first instinct is to give to education, because many witnessed their parents or grandparents work hard. Asians, as you are aware, have a lot of pride in – and put a lot of value on – education. We think it's the best way to motivate and bring up the next generation. But we don't realise that it's not just giving to education, we need to give to education that provides access to jobs, that provides training, that will help people get employed. So, instead of giving to scholarships, do we look at how to promote more vocational training? How do we look at creating more job opportunities? That only comes when there is an institutional set-up, when there is a framework, and that's where AVPN and other networks are good to share where there are unmet needs, where we can partner, where we can collaborate and how we can bring our resources together to get a much better outcome.

Badr Jafar: The AVPN Deal Share Platform makes more than 400 opportunities available for social impact investors and has successfully made hundreds of connections for that purpose. Can you share with us your view on how philanthropists of all ages could be using technology more effectively to boost impact?

Naina Subberwal Batra: Technology is a tool that we have all learned to use more effectively. For example, data.org is a collaborative that was set up in 2019, led by the Rockefeller Foundation and the MasterCard Center for Inclusive Growth, to build data science for social impact. This was particularly crucial during the pandemic, when our members were looking for reliable and accessible information on social issues and non-profit engagement to make decisions on where to give. It was important to use data to be able to connect capital to where it was needed the most.

Besides artificial intelligence, one of the interesting new things that we are seeing in Asia is the use of cryptocurrency. We are finding that philanthropists are starting to consider how this can be used to support non-profits. I don't know whether you're seeing this in other parts of the world, but engagement by the crypto community in philanthropy has taken different forms, such as giving tokens. Vitalik Buterin, a co-founder of Ethereum, has demonstrated the kind of scale at which that's possible. He donated 50 trillion tokens, worth US$1.2 billion, to India's crypto COVID-19 Relief Fund.

We're also seeing things like building financial inclusion in our work. In Asia, in countries like Papua New Guinea, for example, or some of the Pacific Rim countries where they find it difficult to access the international banking system, they are looking at building in financial inclusion through technology by using crypto or crypto tokens with financial inclusion benefits that are built in. It's a very interesting time and I believe that philanthropists, especially next-gen philanthropists, are embracing this kind of technology to look at more innovative ways of how they do their philanthropy.

Badr Jafar: I've witnessed increasing appetite around collaboration with philanthropy since the pandemic, with some great examples of funders connecting and working together. In 2020, you partnered with many grant makers, investors, corporations and governments to form communities around

priority themes such as technology to mitigate the effects of natural disasters and supporting women social entrepreneurs in emerging economies. How effective have you found this experience in multi-sector collaboration and what would you like to see done differently?

Naina Subberwal Batra: We both agree that it's not possible to solve the complex problems that we are trying to solve without multi-sectoral involvement, but we need to build alignment on what we are working towards. So, if you look at bringing people together around the Sustainable Development Goals, or the Paris Agreement on Climate Change, that is something that several stakeholders are aligned on, and are ready to try new approaches and to leverage each other's strengths to build innovative solutions.

In 2020, we supported several collaborations. One in Indonesia was the Gotong Royong [Mutual Assistance] Movement, and it involved many different organisations, including large private-sector foundations, like the Tanoto Foundation, the Indika Foundation, the Djarum Foundation and others. It involved government and, as part of the collaborative, it connected donors and grantees to address social issues arising from the pandemic, mainly focusing on health, safety, employability, livelihoods and education. In a matter of weeks through that collaboration, we found that members had donated more than three million units of medical supplies. They had donated training hours. They had donated capital to those who had found themselves unemployed. We saw a lot of rapid action through collaborative effort around a specific disaster like the pandemic.

We've also seen longer-term collaboratives around specific themes in Asia. An example is the India Climate Collaborative, which is the first collaborative of its kind to address climate change in India. They formed in 2019, supported by large international foundations. Then, for a first in India, they managed to bring in Indian organisations like the Tata Trust, Rohini Nilekani Philanthropies, Mahindra and Swadesh. Before this, especially for climate action, it was tough to get Asian funders to fund.

Through this platform, by creating collaborative collective action, they managed to inspire and motivate Indian philanthropists to look at climate change in India.

Collaboration is a very abused term. We all talk about collaboration, we all talk about people coming together, but it's probably the hardest thing to do. It needs to start with putting egos aside and focusing on a common goal. If you can align those objectives, then I think collaboration becomes slightly easier.

Badr Jafar: You launched Asia's first healthcare unrestricted pooled fund with a mission to respond to the COVID-19 pandemic in Asia, addressing urgent needs from a healthcare and humanitarian perspective. Do you think that the pandemic is changing the way that people think about the role of private philanthropy and philanthropic organisations in helping communities respond to this kind of emergency? In the Middle East and North Africa, the government has been relied on to provide immediate assistance and the philanthropic sector has been a peripheral player at best. Do you see that changing?

Naina Subberwal Batra: I do, and I think the pandemic has played a big role, partly because it's left no one untouched. This is the first global crisis in our living memory where we've all been affected. People have realised that a crisis like this can affect anybody, irrespective of whether you're a rich country or you're a poor country. I'm in Singapore, one of the wealthiest countries in the world, and we are struggling now, with numbers increasing despite having an 88% vaccination ratio. That has caused private-sector philanthropists and philanthropic organisations across Asia to say that we need to step in, because many governments, especially in this part of the world, have struggled. It's not just governments in developing countries; governments in developed countries have also struggled, whether it's been around vaccination take-ups or on the bet that they took about which vaccination to procure – choices to make between livelihoods and life. For the first time, private-sector philanthropy and business have been able to offer value and support government and civil society.

You talked about the pooled fund and unrestricted funding. For me, that was key. We talk about helping organisations on the ground grow, but less than 5% of philanthropic giving is unrestricted or core grants. It's mostly still project grants. I think that, as a network, we need to help encourage our members and philanthropists to be brave. Philanthropy capital is supposed to have a high appetite for risk. It is supposed to be catalytic. It is supposed to enable innovation. If we are so prescriptive, then how are we going to help innovation grow? Every philanthropist who does good does it because there is a non-profit on the ground that is implementing his or her vision. If we don't give them the resources to be brave and to take risks, I think we are being dishonest to the actual aims of philanthropic capital.

> "Every philanthropist who does good does it because there is a non-profit on the ground that is implementing his or her vision."

That is why we launched, and are now on our fourth pooled fund. Every one of them has been unrestricted giving. In their own organisations they will never do unrestricted funding, but when they come together in a pooled fund they feel more confident, and they are much more open to risk-taking. I believe that's the way to go and that's where philanthropy needs to go.

Badr Jafar: AVPN is present on the ground in 13 markets to cater for the local nuances and empower local champions. A report published by the Centre for Strategic Philanthropy at Cambridge highlighted that local recipients of philanthropic investments were increasingly empowered to make their own decisions on use of funds based on their superior knowledge of local needs and imperatives. Are you witnessing this trend and what might this mean for the future of foreign direct philanthropic investment, both in these markets and increasingly from these markets?

Naina Subberwal Batra: Yes, we are seeing these trends. Local organisations are best placed to understand their needs, to understand their cultural context, and therefore be able to design interventions that are likely to have the biggest impact. What we've realised is that the goal of many large international foundations is to use their capital to leverage or to be the first play to inspire local giving. We can use that kind of investment to fund sectors that local philanthropists may initially be reluctant to fund, whether that be advocacy, or gender justice, or climate justice, which local philanthropists initially are uncomfortable funding, at least in Asia. If foreign direct funding starts it, we are finding that local philanthropists are stepping in to take over.

"We need to build more bridges so that both philanthropists and organisations on the ground can share their learnings and their experiences."

Where I think the movement needs to go is sharing those kinds of stories and learnings across different locations and economies. The Cambridge Centre has usefully highlighted models and giving trends in the countries where we need to build more collaborations. We need to build more bridges so that both philanthropists and organisations on the ground can share their learnings and their experiences.

Laurence Lien

Founding CEO, Asia Philanthropy Circle

Laurence Lien is a co-founder and founding CEO of the Asia Philanthropy Circle based in Singapore, and co-founder of the Asia Community Foundation. He is also the chairman of the Lien Foundation, established in 1980 and highly regarded for its forward-thinking approach in the fields of education and elder care. He was the CEO of the National Volunteer and Philanthropy Center in Singapore until 2014. In 2008, he co-founded the Community Foundation of Singapore, which he chaired from 2013 to 2019. He is a board member of the Lien Center for Social Innovation at the Singapore Management University. Prior to his work in the non-profit sector, Lien served in the Singapore Administrative Service, which forms a top echelon of public service leaders in Singapore. He was also a nominated member of parliament in Singapore from 2012 to 2014.

Badr Jafar: Laurence, you've been the CEO of the Asia Philanthropy Circle since 2015. When you co-founded this network, what were you hoping to achieve? What have you learned along the way?

Laurence Lien: When we first started, we wanted philanthropists around the region to have a safe place to come together to exchange and collaborate. We felt that too many people were reinventing the wheel or making the same mistakes. Philanthropy was quite a lonely journey. There were so many networks for businesspeople to talk about business; so, why not something for philanthropists, targeted at principles?

Fast-forward to 2024 and I think we have achieved quite a bit. We have more than 60 families from 12 different markets. We have been elevating philanthropic practice among our members. There's nothing like a network where people share their stories to inspire one another, build a community and create relationships of trust, which can catalyse collaborative impact. Collaboration is not an easy thing. People talk a lot about it, but to really collaborate you need to see yourself working with people week in, week out. If you're doing big-scale, innovative work, things are not linear. They never go exactly the way that you want them to go, so you need relationships of trust. We have developed these relationships and we have even created new NGOs, new impact pathways, whether it's in climate, education, healthcare or dealing with vulnerable communities.

I think what is important is that we are inspiring change at scale. When you work in a collective, you can leverage the power of the collective. You can go to forums with one voice. Eleven of us from the APC attended COP28 (in UAE, December 2023)

"We are inspiring change at scale." and we hosted many events for business and philanthropy. It's because of the APC platform that we were able to bring so many there, but also to increase the voice of Asian philanthropists in global fora and to forge global partnerships.

We are very happy with where we are, but the work is not done. Whatever the achievements, we are only at an early stage. There's so much more to do, whether it's collaboration, or bringing more people in, or deepening the work on the Sustainable Development Goals. Because of the COVID-19 pandemic, unfortunately, progress on some of the SDGs has even gone backwards, and we must double or triple our efforts.

Badr Jafar: Asia includes some of the highest-growth economies in the world. How do you see philanthropy changing as wealth grows in Asia? What do you think are some of the key drivers for more strategic philanthropy in the region and from the region?

Laurence Lien: There's a lot of interest in philanthropy now. I believe we are at an inflection point. People are saying the right things, although I don't think they're doing the right things yet. The good thing is that people want to act. What is driving this? First-generation wealth creators are asking what is beyond just making more money. Philanthropy is always part of the equation. These wealth creators want the next generation to have purpose and meaning, and the next generation is indeed growing up.

We are seeing more interest in philanthropy among wealthy families, as a transition of wealth is happening. But there is also a bifurcation, I feel. The first-generation wealth creators are much more traditionally into charity giving while the next generation are more interested in innovations such as impact investments, or using artificial intelligence for philanthropy, and so

"We are seeing more interest in philanthropy among wealthy families."

on. There is much public good work that needs more investment. We hope that more donors will help build up the ecosystem, because in many of our countries the philanthropy ecosystem – the non-profit ecosystem – is very underdeveloped.

I talk a lot about Asian philanthropists, not because we want to compete with the West for a better model, it's just that the Asian context is different. The way we do things in practice is different; philosophically we are different as well, in terms of values. I think family, religion and government are all big elephants in the room. The way that we evolve will naturally be different. I think we are a bit more community-based, community-driven and more personally engaged. There is this Buddhist concept of *dana*, or generosity. Whether it's Buddhist or even Hindu, *dana* is about quiet giving with no strings attached. That philosophy drives Asian philanthropy in a different direction from the West. Of course, we must work with our respective government in a constructive way too, because government is, as I mentioned, the elephant in the room.

Badr Jafar: What do you think is still missing? In the region's philanthropic infrastructure, are there major intraregional differences? How is Singapore positioning itself as a hub for philanthropy in the region?

Laurence Lien: Of course, there's a danger of overgeneralising when we talk about Asia, because Asia is such a diverse region. I mentioned that the NGO sector is underdeveloped. There are issues of accountability, transparency and governance in a lot of countries. Obviously, closely tied to that is a lack of capacity and lack of talent, so, we need to do a lot more work to support organisations in their growth. Government regulation lags behind. It needs to be much more progressive, forward thinking, regulating the sector but also incentivising philanthropy. In many countries, philanthropy can be hard because of government obstacles such as taxation of donations. All this has made philanthropy a little too slow and too safe. What we need is more enlightened governments and policies. We need more Asian role models. We need to hold each other more accountable, we need more investments in public goods and to build up the ecosystem.

Now, Singapore is a little different. We are a wealth hub. Rather than just being an asset or fund management hub, we have helped set up a lot of family offices, and many wealthy families have moved to Singapore over the past few years. These families want to make decisions around wealth from Singapore, including philanthropy. So, the demand for philanthropy services has risen. Singapore is also a natural melting pot or meeting point for East and West. There is a flow of ideas. It's an innovation hub. Major players like Temasek Trust use their convening power to bring other major players together. All that has created a lot of excitement. Certainly, the government has provided support to build Singapore to be a philanthropy hub. There is intention, there are plans. For example, Temasek Trust has raised more than US$700 million in pledges for the Philanthropy Asia Alliance. Now we have to execute, and make it work.

Badr Jafar: You worked with the Gates Foundation to launch a new foundation for donors – the Asian Community Foundation. What do you hope to achieve with this new foundation? Could you also say more about your philosophy for collaboration between entities and foundations within Asia, but also across the border? How does the collaboration framework work in Asia? How do you hope it will develop and evolve?

Laurence Lien: Leveraging on Singapore becoming the philanthropy hub and sensing that a lot of wealthy families want philanthropy services, several of us from APC started the Asia Community Foundation to make purposeful giving easy. It's not so easy to set up your own foundation, to find the right people to run it and know exactly what to do. Giving across borders, particularly from Singapore, is not easy, because the accountability and transparency [of non-profits] is not there.

If we don't do this, what's going to happen? Philanthropy is not such a high priority for most people that they will do it no matter what. If it's too difficult, they will leave money on the table and things will not get done. This is why we created the foundation. It's a shared infrastructure, like a multi-family office for philanthropy. The Bill & Melinda Gates Foundation has been a great partner, to start this. We provide solutions from philanthropy advisory to grants advisory, grants management or pooled funds. We leverage the community of experienced APC members, because we get the best ideas in terms of the best grantees from people who have been doing it for a long time, who offer a level of validation for newer donors, and who have all these relationships.

We use these relationships, and we crowd-fund from those who are starting out. It's not different from investing. When you want to invest in a company, you find out who is the anchor investor, who has been working with this company and investing in it for a long time. The collaborative effort is linking these people up, connecting the experienced and the less experienced, sharing success and sharing that back-office infrastructure. That's our intent with the Asia Community Foundation. We only launched in September 2023, so it's still early days; but collaboration is in its DNA.

The foundation is collaborating with entities that are within the Singapore ecosystem, but we are always collaborating outside and we have APC members around the world. We want several modes of collaboration. We want to flow funds across borders to support and scale initiatives that work. We want to replicate successful models and we want to build a coalition of players, because some of the problems that we're trying to solve, such as climate change, must be solved at a global level. Climate adaptation has not been a focus at all, particularly in Southeast Asia. We are trying to get our APC members, as well as other

"We want to flow funds across borders to support and scale initiatives that work. We want to replicate successful models and we want to build a coalition of players, because some of the problems that we're trying to solve, such as climate change, must be solved at a global level."

funders, to align their work, so that we can move the needle in these areas.

Badr Jafar: The Asia Philanthropy Circle created a climate collective at the start of 2022, to enable its members to engage more deeply in climate action across Asia. The collective also provides a space for finding solutions to this common threat. How do you see this collective evolving?

Laurence Lien: Actually, the collective came to a natural end in December 2023 because we always intended only a two-year runway. It was targeted at our APC members who were newer to climate philanthropy. It was about building that trusted community of like-minded individuals to learn together, to connect and to collaborate on climate change in Southeast Asia. We decided that we wanted to mainstream the climate work. We want our wider membership to look at climate. Everybody needs to have a climate programme because it is a horizontal and intersectional challenge.

It was primarily a learning platform, but by the end, members of the collective were co-funding each other's programmes. For example, rice production in Vietnam accounts for a sixth of the nation's greenhouse gas emissions. As a result, some of our members came together to start a technical assistance facility to promote climate-smart rice cultivation practices for Vietnamese farmers. We are also working in partnership with other funders outside the circle. For example, we are working to set up a Project Drawdown programme for Asia, creating a roadmap for philanthropists and other decision-makers towards strategic action on climate, and in areas of greater concern like food, agriculture, land use and oceans.

Badr Jafar: Do you believe that philanthropy can play a catalysing role in leveraging more public and business capital for climate mitigation and adaptation strategies across Asia and elsewhere?

Laurence Lien: We definitely believe in philanthropy playing this complementary role. By utilising our entrepreneurial strengths, we can establish a long-term horizon and flexibility, without needing to be accountable to shareholders and investors. In terms of leveraging public capital, I think that the best work philanthropy can do is to improve policy efficacy to help decision-makers make better decisions. Philanthropy can also help to build technical capacity, particularly to help subnational officials implement plans, because quite often national-level officials make commitments and pledges but have no idea how to implement them.

We need research to amplify what works. To leverage private capital, I think we still need a lot more research and innovation. In the early stages where the ROI for commercial returns is not attractive, we need to make more effort to incubate and accelerate start-ups because they need a lot of capacity to grow. We need concessionary capital to bridge the valley of death for start-ups who have initial proof of concept, but who take time to be commercially viable. Already some of our APC members have been doing this. One example is Gree Energy, a biogas-to-energy social enterprise in Indonesia that started with philanthropic capital led by an APC member. We need many more such projects, and I think the opportunities will be there. There's too much waiting for commercial returns downstream. I think there's a lot of work upstream for philanthropic capital before all the downstream opportunities can be unlocked.

Belinda Tanoto

Member of the Board of Trustees, Tanoto Foundation

Belinda Tanoto is a second-generation member of the highly entrepreneurial Indonesian family behind RGE, founded in 1967. Today, the group consists of resource-based manufacturing companies with assets exceeding US$35 billion and a workforce of over 80,000 across Indonesia, China, Brazil, Spain and

Canada. Tanoto is a managing director of the RGE Group, and a member of the group's executive management board.

Belinda's parents Sukanto and Tinah founded Tanoto Foundation in 1981, with the belief that every person should have the opportunity to develop their full potential. The foundation's focus is on developing human capital through early childhood development, basic education and leadership development. For example, it works with teachers and school leaders across Indonesia to promote active learning in basic education, and in the development of future leaders. The foundation has also expanded its footprint to China, where it invests in early childhood and leadership development, and to Singapore, where in 2023, it set up a medical research fund to support discovery and innovation around diseases prevalent in the region.

Tanoto speaks and writes regularly on poverty alleviation, basic education and early childhood education and development. In 2019, she was recognised by Forbes as one of Asia's Heroes of Philanthropy for her work with the Tanoto Foundation.

Badr Jafar: Belinda, you've been involved in your family's philanthropy from an early age. Can you tell us more about your own personal journey into philanthropy, and the foundation's mission to develop human potential?

Belinda Tanoto: I'll start by sharing a bit about my parents' story. My parents started the foundation in the 1980s with the belief that education can change a person's life. My parents never graduated from high school, not because they didn't want to, but because they didn't have the opportunity. So, when they were starting their business and built their first factory, working in very rural areas in Indonesia, they noticed that a lot of people still didn't have access to good-quality education. What started out as building one school next to the factory evolved over many years into what Tanoto Foundation is today, working with government and with other partners to improve access and the quality of education in Indonesia and in China. This means making sure that all our children are in school and learning, because sometimes children are in school but may not be learning. It's really important to tackle that.

In terms of my own journey, giving back, or in my family we call it having a sense of gratitude, is very important. When I was younger, on my birthday instead of getting a birthday party, my parents, my mother especially, would bring us to the orphanage to share our toys because for her it was important that we understood that with great privilege comes great responsibility.

Badr Jafar: Do you think that philanthropy in Indonesia, and more broadly across Asia, has changed over the years? If so, what role do you think the next generation has played in this transition and evolution?

Belinda Tanoto: I think what is interesting is that a lot of the next-generation philanthropists in the region are also active in business. This means that we're bringing our business acumen and our bold entrepreneurial approach to philanthropy. So, it's addressing the root causes of social problems, not just charity. Since we're coming from the business side, a lot of us are also comfortable with bringing a business approach, being data driven, being impact first, and being comfortable with risk and innovation.

> "We're bringing our business acumen and our bold entrepreneurial approach to philanthropy."

Badr Jafar: It's clear you're passionate about partnership development. The Tanoto Foundation has chosen to partner strategically with governments, with international organisations, and with other philanthropic foundations to achieve your goals. Could you tell me more about what partnership models you believe work best to maximise impact in the areas and locations you operate in?

Belinda Tanoto: We reflect a lot about this. Why do we partner? Often, it's not just about pooling the capital; it's also pooling the know-how, the network and the risks. Each party brings something different to the table. In Indonesia, one of our projects is to tackle stunting, and we were one of the founding donors to a multi-donor trust fund with the World Bank. We came in with local knowledge, the World Bank brought the best global practices, given their global footprint, and then the Bill & Melinda Gates Foundation provided support, eventually joining the partnership. Of course, there was also a government partner. We partnered with the Vice President's Office, because the stunting work required coordinating across 11 government agencies and ministries. It was interesting to foster this partnership where we created a platform for democratic stakeholders to come together and discuss the issue openly, and build trust and alignment in our mission.

Badr Jafar: Do you think that networks such as the Asian Venture Philanthropy Network (AVPN) and the Asia Philanthropy Circle play a catalysing role in accelerating the impact of philanthropy in the region? How do you think that philanthropic infrastructure can be reinforced to create a more enabling ecosystem for philanthropy in Asia and elsewhere?

Belinda Tanoto: Yes, for us it's been amazing to be part of AVPN and APC, and we see it creating value in several ways. The first is creating that platform for collaboration and resource sharing to synergise and coordinate efforts. Beyond that, I think, what's nice about giving organisations like APC is that they're made up of philanthropists and foundations of different sizes and scales, and having this peer-to-peer learning has been incredibly useful, especially for somebody like me, who is next generation. The final thing is that these giving circles, or collaborations, help a lot in addressing some of the ecosystem gaps, whether it's talent building or availability of data. We publish a lot of research through APC and AVPN, because in Asia there's not enough information on what's happening in philanthropy. There's not enough information on what's happening in the non-profit world. Being able to come together and pool our knowledge as a one-stop-shop for everybody to refer to is incredibly helpful.

> "Being able to come together and pool our knowledge as a one-stop shop for everybody to refer to is incredibly helpful."

Badr Jafar: You mentioned the lack of data and information, and this is something we also find in the Middle East, a lack of stories that we can capture and present to future generations of philanthropists to take inspiration from and figure out how to do better. Is there a way that you're able to do that yourself? Do you capture the stories of what you do as a foundation, and what you might hear about others in the community doing? Is there a way that you can relay those stories to others within your network and community?

Belinda Tanoto: We work with a few centres, in Asia, Europe and the US, in terms of capturing the best philanthropy practices across different regions. Obviously, our ecosystem is in a nascent stage, and there are not as many players. For example, the reason why we're an operating foundation is that if we were to write a multi-million-dollar cheque, there isn't a ready-made non-profit that's able to absorb that kind of grant. As well as learning best practices from elsewhere, it's important for us to keep in mind the ecosystem in Asia and the innovation that's happening in the region, and to share that with a broader audience.

Tsitsi Masiyiwa

Executive Chair and Co-Founder, Higherlife Foundation

Tsitsi Masiyiwa is chair of the Higherlife Foundation, founded by Tsitsi and her husband Strive Masiyiwa in 1996 in Zimbabwe. The foundation invests in human capital development to build thriving communities, and sustainable livelihoods. Its portfolio encompasses investments in education leadership development, maternal health and neglected tropical diseases. Masiyiwa is a trusted advisor and thought partner to universities, to national leaders and to social entrepreneurs on issues of education, leadership, philanthropy, gender equality and youth empowerment. She is also the chairperson of the End Fund, which mobilises global resources for neglected tropical diseases.

In addition, Masiyiwa is the chair of Co-Impact, a global philanthropic collaborative that supports gender equality and women's leadership. She sits on many other boards and her work has garnered global recognition, including honorary doctorates from Morehouse University in Atlanta, Georgia, and Africa University in Mutare, Zimbabwe, as well as the prestigious Champions for Change Award for Leadership from the International Center for Research on Women. Tsitsi was a founding member of the African Philanthropy Forum (APF), established in 2014 to build a learning community of strategic African philanthropists and social investors. Tsitsi and Strive are signatories to the Giving Pledge.

Badr Jafar: Over the years, the APF has established a strong presence on the African continent, with a footprint in 14 African countries. Tsitsi, you have been personally engaged in building philanthropic infrastructure through the APF to support strategic philanthropy in Africa. I strongly believe in this mission for the global growth markets. Why do you think that infrastructure provides the leverage to accelerate the impact of philanthropy on the African continent? What are some of the gaps that you think still exist in the system?

Tsitsi Masiyiwa: I love philanthropy; it's part and parcel of my DNA. I was the chair of the African Philanthropy Forum, which was founded by the Global Philanthropy Forum as a project, but we were instrumental in turning it from a project into an organisation. The African Philanthropy Forum has now grown to be an important voice that speaks of philanthropy from the perspective of Africans.

Although philanthropy is timeless, as Africans we express philanthropy in a way that is very much influenced by our culture. This is true in other continents as well, but over time the AFP has developed into an organisation that is heavily focused on strategic philanthropy. What do I mean by strategic philanthropy? It's where resources are mobilised to move the needle or cause a systems-change through collaborations with other philanthropists and different types of partnerships.

Where do we see gaps? The first is one of perception. There is still this perception that all philanthropy must be modelled around the philanthropy of the Global North. We forget that in the Global North, legal systems and frameworks are built to encourage and incentivise philanthropy. This doesn't necessarily have to do with love for humanity, but it makes financial sense to give. Those structures sometimes make it difficult to collaborate because there's an expectation that when you go into a collaboration, the Global South philanthropist must put money into a Global North organisation in US dollars. We forget that every country has its own currency, which is equally as valuable, especially when you start spending money or investing. Some of those perception gaps need to close. Another major gap is between the priorities of the communities and the passion of the philanthropist. That gap is very difficult but it's common across the board.

Badr Jafar: The Higherlife Foundation, which you founded in 1996 with Strive, has had a major impact in Zimbabwe and beyond. Could you tell us why you started the foundation and how it's evolved over the past years in terms of its priorities? Can you also tell us more about why you are so passionate about the foundation's mission to develop human potential?

Tsitsi Masiyiwa: The foundation was started as something very personal to us as a family and part of our expression of our faith. It was born at a time when HIV/AIDS was a pandemic, roaring through the world in a heart-breaking manner. Many of us lost family members. I always talk about my aunt who had nine children, all of whom died from HIV and AIDS. At the time, we didn't have money, but we had a strong desire to do something.

We felt education was the best way to contribute towards solving the problem. Our education would be focused on the orphaned children that were left behind. We started the foundation before our business was established as a dream that one day, when we had money, that is where our philanthropy would go. We set up the business in 1998 and the work of the foundation started in 1996. Initially, it was giving that was very much driven by feelings and emotions, and less by being strategic and building systems. But, over time, we brought in professionals who helped us to put in the systems that made the work more efficient, to measure the impact and ensure that resources were put where they should be.

We have evolved to be much more structured and yet remain deeply connected to the communities we serve. We like human capital development. At the end of the day, whether it's health, agriculture, commerce or entrepreneurship, what holds the centre is education. You invest in people and you're able to have the skills and the talents required to tackle the issues of poverty, and to do it in a way that is sustainable over the long term.

"What holds the centre is education."

Badr Jafar: Do you think that philanthropy in Africa has changed since you began your own journey? What role do you believe is being played by the next generation, who are inheriting wealth and beginning their respective giving journeys?

Tsitsi Masiyiwa: Philanthropy has changed a lot. There's a lot more collaboration than before among local philanthropists, and among philanthropists from different regions. It's something that young people are aspiring to do. It's more common to hear young people say that when they are successful, they would love to

become a philanthropist. It's something people admire. We've always
been generous people. In Africa, this
generosity is our hallmark. Philanthropy allows us to express our generosity in ways that are more impactful,
and where there are more resources
to do it at scale.

"Philanthropy allows us to express our generosity in ways that are more impactful, and where there are more resources to do it at scale."

These are some of the changes we have seen from focusing on education as the primary way in which we do our philanthropy, but in different sectors. There is more wealth and more high-net-worth individuals than we've ever seen. Personally, I wish people would be more generous. Wealthy individuals are focused on what they love to do in their communities, and on something that is directly related to them. I wish that there would be more exploration of areas where we have no vested interest. I believe in the importance of partnering with the government and aligning with the government's priorities, because if you have your own priorities that are unrelated to what the government is focusing on, you won't achieve much.

Philanthropy fills in the gaps. To do that effectively, you must marry your vision and the national vision. You can also make use of the organisations that have data, and that are focused on feeding into national strategies. For example, the World Health Organization, and many others in finance, agriculture and education, provide data that can be broken down to national level. Philanthropy can also use flexible funding and long-term funding to do the things that government cannot do. I think philanthropists have become a lot smarter and more effective by not trying to copy what the government is doing, but complementing and filling in the gaps. They play a very important catalytic role that I've seen happen time and time again.

With the next generation, I think we are still in the early stages. The next generation has a growing voice in amplifying issues that our generation has not been able to solve, especially issues that arise because of race and colonialism. They are bolder. Perhaps within the coming decade we'll see a real shift of wealth to the next generation, and the ability to decide how resources are allocated. They are more bullish than we are. There's an impatience in the way they want to bring about change.

Badr Jafar: You spoke about collaboration. I know that you're passionate about working with partners. Higherlife works closely with other organisations, including another one of your family's organisations, Delta Philanthropies, to implement your programmes. Can you tell me more about what partnership models you believe work best to maximise impact? What do you think are the possibilities for more collaborative or pooled funds in the future within Africa's philanthropic landscape?

Tsitsi Masiyiwa: Collaboration is happening at all levels. At one level, you have crowdfunding, where individuals are giving small amounts collectively. We have millions and millions of people who are doing that. They do it also through their churches or places of worship. They do it through their communities and networks, which has really been impactful. At another level of giving, we find small grants to communities that lack resources. Small communities and women entrepreneurs need small loans for whatever projects they do, such as small agricultural projects. There are many grant makers who will give those small loans without an expectation of financial sustainability; that is an important model.

The next level is project giving, which we are now finding very common among donor agencies, such as USAID and various aid agencies from different parts of the world. They tend to give large amounts but it's project funding. When the money runs out, that's the end of the project, and people disperse. Sometimes the project ends before the impact or goal has been achieved, which is sad. It's still a model that's important, but I think growing less and less in importance. At a higher level, there is impact or systemic change funding. This is what we do in neglected tropical diseases, where our goal is to eliminate certain diseases like elephantiasis or river blindness. The big philanthropists, such as the Gates Foundation, Reaching the Last Mile, the ELMA Philanthropies and the Dangote Foundation, tackle these big issues that require a lot of resources and long-term funding. I've seen that be very impactful. We have seen different models of collaboration for impact such as Blue Meridian and Co-Impact. The Audacious Project is another one. All these different models are quite effective. We see the impact and the effectiveness of recognising that all the different types of giving are important. Some can target small communities; others target whole sectors or nations or regions. Whichever model it is, it's important, and it's part and parcel of what our societies need to bring the transformation we need to see prosperity in our communities.

Badr Jafar: Do you see a promising future for impact investing and other social finance approaches in Africa? Is that something that you think is becoming more popular over time and with the next generation?

Tsitsi Masiyiwa: We went through a season when there was a lot of momentum around impact investment. Now I see that things have plateaued a bit. Philanthropists practising pure philanthropy where there's no expectation of financial return find it difficult to have discussions around financial return and profit because their philanthropy is targeting the most vulnerable. To bring in a profit motive, even if the returns are much lower than what we normally find in a for-profit business, is not easy to do. I think much of the leadership that drives impact investment is coming from the private sector. Not enough leaders have a mixture of strong private-sector experience and experience in the not-for-profit sector.

Once those numbers grow, the narrative is likely to change. We are going to find it easier, whether it's at family foundation level or at board level. In most of the circles that I engage with, there is difficulty marrying the two. Many philanthropists set up the non-profit arm of their philanthropy, and a separate arm for impact investment, and there's always more that goes to philanthropy. There's also a discomfort in society. Even if our

aspirations and impact investments are aligned with philanthropy, I think society generally has an expectation that if you
talk about investing, even the mention of profit makes the
approach lose its shine and authenticity. So, we've got to change
the narrative. If you have a strong mix of for-profit and
non-profit leadership running some of these impact investment
funds, we can have more impact and see the growth that is so
needed, because the demand for help is huge and the resources
are too few.

CLOSING THOUGHTS

The stories told in the preceding chapters provide compelling evidence that individual philanthropists, business leaders and international funders are already having a significant impact on many of the world's challenges. However, if one theme comes through more clearly than any other, it is that this potential for impact is multiplied when philanthropists collaborate with one another, and with business and government. Almost all the donors I spoke to acknowledged the power and necessity of working with others, rather than in isolation. Whether it is international funders increasingly collaborating with local players in various countries, or businesses working with non-profits, or governments taking action to support the efforts of individual givers, strategic philanthropy is consistently more impactful when it is amplified through collaboration. For me, the most immediate question is: What are the best ways to accelerate the adoption of collaborative models that will generate greater impact? As I argued in the preface to this book, and touched on in many of these conversations, we urgently need a more enabling environment that leverages and promotes strategic philanthropy – particularly in the global growth markets where the philanthropic sector is burgeoning.

I see four elements to this enabling environment: one, stronger and more active local and regional networks; two, simpler and more efficient regulation; three, better philanthropic governance, supported by solid data and research-based evidence; and four, a well-informed media covering the sector and strengthening the narrative around philanthropy.

The introduction of more flexible and enabling regulation of philanthropic activity and the non-profit sector in several jurisdictions would contribute significantly to the development of more effective philanthropy. While philanthropic networks do an important job of advocating for more efficient regulation, fuzzy or incomplete legal frameworks in many countries continue to slow the development of foundations and civil society organisations. In many countries, there are no frameworks for establishing a foundation or similar grant-making vehicles. In other countries, the legal requirements are burdensome and restrictive, and fiscal incentives for giving are absent or insufficient. Receiving money from outside the region or moving funds between countries is often an arduous task. New digital platforms and channels for giving are difficult if not impossible to establish in many jurisdictions. All these factors have a stifling effect on the transparent flow and ultimate impact of philanthropic capital.

That said, it is also a two-way street. The philanthropic sector must demonstrate its own commitment to greater accountability and transparency to encourage a better enabling environment and more conducive regulatory frameworks. This includes voluntarily adopting standards of philanthropic practice with a commitment to open communication about the flows of philanthropic capital – how much, to whom and for what purpose. Additionally, more effective measurement and reporting of outcomes over time would help to strengthen trust between donors, recipients, regulators and the public, so that all stakeholders can be better informed about the difference that philanthropic capital is making – including coming clean about what's working, and what isn't. Again, the development of a stronger philanthropic ecosystem will help to build and embed these practices more rapidly and more widely.

Greater transparency will also enable increased sharing of data and evidence. This underpins all our efforts. Without data, our networks are blind. Without evidence, philanthropists cannot make fully informed decisions about the allocation of their capital or the weighing up of strategic options. By collecting and sharing data, working in collaboration with experts within our academic and professional networks, and using knowledge for better advocacy, philanthropy will be able to harness more of its potential to generate meaningful impact.

One final and essential part of an enabling philanthropic infrastructure is well-informed journalism focused on philanthropy and social impact. I believe that the full story of the dynamic growth of philanthropy in emerging markets remains to be told. We require creative media partnerships between philanthropists and local journalists to encourage greater exchange of ideas and perspectives between philanthropic voices from around the globe, and to showcase local champions. This can inspire and enhance philanthropic practice within the world's fastest-growing regions.

Efforts to build the philanthropic infrastructure across all of these fronts promise to boost the business of philanthropy and enable us to realise more of the important benefits of practising strategic philanthropy with global impact. After speaking to the diverse philanthropic leaders featured in this book, and listening to their inspiring stories, I am more optimistic than ever that philanthropy can be the glue that binds business, government and civil society together in concerted action. Philanthropy, giving of any kind for the love of humanity and our habitat, is accessible to all of us who are motivated to give to our societies and to our common future. The opportunities to engage are limited only by our imagination. What these stories demonstrate is that we can all generate impact in different ways. By working together, across borders and sectors, we can give ourselves the best possible chance of creating a more inclusive, equitable and sustainable future for generations to come.

ACKNOWLEDGEMENTS

This book would not have been possible without the dedication, wisdom and kind cooperation of all the amazing interviewees, as well as the great support of the following individuals*: Charlie Brotherstone, Charles Keidan, Hannah Lonergan, Anita Manek, Hilary Pearson and Daniel Slack-Smith.

* Listed alphabetically

REFERENCES

2. The Future of Global Philanthropy

1. Pierre-Olivier Gourinchas (25 July 2023), 'Global Economy on Track but Not Yet Out of the Woods', IMF Blog. https://www.imf .org/en/Blogs/Articles/2023/07/25/global-economy-on-track-but -not-yet-out-of-the-woods

2. The Cerulli Report (2021), 'U.S. High-Net-Worth and Ultra-High-Net-Worth Markets'. https://www.cerulli.com/reports/us-high -net-worth-and-ultra-high-net-worth-markets-2023

3. IMF Datamapper (2022), 'Real GDP Growth'. www.imf.org /external/datamapper/NGDP_RPCH@WEO/OEMDC/ADVEC /WEOWORLD

4. OECD (2021), *Private Philanthropy for Development – Second Edition*. Paris: OECD Publishing.

5. Harvard Kennedy School of Government (2018), *Global Philanthropy Report – Perspectives on the Global Foundation Sector*. https://cpl.hks.harvard.edu/files/cpl/files/global_philanthropy _report_final_april_2018.pdf

6. A. Sheth, R. Shridharan, N. Nundy, P. Dastoor and P. Pal (2022), *India Philanthropy Report 2022*, Bain & Company/Dasra. https://www.bain.com/insights/india-philanthropy-report-2022/

7. Amounts of annual global *zakat* and *sadaqah* giving are very difficult to estimate because of lack of accurate estimates of wealth

for Muslim countries. See H. Ahmed, 'Potential Global Zakat Pool: Demystifying the Numbers', online blog, National Zakat Foundation. https://nzfworldwide.com/potential-global-Zakat-pool-demystifying-the-numbers/

8. This wide range in estimate is due to the fact that there is very little combined data on *zakat* and *sadaqah* giving.

9. Charities Aid Foundation (2022), *World Giving Index 2022*. https://www.cafonline.org/docs/default-source/about-us-research/caf_world_giving_index_2022_210922-final.pdf

10. Hilary McConnaughey and Sokal Shtylla (2020), *Stepping Off The Sidelines*, The Milken Institute. https://milkeninstitute.org/sites/default/files/reports-pdf/MI_SteppingOfftheSidelines_Report_FINAL_1_0.pdf

11. African Union Commission (2019), 'Africa's Future: Youth and the Date Defining Their Lives'. https://www.prb.org/wp-content/uploads/2019/10/Status-of-African-Youth-SPEC.pdf

3. Philanthropy and the Polycrisis

1. Scott Janzwood and Thomas Homer-Dixon (2022), 'What Is a Global Polycrisis?' Discussion Paper #2022–4, Cascade Institute. https://cascadeinstitute.org/technical-paper/what-is-a-global-polycrisis/

8. Catalysing Social Innovation

1. J. A. Phills Jr., K. Deiglmeier and D. T. Miller (2008), 'Rediscovering Social Innovation', *Stanford Social Innovation Review*, 6(4), 34–43. https://doi.org/10.48558/GBJY-GJ471.